Wolf

A Memoir of ̖
and Atoneme̖

"Carter's memoir is a beautiful and moving story, full of truths and hard-earned wisdom."

– Carolyn Holbrook, author of
Tell Me Your Names and I will Testify, winner of
the 2021 MN Book Award in Memoir and Creative Nonfiction

"The delicacy of the writing and purposeful language are only enhanced by the excellent pace. . . . He cares enough about becoming a better person that he immerses himself in learning what has made him tick and ultimately, what will make him a better (and happier) person, husband, father and friend."

– Debbie Burke, author and editor

"Carter has crafted a complex memoir, skillfully weaving powerful vignettes from a brutally traumatic experience into a parallel, extended tale of personal evasion, reflection and discovery. . . . an invaluable guide to anyone dealing with the lasting impact of almost any past trauma. All in all, a phenomenal piece of work!"

– Ken Kaliher, journalist

"From childhood trauma and traumatic stress, to healing and resolution through confession and atonement, . . . it's a profound story of Carter's experience and journey into an authentic self."

– Jim Smith, organization and human development consultant

Wolf

A Memoir of Love and Atonement

By Carter McNamara

Authenticity Consulting, LLC

Trademarks
LEGO is a trademark and copyright of the LEGO Group.
Vicks and VapoRub are trademarks of The Procter & Gamble Company.
Kent is a trademark of Lorillard Licensing Company LLC.

Credits
Cover background image by Jack Redgate, Pexels.com.
All other photographs are from the author's personal collection.
Cover design by Erin Scott/Wylde Hare, LLC, Woodbury, Minnesota.

Publisher's Cataloging in Publication Data
McNamara, Carter, 1953 -
Wolf: A Memoir of Love and Atonement / by Carter McNamara

ISBN 978-1-933719-40-5 - paperback
ISBN 978-1-933719-41-2 - ebook

1. McNamara, Carter – childhood, marriage. 2. Authors, American – 21st Century – Biography 3. Recovery - ACoA, PTSD. I. Title

Printed in the United States of America
10 9 8 7 6

To
Mac, Renee, Faith,
Darienne, and Ian

"The wise try to adjust themselves to the truth,
while fools try to adjust the truth
to themselves."

– Thibaut

Table of Contents

Introduction

In her book *The Art of Memoir*, Mary Karr writes, "In some ways, writing a memoir is knocking yourself out with your own fist. But nobody I know who's written a great one describes it as anything less than a major-league shit-eating contest." I wholeheartedly agree.

I grew up in a culture where people rarely talked about their personal problems. That was fine with me. I worked hard to hide my deep shame and guilt about my traumatic past. Thus, one can only imagine my soul-ripping experience when writing a God's honest truth about my trauma and the crisis it took for me to finally recover—and to write about the damage I had done to my family and what it took for me to atone for what I had done.

If someone like me can go through all of that, then you or your loved one might as well. My story is one example of how it could be done. As I write this memoir, my wife and I have had forty-one years together.

If you've been traumatized in childhood or adulthood and are working hard to hide it, then this story is an example of how you can face your demons and go on to partner with a loved one in a healthy relationship. If you've harmed others when dealing with your symptoms, then here's an example of how you could gain forgiveness from them—and perhaps from yourself. If you're working hard to help a partner deal with their trauma, then here's an example of how you can protect your own health while working to help them.

Readers will notice that I do a lot of personal reflection—thinking to myself—in the story. This is common among traumatized people: always wondering if they're safe and if they're coming across as normal to other people. I ask for your patience where I might seem self-absorbed in this regard.

1

Author's Note

In a memoir, the accuracy of the story is extremely important. I wrote the dialogue in the story to the best of my memory as to what could reasonably have been said and by whom. My wife closely reviewed the manuscript to ensure it was accurate. My siblings reviewed it and agreed that the experiences I described with our mother were entirely believable based on their own experiences with her. I changed the names of characters, other than family members and teachers, where it would protect their privacy and reputations. For the sake of brevity and clarity in the story, I wrote the character of Lloyd as a composite of two close friends. The character of Astrid is a composite of two therapists who helped me in my recovery.

Instant breakthroughs in therapy as depicted in stories— including this one—are actually quite rare. It is much more common that recovery like mine is a slow, complex, and difficult process that is difficult to describe in a manner that would hold the reader's interest. Thus, my therapy sessions were reduced to a number that would include the highlights from all of the sessions in the time frame of this story.

None of the above changes detracts from the true arc and essence of my actual story.

This book does not provide professional advice about recovering from trauma. Readers seeking that type of help should contact a professional therapist.

Prologue – "Don't Lie to Me!"

My best friend, Gordon, wants the money that I borrowed from him to buy my BB gun. I go into my room to get the money I saved from selling pop bottles. I keep it in my secret hiding spot behind my underwear in my bottom drawer. But now it's gone.

I run into Mommy's room. She's sitting on her bed, reading another paperback and smoking a Kent cigarette. The room stinks. I hate it. Her red hair is up in a bun on her head. She's wearing those eyeglasses that have sharp corners. She calls them cat-eye glasses. They're weird.

"Mommy, my money is gone."

She doesn't look at me. She never does.

"Yes, uh hum." Her thumbs twitch. "Maybe Barney took it." Barney is one of the men that comes to the loud drinking parties at our house.

I step closer. "Barney hasn't been here since I counted it the last time. It couldn't be him. Gordon wants his money now to buy BBs for his gun."

"Barney took your eight dollars," she quietly mumbles, still staring at her book.

I step closer. "Mommy, how did you know there were eight dollars there? I didn't tell anyone."

"Uh hum, you go play now . . ."

She's lying to me again. My face gets really hot and my heart beats so hard I'm afraid I'll die. My sisters say when I get really mad at her, I yell lots of words at her. But I get really mad 'cause she's so mean to us. She lies. She steals. Mostly, she blames us kids for it.

When I yell for a long time, I can't breathe and then I start to cry really hard. Sometimes that makes me throw up, and it stinks like Mommy's throw-ups always do. I try really hard not to cry. This time I can't help it. I start to cry.

"Don't cry. Big boys don't cry."

She always says that.

I step closer. "But you took my money! You tell me not to lie, but you lie all the time! You get drunk in bed for days and I can't wake you and our house stinks like throw-up so I can't have friends in our house. My friends—their moms don't do that. You say you're so smart, but you're stupid because I have to watch everything so nothing goes wrong. I'm only ten. None of the other moms do this! I want a good mom, a normal mom. I hate you!"

Her head and arms start trembling and she cries softly.

"How can you be so mean to me?"

She always says this when I get mad. She doesn't look at me when she says it.

I rush up to her, grab her book, tear it in half and throw it on the floor.

She looks at the pieces on the floor and her eyes get big.

"No!"

She still doesn't look at me.

I turn and run out the back door all the way down to Cherry Creek, where I'm safe from her drinking, her lies, and her throw-ups. The creek is just the worms, the bugs, and the fish.

When I get to the creek, I find my little cave. I dug it with an empty coffee can. It's a tiny hole in a hill by the water. It's just big enough for me to back into. I keep it covered with a bush, so no one knows it's there. I move the bush back into the hole and cover it again. Now I can cry and no one will hear me. I'm safe here.

After a while, I don't feel so mad at Mommy anymore. I start feeling mad at myself because I made her cry. Sometimes I don't remember what I yelled. I hope nobody finds out how mean I am and that I'm not normal. That I attack like a wolf. I'm never gonna tell anyone.

Carter McNamara

Part 1
Something's Wrong with Me

(1981-1982)

"Nobody realizes that some people expend
tremendous energy merely to be normal."

– Albert Camus

Carter McNamara

"Who Are You?"

It was the first week of August 1981, typically the hottest month in Minnesota. Muggy, sticky, oppressive. Didn't matter. I was in a loving relationship with my wife. One that was open, honest, and trusting. One where I would do whatever it took to hide my past from her.

It had been another long day at work as a software engineer—a job that made me feel like I'd finally arrived, but at the wrong location. I wanted to teach philosophy, but I'd opted for the more lucrative career rather than the more satisfying one.

I pulled the car into the condo parking lot around seven-thirty p.m. I loved coming home to Teri, my wife. She felt like the safe zone in the game of tag. When you're with her, no one could tag you out. Coming home always restarted my day. Maybe this was what normal was. She had been waiting for me and gave me a big hug.

"You look so tired, Carter. I'm glad I'm not working in your department."

Although we'd graduated three months ago with four-year degrees in computer science and now worked for the same technology company, we had quite different jobs. I worked to get products to demanding customers. She enjoyed providing software to fellow employees.

Now that she was home, she was already out of her professional attire. She was clad in a loose purple T-shirt with the words "Baby Lives Here" on the belly. She loved being pregnant and relished the thought of being a mom in five months. She radiated motherhood. Me? I'd never had a father, so I'd spent another lunch hour at the library, reading about being one. I should tell her about my fears of being a dad, but I didn't want her to feel like she'd married a freak who didn't know what a dad was.

I turned to drop my khaki sports coat on the back of the dinette chair and sat down at the table.

I said, "Love, I'm wiped out. My brain died around six o'clock. I was hoping to watch Magnum PI. I need to feel like I'm a hunky-looking male living the good life in Hawaii, solving crimes, you know?" I smiled at her, hoping she'd cooperate. She gently placed the chicken platter and silverware in front of me. Mashed potatoes with skins. Green beans. Ice cold milk. Always a balanced diet with her.

"You already ate?"

She nodded.

She brought her cup of peppermint tea, sat down next to me, and said, "We did a fun exercise at work today. I want us to do it tonight, too." She sounded hopeful, like a child going to the zoo.

The exercise was meant to build teamwork, she explained. They were given a list of questions and asked to look at them alone for five minutes. Then, in groups of three, each person was supposed to ask one question to the other two. The other two did the same, but had to pick a different question.

"I thought it would be goofy and maybe a waste of time. But it actually helped us to get to know each other." She smiled and used her horror movie voice. "You and I will share our inner secrets." She laughed at her play-acting.

Our deepest secrets? How would I get out of this? I tried to maneuver into my best pouting look: furrowed brow, sagging shoulders, corners of my mouth turned down. I looked at her. "Love, really. I just want to be brain-dead tonight."

She ignored me. "Let's pretend you and I are building our own little team—our marriage. What do you think?" She was selling me something and I wasn't buying it. I could feel my heart starting to race and my face getting red. I needed to watch my temper.

She pulled her chair closer, then pretended to look official: sitting upright, shoulders back, both hands on the list of questions. "I'll ask the first question. How about since you're the quieter one, you answer a question first?" She chuckled, still having fun teasing me.

Holding my fork in mid-air, I said, "Love, can't we wait until I finish eating?" Maybe by then, she'd have forgotten this silly, irritating exercise. Why couldn't she see I didn't want to do this? This wasn't all about her.

She was undeterred. "Okay, here we go. This is an easy one. In five sentences or less, describe how others see you when working in teams." She looked up at me and chuckled again. She was enjoying this.

Now I was infuriated because I'd been ignored. I felt threatened because she was so persistent. Where would these questions go? I dropped my fork and glared. "You've known me for almost a year. Why don't you answer that? You're the one who's doing this damned inquisition. I just want to eat my damned dinner. I live here, too, you know."

Her head jerked back, her jaw dropped, and her eyes teared up. She laid the list on her lap and looked away. I felt terrified, ambushed by my outburst. I felt like two different people—Dr. Jekyll and Mr. Hyde. I was trying so hard to have a fresh start with her, to control my rages. I was trying desperately not to be like I was with Amy, my previous girlfriend who'd put up with three years of my tantrums.

I felt as if I'd physically assaulted Teri, but I would never do that. I had never done that. What should I do? Try to calm her down? Distract her and diffuse the situation? Try to get back to a playful and affectionate evening? I needed to remind myself that she knew little about me. We'd been dating for only five months before we got married. We'd been married for only two weeks. During that time, I'd been hiding as much as possible from her. She deserved to know more information about me. Fine, I'd answer some of her questions, but in the safest way possible.

I put my hand on hers. "I'm sorry I got so irritable. I'm tired, hungry, and work is so stressful. You're right. It could be fun to do this. Better than sitting here feeling sorry for myself." I forced a smile, trying to look more committed.

Now she looked like she wasn't sure about doing the questions. Her cheeks were taut, lips pressed together. She wasn't giggling anymore. I'd better change the mood and fast.

"So, Teri, let me answer that question." I cleared my throat as if getting ready to give a speech. I stood up, hands on hips and struck a pose. "I'm a white, male Caucasian. Six foot three. A hundred eighty pounds. Hopeful and focused, yet cynical and confused. And . . . I have a wee bit of a temper." Whew. I'd struck the right balance between playful and thoughtful.

I sat down and looked for applause. There was none. She was far too serious to feign a response. In an instant, she'd pivoted from fanciful to hurt. I leaned forward, trying to look interested and asked her the same question she'd asked me.

With the list on her lap, she carefully picked up her cup, took a sip, looked at me, and said, "Okay, if you're sure."

I nodded.

"So. How would my team see me? That I'm a dedicated employee—who says I'm a very lucky woman to have such a loving husband who will be such a loving father, too—and he'll share with me, so we both can grow together." Her emphasis on the word "share" wasn't lost on me.

She'd said a lot. That I needed to open up about myself. It would take time, but she'd support me in doing it. I looked her in the eyes and, although I wouldn't say I agreed with her, I gave her a long smile as if I had. Then I turned back to my food.

Her instinct for fun—and her own wisdom—had saved us both. She straightened herself in the chair, looked at her list, and asked the next question, "How do you like to communicate with teams?" She chuckled. I was relieved. She was having fun again.

First of all, I thought to myself, I don't like working in teams. I don't like counting on other people. No, I'd better not say that.

"Carter?"

I set my fork down, smiled, and said, "You actually mean how do I communicate with the team you call our marriage, don't you? Well, I'd always get team members' ideas for what they wanted to do with the team." Had she gotten the clue that I just wanted to be left alone now, not to be analyzed? Just to be sure she got my point, I added, "I'd know that each team member is different and might want to participate differently than the others." There. That should've made my point. "Your turn?"

"I agree it's important to get each member's feedback and that everyone is different, but the team needs a common goal. I'd be sure everyone knew what it was and how important it was to participate in achieving it." She said that very seriously to be sure I'd gotten her point. I had.

"I'm just tired, love. Now, I'm going to eat and when I finish, I'll see what Magnum is up to. I love you." I finished with a crooked smile.

"I love you, too, Carter." She sat there, her mouth open slightly as if to say something more. Then she got up, touched me on the shoulder, went into the kitchen, and started loading the dishwasher.

I sat there, slowly eating my dinner, feeling like an imposter without a plan.

Mom Wants to Make Fudge

I love fishing by myself. I'm lucky that Cherry Creek is full of fish—bullheads, suckers, and sometimes trout, too! The creek is a mile from our house. I always feel good there. I can get there really fast—faster if I run. I run faster than anyone in the first grade.

I take my tackle box down from the shelf in our shed. The shed is a tiny room connected to our back door. My box has all the stuff I need. Every size of hooks and bobbers. I love how the box smells like fish. It's heavy and makes a rattling noise when I run.

My fishing rod has never broken, not like my friends' rods. I have to be really careful, so the fishing line doesn't get all wrapped around itself in the reel. And I have to be really careful 'cause the fishing hooks are very sharp. Gordon's sister, Sandy, got one stuck in her little finger and she screamed like heck. The doctor had to get it out. But I never stick myself.

I turn to go, but Mommy sticks her head out the door and yells, "Carter, come in here now! We're gonna make hard fudge."

Oh, no. Not now. She always does this. She gets these crazy ideas out of the blue. She says we'll have fun, but we never do. She always yells at us and we get into a big fight.

I say, "No, I'm going fishing."

She ignores me and steps into the shed. "Carter, get in here! Here, give me that box." She takes my box and puts it up on the shelf.

"Goddammit," I yell. Mommy says I cuss too much. I don't care.

I go into the kitchen feeling very sad. Now Mommy and my sister, Renee, are standing there by the stove. Mommy is stirring the pot and telling Renee things about sugar and eggs. Renee's looking down into the pot and listening. Renee is eighteen years old. She's beautiful, with long dark hair and a smile that makes me feel good. She smiles a lot.

My sister, Faith, is fourteen. She's standing farther away, but she's trying to get closer to see the fudge. She's wearing a white blouse tucked into a black skirt. She's got black shoes and white socks rolled down over her ankles—almost like a uniform or something. She's holding a small pan in her hand. She asks Mommy if she can learn, too. Mommy turns and yells, "Don't bother us!"

Faith's eyes get big and her head pops back. She steps backward five steps. She's still holding her empty pan at her side. Now there are tears in her eyes.

Mommy hurt Faith's feelings really bad. I feel tears stinging in my eyes, too, when I watch Faith. I won't cry because Mommy says big boys don't cry. But why won't Mommy let Faith help?

I want to run out the door because my heart hurts so bad. Instead, I say, "Mommy, say you're sorry. Let Faith help."

"Here, put the sugar back in the cabinet," she tells me. I start climbing on the counter so I can reach the cabinet. Then I'll leave to go fishing.

Mommy starts acting like nothing happened. She does that sometimes. Now she starts singing, "The Bobolink says, well what do you think? Spring is here! Spring is here! Spring is here!" The singing makes me even madder because she's still ignoring Faith. She should say "I'm sorry" to Faith instead.

I tell Mommy, "Just be quiet!" She doesn't look at me or say anything. I feel so hot and mad that I grab the spoon out of the boiling pot and flick the fudge all over the wall behind the stove. I want Faith to fight with her. Then I look at Mommy. She sees me do it but doesn't do anything. She just stares at the spots of fudge on the wall. So I do it again. Still, Mommy does nothing. She just ignores me like she always does.

I start yelling, "Spank me, Mommy! Spank me! I dare you! Do it! Don't you see what I did?"

Mommy just starts shaking her head really slow. She doesn't say anything. She turns off the stove and walks away into her bedroom. Renee and Faith just stand there, looking at the counter.

I feel bad, but I'm going fishing anyway. I'll get my tackle box and never come back.

See Me!

Lonny, my supervisor, was six feet, five inches tall with a completely bald head. He sauntered when he walked like a tranquil giant. He'd slowly roll his massive head side to side like it was anchored on a loose spring. He clearly had his favorites, those he spoke to and those he didn't. He rarely smiled. Maybe his sheer bulk and total indifference were why so many of us were afraid of him.

Our work culture was intense. Tight schedules and fixed deadlines. Hours of concentration on minute details. Highly intelligent people, few with strong people skills. Not the type of culture that especially suited me. I favored relaxed and creative environments with engaging people.

We software engineers sat in bays of four desks apiece. If you looked hard enough, you could see each of us behind stacks of computer printouts. Two or three times a day, Lonny would drift into our bay. He always looked intent, like he had extremely important news to share. He often addressed people formally, using "Mr." or "Mrs." and their last name. He'd talk to the other three people in my bay, never looking at me. I'd try enticing him by leaning into his field of view without seeming overly eager.

My current assignment was to help develop the software for a navigation device for one of the company's largest customers. The customer kept asking if the device would be done on time and our company kept saying yes, even though we were already well behind schedule. For two weeks, our team had been working twelve- to fourteen-hour days, six days a week to get back on schedule. All that time, Lonny never looked at me once.

On Friday, August 14th, my bay mates and I returned from a short walk in the oppressive heat, our shirts still sticking to our bodies. On a whim, before we went back into our bay, I pulled Jack aside. He was the senior engineer among us. I put it to him bluntly. "Doesn't Lonny like me?" I explained what I'd seen and felt since May and how much it irritated me.

Jack was about five feet, eight inches tall with an angular head. Whenever you encountered him, you'd spend the first few seconds trying not to stare at it. He bent slightly forward when he walked, like he was on a mission to get to the bathroom. Whenever he spoke, he'd start with a small grunt to clear his throat. Then he'd pause with hands in pockets, head tilted to the right. He'd look down, pause, then finally speak as if issuing a carefully computed conclusion.

He looked up at me. "Carter, you've only been here for a month. I'd encourage you to give it more time. Perhaps he looks at you, but you don't notice."

No, Jack, I've been here at least three months. Why don't people see me?

Jack turned away and went on talking with the others about his new Ford Fiesta as if our conversation had never occurred. Should I simply believe Jack and ignore my lying eyes? I felt like a juror being told by the judge, "Please disregard that evidence."

Two days later, the final project report was delivered. It was clear we'd met the deadline. Finally, we could relax. We were proud and relieved.

Lonny drifted into our bay. He was actually smiling—it was like meeting him for the first time. He looked at each of my bay mates, Jack, Wally, and Ira, then said, "Gentleman, I commend each of you for your efforts. I, along with the other managers here, am glad you're on our team. I speak for them when I say a sincere 'thank you!'" He looked down and smiled, perhaps pleased with himself that he'd actually sounded appreciative. Then he drifted out.

I gasped out loud and held my breath. He hadn't even looked at me. I stared at the entrance to the bay, waiting for him to come back and attempt an apology. It didn't happen. I turned to my coworkers. They were smiling, enjoying the rare moment of gratitude that had come their way.

This time, no eager puppy routine. I felt the familiar heat rising up. I wasn't afraid of it. I needed it. Lonny didn't think I was important enough to even see me. I didn't exist to him. I wasn't real.

However, he was my boss. I tried hard to think about what to do. Tolerate the situation as a "professional," not make waves, and continue the indignity of being ignored? Or confront him and hold him responsible, and risk getting fired?

My body took over as it had so many times in the past. I strode straight into his office and in a voice like a teacher scolding a pupil, I said, "Lonny?"

He looked up at me and bellowed, "Don't you ever come charging into my office! If you want something from me, you'll talk to me when I'm in your bay!"

For a second, I felt sorry for him. He didn't know that when I was enraged, no one else existed except me.

I stepped forward. "Lonny, you suck at being a boss. You could at least pretend you actually see someone right there in front of your face, especially if it's a new employee who desperately needs your approval. If you don't understand what I'm talking about or if it doesn't seem important enough for you to do, then you might schedule a meeting with Human Resources and ask for some help." I was smiling now.

I stepped closer. "And if you have an issue with me, at least have the courage to say so to my face. If you can't find me, I'm in the first bay down the aisle. You walk right past me every time you come in to talk to my bay mates. Do you understand?"

I stood there staring at him to be sure he'd gotten my message. It seemed he had. His head was tipped back and his mouth was open as if getting ready for the dentist. Then I turned and deliberately drifted out of his office, making a show of slowly rolling my head side to side.

I returned to my bay completely composed. It felt good to finally stand up for myself. I couldn't care less now about what happened to me. I sat down, picked up my latest assignment, and started reading as if I hadn't engaged with him at all.

A half hour later, Wally approached me at the coffee machine. He walked up with his mouth wide open, shaking his head. He seemed to struggle with his breathing, making small gasping sounds. Then he looked both ways to make sure no one was within earshot and whispered, "What was that about? We heard you all the way across the aisle. I might as well say 'goodbye' to you right now, because Lonny will spit you out the door!" He said it like a child taunting another with a secret.

What was he expecting me to say?

"Okay," I said casually, meeting his gaze. He lowered his eyebrows and squinted like he was trying to see inside my head.

"Sorry, Wally. That's all I got." I stepped around him and sauntered away.

He didn't understand. I wanted to be fired. I'd treat this experience as one big mistake. I wasn't meant for this job, anyway. I'd get a new one, working for some small business that would appreciate my skills, where people respected each other, where the bosses actually saw their employees. I felt like I'd gotten out of prison!

Released

Instead of working late, I headed home at five p.m., anticipating the usual long-lasting hug from Teri. This time, though, it would feel like I'd hit the walk-off home run and won the ball game.

She knew my problems with Lonny, so I was excited to tell her my decision. I burst through the door and announced right away, "Love? I'm home. We need to talk! I finally quit my job!" I waited, holding my breath. This will be great!

She came out of the bedroom, walking slowly as if approaching a bonfire. She frowned as if I'd spoken in Swahili. "What did you just say?"

I repeated what I'd said, sure she'd feel greatly relieved. Instead, she leaned forward, hands on hips, and stared deeply into my eyes. She looked pale. Is she actually angry at me? What for? This isn't going like I'd planned.

"Love, I need you to listen to me, to see me." My voice was soft and even, trying to sound calm. I walked with purpose to the couch and patted the cushion next to me. This time, I was speaking English. What doesn't she understand? I patted the cushion again and tried to seem my most inviting, my voice a little chipper and smiling just a little. She strode to the couch, looking like she couldn't decide whether to sit far apart or next to me. So she sat in the middle. I put my hand on her knee.

"Just let me explain, okay?" I told her how Lonny had utterly ignored me and how I'd given him a piece of my mind.

At first, she looked like Lonny when I walked out of his office. Then she was glowering. Then her jaw seemed to sag. She took a deep breath, shook her head and said, "Carter, I can't believe this is happening."

She'd finally caught up with me. She couldn't believe Lonny had been such a jerk today. "Oh, yeah. He's that big of a jerk. Hard to believe, right?"

"Did you actually say that to him? Did you?"

By now, I was losing track. What had I actually said? I'm not sure I remembered. Had I blacked out or something? This wasn't going the way I thought it would.

She was just sitting there staring at the carpet, her eyes teared up and hands squeezed together. The more I watched her, the more confused I got. What's going on? Didn't she understand what I'd been through?

"Teri? This might be one of those times you actually have to give me a reply. I was hoping you'd understand and be glad for me." I was getting pissed. That couldn't happen. One of us needed to stay calm here.

She finally looked up at me. "I'm trying, but I don't know what to say. I feel like you . . ."

Now my heart was ramping up, my breathing getting faster. I wanted to hear her say it. "Like I what? I was yelling too many words? I was hurting people? I was being so mean, so cruel?"

She let out a deep sigh, put up her hands, and said, "You know I'm pregnant. I have to manage my stress and right now, I'm ready to scream. Let's just make dinner and slow all of this down." She stood up and strode into the kitchen.

Clearly, she didn't understand. I followed her into the kitchen and tried to get lost in our kitchen routine. I did the salads. They don't take much skill to do. Lettuce, croutons, cheddar cheese, and dressing. Done. Then two bowls—the off-white ceramic ones, the ones she'd salvaged from her divorce. Done. I made sure she knew I wasn't happy. I didn't have to tell her. I banged the bowls around and tossed the forks on the table to make my point.

She did the rest. Today, it's chicken—that's the meat, or protein portion, as she calls it. Chicken, it's low fat ... and low-cost in case Daddy doesn't have a job. Potatoes baked from the microwave. She hated that because the skins tasted like leather. Tough.

We didn't talk. We tried, but it felt like a bad high school play. What did she think would happen? HR would move me to a different department? I'd get a letter in my personnel file? I'd get sentenced to an anger management workshop?

About fifteen minutes later, she set down her fork and rested her elbows on the table. She folded her hands as if lecturing a small child. "I was at the desk, thinking of how lucky we were to have each other. Now, you're telling me you're quitting your job? Yeah, sounds like you'll have to. Carter, you can't talk to a supervisor like that. Sometimes, it seems like you get so angry inside, even I'm afraid of you. You start this . . . what do I call it? Verbal vomit. Sometimes you don't even remember what you've said." She'd noticed all that?

I sat there in shock. I dropped my fork on my plate. It sounded like a ring of keys turning in a lock. I took another gulp of my water. I was all alone in this. In an attempt at a calm voice, I said, "Okay. Tell me, what do you think I should do? I'm listening." No, I was not. I was thinking about how to get the hell out of here. Out of all of it.

In a carefully measured tone, she said, "First, I think you should apologize. Lonny is an ass, but he didn't deserve all that. He didn't. Carter, you were just being mean." Well, there's that familiar phrase my mom used to say.

"Apologize? And things go back to the way they were? I can't work with someone like that!" Shaking my head, I added, "I won't."

She took a deep breath. "I love you. I will support you in whatever you do. But you just can't quit. Not now. You need at least two years at this job before any company will believe you're stable enough to hire you." Then she picked up her plate, glass, and silverware and headed to the kitchen. I'd been dismissed.

That was it. I'd had enough. "Okay. I'll go back to work Monday to apologize. I'll say I have a mental illness, a problem with rage. That I talked to my wife and she set me straight. She's so much wiser than I am, but I'm so lucky 'cause, gosh, she loves me so much! Then I'll get on my knees and beg his forgiveness. Then you can have your fucking little nest back. You can go on buying your favorite baby clothes. We'll all be so normal again!"

I wanted to explode. Desecrate. Destroy. Scratch at myself. She's so goddamned calm as if she's just parenting me, like I'm a spoiled brat having a tantrum.

She set down the plate, glass, and silverware, then pointed at me. "There, that, Carter. That's what I mean. What you just said to me. You spew out all that hatred at people and it's just . . . mean."

My mind went blank, but my body knew just what to do. I stood up, charged into the bedroom and grabbed what I hoped were some shirts, pants, and underwear. I stuffed them into a bag and barged toward the door. It felt so good, so freeing.

On the way out, I grabbed the car keys, turned, and pretended I was calm. I said, "I love you, but this isn't for me."

There. That was a grand exit. I got her good.

It felt so good to be driving away. Free from that cage. No more role of "husband." No more pretending. I opened my car window to let in the fresh air. I cranked up the radio as loud as it would go. Sure, there'd be details to work out, but I was a survivor if ever there was one.

Fortunately, we still had the apartment we'd lived in before we bought the condo. We'd only been in the apartment three months after graduating from college in mid-May. We still had one month on the lease. That's where I was headed: freedom.

But You Can't Hide

I'm in a recurring lucid dream. The dream of the wolf.

It's always dusk and a full moon is rising. It's warm and comfortable. I'm in the middle of a small meadow. The grass feels lush and soft like a lawn that's not been mowed.

There's a dark blue line of pine trees around me. They circle me like bystanders who know I belong with them. I hear a soft breeze gently brushing across their tops. The air smells like damp moss with a faint touch of mint.

I hear the sounds of rippling water, probably a creek. I turn and head across the meadow toward it. On the way, I realize I'm loping low to the ground. I look down and notice I have paws—small, furry, turned-down toes.

Soon I enter the woods, but now I'm moving along far too fast, gliding low among the trees. They have large roots like mangroves, but I don't smash into any of them. I feel so safe, natural, and free.

The ground slopes down to reveal a small, gently flowing creek about five feet wide bordered by boulders worn smooth from centuries of running water. I hear a symphony of croaking frogs in the background.

I work my way down to the water's edge and look into it. There's the face of a wolf staring back at me. I know it's important for me to study that image, but I don't want to.

I try to turn away, but it feels like a firm hand is pushing my head down, making me look. I yearn for a clearer image, but the moving water warps my portrait.

I give up. I don't want to look at myself. I turn to my left and trot away. It feels colder now.

Who Am I?

I had served my time, been released from that domestic cage. Now I had my freedom.

On the way to the apartment, I drove past downtown Minneapolis. The Jeweled City of the North. Skyscrapers spearing the sky full of endless offices. Places I could find work. "Find work." Now there was a North Dakota phrase. I laughed at myself.

I parked the car, grabbed my clothes, and walked into the familiar place, now almost empty. It was like every other new apartment. The chemical smell of new carpet. White walls everywhere as if you're stuck in a snowstorm. Rhythmic thuds outside the door when someone walks down the hall. We hadn't been living in the apartment for a few weeks now, but it already felt like years to me. We'd left the air conditioner on and now it was damn chilly in here. I turned it off.

Even though I was still angry, I instantly missed Teri when I stepped in. I fought the feeling. I can't go there if I'm to remain free, so I immersed myself in hanging up my clothes. The new fridge was vacant and still smelled like plastic. I'd get plenty of food tomorrow, Saturday.

I sat back in "our" huge, gray, overstuffed lounge chair. It was one of those chairs that, when they were making it, they must have been in a fever of upholstering because they kept stuffing it with cotton. As I sat in it, I realized this was the closest thing to a hug I would get for a long time. For now, it'd have to remain my seclusion, like my den back at Cherry Creek.

I chuckled, remembering the fun we'd had getting that damn chair. She'd seen it when we drove by a yard sale. "Stop! Look at that thing. I think it's a chair! Go back! Go back!" So I drove around the block in our blue and white 1969 Chrysler Newport. We bought the car used from a friend back in Belfield, North Dakota, where I graduated from high school. He wanted two hundred and fifty dollars for it. I liked the guy, so we bargained him up to three hundred. Teri and I laughed every time we thought of that negotiation.

We'd furnished our new condo the same way, driving around town until Teri would yell, "Stop. Go Back! Go back!" She'd have spied some treasure trove of furnishings. We'd haul another load back to the apartment or condo. Back then, I acted like it was a pain, but it really had been pure pleasure. We'd done amazing things together.

Now, sadness and guilt moved over me like an eclipse. I felt like a child whose puppy had died—and I was the one who had killed it. I was beginning to wish I could push a button and instantly be back in the condo, no matter who was right or who was wrong. Instead, here I was sitting in our chair, all alone.

I must have sat there for an hour, trying to convince myself that I had not flown into another blind rage. It was my worst fear: my body waging war and leaving me to deal with the carnage. With Amy, we'd pretended that never happened, but it did, and it took a toll on both of us.

I ached for the bright, happy feelings of Renee's home in Belfield. I daydreamed about the Badlands fifteen miles from her home. Those clay hills always felt more like home than anywhere else. They embraced me like a mother, crazy as that sounds. Rolling mounds of smoke-colored clay with deep, craggy canyons between them. Each hill stacked with bold bands of different colors: coal black, brick red, and burnt orange. I remembered Teri's tears of wonder the first time I was there with her. I never had tantrums—rages—blow-ups—back there.

By now, I was beginning to feel awfully heavy down in that damn chair. My back hurt like it always did when I sat in it, but this heaviness was from far more than physical discomfort. I'd dug myself another hole and this time, I was falling far into it.

My mind kept racing with questions that had no answers. Did she really love me? If so, why hadn't she listened to me? Did I really love her? If I did, then what was I doing here? Was it my fault? Hers? It's got to be somebody's fault. This had to make sense somehow. I missed my black-and-white view of the world. It was usually so clear, but now it was so gray. Before, all the questions were answered with "yes" or "no." Now, they're also answered with "yes and no" and even "maybe."

The phone rang. We'd left it connected in case we needed it when we were moving things out. It kept ringing. I knew it was her, but I couldn't talk to her. Not now. It was too soon. If I picked it up now, my raging anger might come back. More likely, I'd start apologizing just to get all of this over with.

I wanted to feel good again right now. I called my old friend, Lloyd. Whenever we talked to each other, we'd end up laughing. We shared the same irreverent views about the world. We both had mothers who few people would call normal. We had no fathers to temper our crazy mothers, so we did the best we could. We saw ourselves as the normal ones and the rest of humanity as clowns on a stage.

Lloyd had been known to take a strong stance in his advice to me, but afterward, if things turned to shit for me, he'd deny that he ever shared an opinion. "You should go to therapy!" "Oh, it didn't work out? I told you not to go!" So I often had to take him with a grain of salt.

"Hello? Oh . . . Lloyd, huh? Sorry, I must have dialed the wrong number. Well, since I accidentally called you, we might as well talk." It was so good to be so irreverent.

He was already laughing. "You calling this late, you must be in trouble. What did you do? I bet it's with your wife, right?"

I felt my anxiety ebb and my shoulders relax.

"It'd be hard to explain, especially to you, but I'll just jump right in and get to the point." I paused for effect. "Yeah, it's with my wife. I'm right, she's wrong. There. Done."

Now he was laughing even harder. "Yeah, I wish it was that easy with my wife. From now on, I'll just say to her, 'Carter says I'm right and you're wrong, so there!' She'll say to me what I've always said should be on your tombstone: 'Here Lies Carter McNamara, the Bastard.'"

"Okay, Lloyd. I need to explain this situation. I've even confused myself. We need to get serious." The word "serious" always sent us into hysterics and now was no different. After we calmed down, I said, "C'mon, put that graduate degree in therapy to use. It's time to give me some help. I mentioned my boss, Humpty Dumpty, to you before. Lonny? How he thinks I'm invisible? I've been telling you for weeks I'm gonna confront him big time. Well, I finally did it."

By now, he was in hysterics again. As he tried to catch his breath, he squeaked out, "Okay, so now you're without a job. Are you without a wife, too?" More laughter.

"Well, I'd like to tell you I quit and Teri agrees with me completely, but . . ."

Between guffaws, he finished my sentence for me. "But that's not true!"

"Well, Lloyd, before you so rudely interrupted me, I was gonna say the same thing. Now, if you'll just listen, I'll explain the situation so you can give me the simple answer, and I can go home and get back to work on Monday."

"Okay, I'm listening."

That was hard to believe because he was still laughing, if only a bit more softly.

I took advantage of the lull and said, "I told him off. I told him that his ignoring me was certainly not a state-of-the-art management technique. But he didn't need to panic because he could always take a course in people skills."

Lloyd howled. I realized that this was not what I'd said to Lonny, but I couldn't remember what I'd actually said.

He settled down enough to ask, "What does Teri think?"

"Well, that's not all of it." I waited for Lloyd to start up again, but he didn't. He realized I was in far bigger trouble than I'd said. "I came home and told Teri I was quitting my job."

There was a long pause. He was no longer laughing. "So you really are without a job and a wife. You're not staying with me, you know."

This time, I didn't respond with "seriously" because I genuinely needed him to be serious.

"I'm sitting in my old apartment feeling like a total fuck-up. I'm not worried about the job. I'm worried about . . ." What was I worried about? Face it. I was most worried about losing Teri. I wasn't hours ago, but I was now. "I'm worried Teri's seen a side of me that she can't forgive. Until now, she thought I was this wise, worldly person who she was so lucky to be married to."

"No. She's not that dumb. Seriously." This time, neither of us was laughing. "My advice? Come back home to Bismarck for a week. Get some space. Take some time for yourself. Pretend you're not even married if you have to. Figure out how you got yourself into such a shitty job and with a wife who won't even let you leave it. And, if you get a divorce, get a good lawyer. Good night."

It took me a while to absorb his advice. It felt affirming to have someone agree with me to just take flight. The challenge would be living with myself afterward. I felt like I was stuck in that middle ground between the thoughts in your head and the feelings in your heart.

What about my heart? To deal with that, I needed to call Renee. Whether she knew it or not, everything good I'd learned about life, I learned from her. She was a mentor to me. She'd worked hard to stop passing the craziness down through our families.

As I was dialing, I realized it was late there. She might be sleeping. How could I get any compassion if she was pissed at me?

"Hmm, hello?"

We knew each other's voices so well there was no need to identify ourselves. In my most apologetic voice, I said, "I woke you up, didn't I?"

"No, I was just reading." No, she wasn't. I see she's still the people-pleasing sister. "Are you okay?" She was always concerned about me.

"No." I launched into my story. Lonny the jerk. Me hating my job. Teri not letting me quit. Me here alone back in the apartment. Should I leave my marriage?

Renee never directly gave me advice. She didn't want to insult me by acting like she had all the answers and I didn't. "Carter, you've got a partner, an Old Soul, like a wise old friend. It's gotten you through times that would've crushed most people. I'm sure you'll do what's best for you and your family. You don't want them to go through what we kids did. At first, it might be tough to do what's right, but you'll be glad you did." Then she paused for that to sink in. "I love you. Good night."

She had just alluded to what might be best for me and assumed I would hear it if I was ready for it. In Renee-speak, she had told me to get back home.

I hung up and sat there mulling over the advice from Renee and Lloyd. My thoughts were disjointed. What should I do? Go back to the marriage and that awful job or claim the freedom I had now? That freedom was beginning to feel like an illusion. I actually thought I'd drive away and turn off my love for Teri like a faucet and then I'd see the baby every other weekend. What was wrong with me? I felt guilty for blindsiding her with that terrifying rage. I wondered how confused and frightened she must be, how worried about me she must be feeling. I needed to take a good, long look at myself.

What should I do? How do people decide these things? List the pros and cons? Do a spreadsheet? Throw darts? Talk to a friend? Go with your gut? Ask your dad for advice? Well, that's not an option.

I needed a win-win situation where I wouldn't have to apologize or admit I was wrong. I hadn't figured out how to make that happen yet. For now, the best option was to go back home tomorrow and pretend none of this had happened. Get back to being normal.

I'm Busted

The next morning, Saturday, August 15th, I stood outside our condo building. I felt like I was facing a minefield and on the other side was our relationship.

I was hoping she'd still be sleeping so I could sneak in without having a fuss. Instead, when I quietly opened the front door, she was standing right there in our walk-through kitchen making tea. She hadn't brushed her hair yet. She moved in slow motion. Her head down. Eyes blinking slowly. No eye contact.

Without turning to me, she said simply, "Good morning." She squeezed the tea bag, took it out of the cup and tossed it in the garbage.

"Good morning," I responded evenly, trying to set the tone. I just wanted things back to normal, to joke around, maybe even bump into each other a few times until we could do a heart-felt hug. But that would have to wait. Who knows? Maybe she understood by now that I needed to quit my job. I didn't want to keep explaining it to her.

I had to get her away from the scene of the crime. Loud restaurants are a great way to avoid conversation. "Let's just have some breakfast. Let's go out."

For a long moment she acted like she hadn't heard me. Then, still without looking at me, she replied, "That sounded good, but I've got a bit of a headache again. Sorry. How about I make some eggs." That didn't sound like a question. This was not going well.

We sat through the breakfast she had made just the way I liked it: two eggs over easy and runny so I could smear my dry wheat toast through it. My gut took over when my brain would not. I was famished.

I began to feel normal again, confident we could get back to what we had before. We'd joke about having a screaming baby and who would take care of it during the night. We'd rush through our routine to get to work. Before leaving, we'd look back and marvel at how beautiful our new home had become. Then we'd look at each other, smile, and glide out the door.

After setting the dishes in the sink, she came up behind me, touched my shoulder, and said, "I'm glad you're home." She paused. "I don't want to fight like that ever again." Another pause. "But I do want to talk about your job. It doesn't have to be a fight. I just want to understand. Okay? Did you stay in the apartment last night?" I hoped I'd get back in without a hassle. Damn. She's not gonna let that happen.

"Yeah, I wanted to be alone and think." I wanted to sound reasonable, like I had a good excuse for barging out the door. Instead, I sounded lame and felt embarrassed. I wanted to come off better than that, so I turned to her and said, "Look. I want to start by apologizing for barging out. I was so wound up from Lonny ignoring me." There, I even apologized. Maybe that'll steer this discussion to Lonny and not me.

That didn't happen.

"I agree. You've been very patient. I'm so lucky that my boss is a reasonable human being. I like him. But I'm hoping we can talk about us now. Do you realize we've been married less than a month? We've known each other longer, sure. But, even for me having been married before, this is a newly committed relationship. Thanks for putting up with me."

I didn't get the feeling that she was leading up to an apology. That last sentence sounded like there'd be a "but" after it. This is like the part in a trial where the judge says, "Although you've been a good citizen, sentencing guidelines still apply."

"Carter, I just want to understand something." She sat down and took my hand. "First, I want to know if coming back here today means you're totally committed to me, to this marriage, and our lives together. I don't want to take us for granted, but I want to be able to count on us."

I thought of a myriad of ways to detract, distract, and delay. Then I remembered how lonely I had felt back in the apartment. I had ached to be with her. I remembered the hard questions that I asked myself, none with any answers. Most of all, I remembered Renee's soulful advice.

I squeezed Teri's hand. "Love, you can count on me. I am committed to you, our marriage, and our lives together . . . and that scares the shit out of me." Now I had that dreaded stinging in my eyes that meant I would cry. I couldn't. Ever.

She squeezed my hand in return. "I'm scared, too, but I'd have you. I'd have us and we'd have each other." She'd said it like she was reminding me of something quite important that I had forgotten . . . and I had. "And since you're committed to me, then I need you to involve me in anything that will affect us. No more impulsive decisions. No more deciding to quit your job and then letting me know afterward. No more fights like that. They terrify me. When you are angry, let me know why right away. But without the yelling and the sarcasm."

Without thinking, I said, "Yes. I promise."

She tilted her head sideways as if she hadn't heard me. Before I could repeat myself, she asked, "Carter, do you really? You know what this means?"

I thought about what she was asking of me. Involve her in my decision-making? Sure, I could get better at that. Handle my anger better and avoid more fights like this? I wasn't so sure. That rage was buried deep in my body, stemming from a childhood she would never know about. She had asked about my childhood before, but I had successfully avoided any truthful answers.

"I'll try really hard . . . and I'll keep on trying." I couldn't have sounded more truthful because it was the truth.

"Thank you." She got up, kissed the top of my head, and said, "Now let's do the dishes together."

Maybe we were back to normal.

Out in the Cold

Bang! Bang! Bang!

It's the middle of the night. What's she doing this time? I thought she was passed out. I hate nighttime. It's always when Mom gets weird.

I push myself out of my bed and wrap my old gray robe around me. I'm twelve and tall for my age. I've had this robe since I was nine, so now it looks more like a small shirt on me.

I find her in our tiny kitchen. It's like a small hallway with a little table and three chairs squeezed against one side and with a counter, sink, and stove crammed onto the other.

She's standing over the table, wearing her dingy old pink nightgown, the one with a strap hanging down from her shoulder. Her arm is raised and she's holding a small metal saucepan. She looks like a pale statue with thin straggly hair.

Her head is down near the top of the table, as if she's carefully looking for something on it. She isn't wearing her glasses, so she's squinting hard.

"Gotta kill the grasshoppers," she mumbles. It's hard to understand her. Her mouth is very dry and keeps making smacking noises like pulling sticks out of the mud.

She stops, stares at a spot on the table, and then slams the pan down on it. Without looking at me, she tells me, "Go get Axel." He's her brother who's been dead for seventeen years.

When I was too young to go to school, I felt sorry for her because she was so sick in bed all the time. She'd say it was because she had "nerves" and because people had been "so cruel to her." I got older and now I know it's because she drinks and takes drugs all the time. I don't feel sorry for her anymore.

I gently put my hand on her shoulder and tell her the grasshoppers are gone now. I take the pan and set it down, then take her back to her bedroom. It's a small room with no doors. The smell of her piss hits me the moment we come in. If I don't change the bed now, the smell will be all over the house.

My sister Faith lives with us, but she's working an overnight shift. Besides, she's so good at just ignoring Mom.

I sit Mom down onto the tiny stool by her dresser and tell her to stay there. I can do this bed routine in my sleep. If I do it quick enough, I'll forget about it in the morning. I hate touching anything on her bed. It reminds me of when I grabbed a dead old bird one time when I was bagging leaves. My fingers went into the bird and I almost threw up.

I grab the jug of bleach and a rag from the kitchen. I pull off the quilt and blanket and toss them onto the floor. I carefully peel off the wet sheet, take it through the kitchen and out the back door into the shed.

It's winter in North Dakota. When you're outside, it's so cold you can see your breath. It comes out in small misty clouds. If you don't wear your parka with the hood up, you can freeze your ears off. Same with your fingers if you don't wear your mittens. The wet sheet will freeze soon, but we still don't have a washing machine. I'll deal with the sheet later.

When I come back in, I find her standing and holding the jug of bleach. My fault. I should've been more careful. She could've drunk it and killed herself.

I take the jug, sit her back down, and tell her to stay there. I pull off the yellow plastic shower curtain that we put onto her mattress so it won't get wet if she pisses her bed again. I grab the jug and rag and start wiping down the curtain. The bleach always stings my nose and makes my eyes water.

Mom starts mumbling again, this time louder, about being a genius, doing so much for everyone, and that no one understands her. Then she stands up, grabs me, and pulls me backward. I spill some of the bleach onto the worn-out carpet. It'll make a white spot. Who cares? I sit her back down onto the stool, harder this time. I grab another sheet to put back on the bed.

She stands up again. Now she's yelling for my sister, Renee. She used to be the one who took care of Mom, but she moved out when she got married six years ago. Good for her. My brother Mac quit high school just so he could get out.

I tell Mom that Renee isn't here and I sit her back down onto the stool, harder. She gets up again and pushes me, yelling at me to stop being so cruel.

My heart is racing and my face is really hot. I get Mom's coat from the closet, wrap it around her, pull her through the kitchen, and shove her out into the shed. She falls down onto her hands and knees.

"Stay there!"

I just need one more minute. I lock the shed door and walk back into the bedroom. I put the curtain and new sheet onto the bed, then throw the blanket and quilt back onto it. Done.

I sit down onto the stool. If I can calm myself down without her in here, maybe I can get back to sleep and go to school tomorrow. Before I leave her bedroom, I remember to look around for wine bottles. We always pour them out. My sisters and I think that men bring them to her when we're not home. I don't find any, so I make my way back to my bed, take off my robe, and collapse on my bed. I promise myself that next time, I'll just lock her outside right away so I can get the job done sooner.

I lie down and close my eyes. Then I remember. She's still outside. I jump up to get her back in. She could freeze to death out there. How could I have forgotten her? I get so angry sometimes that I don't know what I'm doing.

What if I don't get her? She'd be out of our lives forever. Even when she's sober, she just sits in her bedroom reading her tiny paperback books, smoking her stinky Kent cigarettes. When we get home, we never know if she'll be passed out and pissing herself, or vomiting again. When she sobers up, she'll blame it all on us and the world for being so cruel to her.

But if she dies, the cops could blame it on me. They could put me in the state hospital and give me shocks on my brain like Mom said they did to her. I have to learn to not get so angry or I'll get in trouble.

I rush out to get her. When I open the door, she's in the corner of the shed curled into a little ball, her knees up to her chest and her arms wrapped around them. At first, I worry that she's dead because her eyes are closed. As I get closer, I see she's shivering, so I know she's alive.

She whispers, "It's so cold. It's so cold."

I pull her up and drag her into the house. I pull back the blanket and then put her on her bed. I keep her coat on her and cover her up again.

I go back to my own bed. Now I'm wide awake. Maybe I don't need to wait until I am old enough to move out. Maybe there's another way to get out of this mess. I need to figure out how to get away with it.

Mom always tells us, "Don't tell other people about what goes on in our house." Now I know why she says that.

Exposed

After my heart-to-heart with Teri about my blow-up with Lonny, our weekend was normal. Meals, shopping, TV, and hugging. I kept thinking of the parable of the leaky roof. When it's raining, it's too wet to fix the roof. The best time to fix it is when it's dry. I was the leaky roof—and it wasn't raining. The best time to fix my blow-ups was when I wasn't having one, but what do I do about them?

I should've felt guilt, fear, and dread about going into work, but I didn't because whether or not I was fired, I still had Teri.

The following Monday, I went in, expecting to find the pink slip on my desk telling me to "go straight to Human Resources." No problem. That would be the first step to getting out of here.

There was indeed a note on my desk. "Mr. McNamara, please come to my office." Signed, Lonny. My bay mates had probably seen Lonny leave the note. No one looked at me, no one greeted me. Like soldiers being careful about getting too close to each other in case one of them got killed, my colleagues were steering clear of a casualty.

I set down my satchel, picked up the note, and started toward his office. I wasn't afraid. I knew this was for the best. I'd stand in his office and let him get his pound of flesh. I'd remind myself that I survived worse and this is for the best. Then I'm outta here. After all, I only said to Lonny what he needed to hear, but he didn't need to hear it the way I said it. I'd apologize for that. Then Lonny and HR could do their thing.

I slowed down. What if I just walked out the door? That would save everyone a lot of drama. I could spend the day alone while Teri was at work. I could write my resignation letter. I could write that I was fed up with Lonny, that I'd decided to just quit. I'd do like my mother, blame it on someone else. Then I'd polish my resume and drop off copies at other companies. I'd tell Teri what I did when she got home. She'd be pissed because I violated the pact I'd made with her days earlier.

I paused, conflicted. Nothing to gain if I go in, but something to lose if I don't. Teri would be disappointed. She'd wish I had done what I promised. I'd better stay in her good graces.

I walked into his office, feeling like a child sent to apologize for stealing candy. Lonny was in his chair, looking at some paperwork, the palm of each hand on a cheek, like he was struggling to read. He looked up.

"Good morning, Mr. McNamara. Please come in. Close the door."

I did as he ordered. Then he sat back in his chair and said, "You can be a frightening fella." He'd said it in a pleasant but offhanded kind of way, like, "I had a good lunch today."

I didn't know how to respond. First of all, I was stunned that somebody—my boss who did my performance evaluations—had confronted me about my anger. Second, I hadn't expected this hulk of a man to be afraid of me.

"Lonny, I'm sorry for being so disrespectful. I shouldn't have been sarcastic. I can understand you don't want someone like me on your team."

He sat forward and put out the palm of his hand to stop me. Now I was genuinely confused. I was trying to help him fire me. Why had he stopped me?

He sat back again, put his massive hands on his stomach, and took a deep breath. "I thought about what you said about my needing people skills. Interesting you should say that because HR told me the same thing. I was a damn good engineer. I got promoted to supervisor because of that. But this job is completely different. This job is working with people and not with numbers." He sounded reflective, not angry. "So I suppose I should be grateful you reminded me that I needed to improve."

He sat forward again. He suddenly sounded stern. "But I don't appreciate how you said it. You were just plain mean." Then he waited for that to sink in. It did. I'd been trying for years to escape that label. Evidently, I wasn't very good at it.

"Carter, I'm being patient and forgiving about how you talked to me. I deserve to be as frank with you now as you were with me, but I'll do it differently." He paused for effect. "You were in some kind of rage back there. Words were coming out of your mouth like wildfire. Carter, you attacked me like some kind of animal, like a wolf. I'll admit, it scared me—and it should scare you. You're a good engineer. You'll be a better man if you can take care of that problem of yours. I hope you'll seriously think about it and do something about it." Then he sat forward and looked down at his papers. I'd been dismissed.

That goddamned stinging started in my eyes, so I rose to my feet and turned to walk away. I stopped just inside his door, turned, and said sincerely, "Thank you, Lonny."

When I got home that evening, Teri was waiting expectantly for my report. I was still so baffled that Lonny hadn't fired me, I didn't know what to say.

"Well, did you get fired or what?"

"No, I didn't get fired. In fact, he even admitted I was right, that he needed better people skills. He also said, though, he didn't appreciate how I talked to him. Then he told me to get back to work. But I did apologize to him today, and I still have my job." I didn't say that he told me I had a problem with my anger and that I needed to take care of it. I didn't need to tell Teri that. She already knew.

"Carter, that's such a relief. You need to be careful about your anger."

I looked away in frustration and shame. I was still that cruel child despite my efforts to hide it. I felt exposed.

Two Sides to the Story

Labor Day weekend, 1981. I'd have to be on top of my game to survive this trip.

Teri and I were driving west to Belfield where Renee lived. Teri would be meeting my sister Faith for the first time. Faith's mission in life was to convince Renee and me that Mom wasn't all that bad, that she had her good side, too. I fervently hoped Faith would leave her campaign out of this visit.

I loved long trips in the car—the feeling of distance and movement with changing lanes between cars all going the same direction. I sipped my coffee, strong and nutty with a hint of vanilla. The aroma permeated the air. Silence and serenity. No one could intervene.

Teri was five months pregnant and uncomfortable. She was constantly moving forward, backward, sideways, then forward again.

"Should we just pull over and pop that little person out?" I asked her.

She was too involved in her situation to laugh at my joke.

Finally, she sat back and sighed, as if to give up. Looking at the road ahead of us, she said, "I've met Renee, but not Mac. His real name is Dion, right?"

Oh no, not more digging into my family. Sure, she deserved to know more, but not right now. "Honey, can we talk later? I love this drive. The rolling green hills are so peaceful." I stressed the word *peaceful*. I turned back to the road again. We'd see if she got my message.

She stayed quiet, then started shuffling around again. I wished I could help somehow, so I acquiesced.

"Let's see. What about Mac?" I laughed. "Think of the Peanuts character Charlie Brown. He has some failures in life. They frustrate him a lot, but he keeps on trying. Everybody who knows him likes him. That's Mac. I barely remember him; he was so much older than me. I hope you get to meet him sometime."

I didn't add that he loved his Budweiser. He could drink a six-pack in the time it took someone else to drink two beers. The first couple he'd be smiling, strumming his guitar. Then he'd sink into a dark place. Cursing, snapping, yelling, then leaving. When he was home, he and Mom fought constantly. I'd run out the door and down to the creek. Renee remembers Mac as a boy, pleading with Mom not to hit him with the baseball bat. If she'd tried that with me, the bat would've been on Mom.

"I do, too. I know I'll love him if he's like you. What about Faith?"

Dammit, Teri! Faith is more difficult to talk about.

"So, what about Faith? Right. When she was nineteen, she started working as a bookkeeper. She learned the books on her own. She's got two kids. Darilyn is twelve and Dion is nine. Faith is authentic. What you see is what you get. She says what's on her mind. Sometimes the discussion might bounce around a lot and you'll hear me try to get things back on track. Still, you'll like her a lot." I meant what I said.

I thought about what I would not say. Faith was amazingly good at staying away from Mom. When Mom did notice her, she'd start criticizing or raging on her. Faith started taking diet pills in 1965 or 1966. They turned her into a raving lunatic. She'd rush around the house in jerky motions, sometimes talking to herself. Renee helped Faith move out in 1967. Frankly, I was pleased to see her go. It was much quieter that way.

I noticed two combines harvesting a crop. Wheat? I rolled down my window just enough to smell the cut straw—like freshly cut grass, but mustier. I rolled it back up and let my mind wander. Working on farms was far from studying computer printouts like I was doing now. I wanted a job like farming—nurturing, making a difference for people. Now was not the time to say that. No, now we needed stability. I'd been sentenced to at least two years in this job. I looked back at the road and forced my mind to think of better things.

"What am I going to do with this?" she asked, squirming and pointing to the bump on her belly. We both laughed. Maybe the questions are over now.

"So what about your mother? She's my mother-in-law and I don't know anything about her."

Dammit, Teri! This will be the most difficult to talk about. "Love, I hadn't seen much of her before she died five years ago. She stayed home and read a lot. Loved Kent cigarettes. Drank coffee so thick, the grounds stuck in her teeth. Then she'd complain she couldn't sleep." I forced a chuckle, trying to sound affectionate.

"If she didn't work, then where did you get money to live on?"

"We were on welfare, but that usually ran out before the end of the month. I'd catch fish and bring them home. Sometimes the baker would let me sweep floors and pay me with old bread. We'd get some government subsidy food like big tubs of peanut butter and powdered milk. Once in a while, she sold a painting or some poems. Maybe Mac, Renee, or Faith chipped in."

"I hated powdered milk when we had to use it. That must have been tough, but it sounds like you and your mom were resourceful. What else did you learn from her?" I'd never been asked that before. I glanced at her. She was looking at me, her head tipped to the side with a slight smile.

I needed the perfect answer, believable for her and truthful for me. "She taught me the importance of always being honest, respectful, and taking responsibility for yourself."

"She sounds wonderful."

We pulled into Belfield nine hours after we'd left home. When I got out of the car, my legs felt like clay. Everything moved slower, including my thoughts. It looked like every grasshopper in North Dakota had slammed against our windshield.

Teri and I slogged into the house where Renee, her husband, LeeRoy, and Faith were sitting at the kitchen table. Our entrance caused a commotion of scraping chairs and congestion at the door. My first priority was to introduce Teri to Faith.

She'd already experienced LeeRoy's charm during a visit back in April. He told me she was "beautiful and smart, too." I felt like he was saying that privately, one man to another, even though it was a sexist thing to say.

I put my arm on Teri's shoulder and introduced her to Faith. Faith gushed and Teri glowed. LeeRoy bellowed, "Well, hello there. What happened to your tummy?" He patted the bump, then hugged her. I stood there and watched the beautiful dance of welcome. My family.

LeeRoy reached out to shake my hand. He and Renee had taken me in during my last three years of high school when Mom was committed to the state hospital again. During those years, Renee had been her usual nurturing self. LeeRoy, a broad-shouldered and muscular man, had been brusque and impersonal. He was the only father figure I'd ever had, and I was terrified of him. Standing there shaking his hand now, I felt seen and affirmed.

Renee approached me for her hug. She was five feet, five inches tall with soft hazel eyes and chestnut hair. I wrapped my arms around her and held her in my heart. Next was Faith. Her hugs were always sincere . . . long and close. She was the same height as Renee, but with more striking features. Hazel eyes, larger and more penetrating. Darker hair, tinged in red, more like our mother's. Where Renee was reserved, Faith thought out loud.

I said, "It's good to be together." This was one of the few times the three of us had been together since Mom died five years before.

LeeRoy took the cue. "I'm going for coffee. How long will you folks be here?"

"For two full days, leaving Monday morning," I replied. He nodded, then was out the door. He always marched to his own drummer.

Renee had already made coffee and her homemade caramel rolls were on the table. Her rolls were always soft, sweet, puffy, and moist. Perfect with strong black coffee. But Belfield coffee was more like dirty water. When served in a white cup, you could see through to the bottom.

"Anyone heard from Mac?" I asked.

"No, I assume he's still working at the Farmers Union in Williston," Renee replied.

"Oh, poor Mac," Faith sighed. There wasn't much to say about Mac. This was our refrain. He dealt with chaos and conflict by walking out the door. We hardly knew him.

The next few hours were sounds of family: short stories, quick questions, and laughter. Renee shared updates about her girls, Adrienne, LaRae, and Rhonda, ages ten, thirteen, and sixteen. My sisters caught up on their children's lives.

Thankfully, Faith hadn't started any speeches about Mom. I thought about pulling her aside, asking her to keep it that way.

"How's the pregnancy going?" Renee asked.

Teri rolled her eyes at the annoyance of the symptoms. As she mentioned each one, she'd point to it. Heartburn, headaches, back pain, leg cramps. To feign the drama of it all, she looked up and ran the back of her hand across her forehead with a deep sigh. Then we all burst out laughing. This must be what family is like . . . and I had one. I just needed to get used to it.

My reverie was broken when Faith suddenly asked, "Carter, remember when Mom used to play checkers with you? You both loved that!" Her tone was pleading for me to agree.

I snapped at her. "Yeah, Faith, I remember winning all the time. I asked Mom if she was letting me win and she'd said no. I also remember Renee telling Mom that she should quit letting me win and Mom said there was no harm in that. I remember my sadness and never wanting to play with her again."

I glanced quickly at Teri, afraid she noticed my tone. She had. She was frowning at me as if to say, "What the hell was that about?"

I'd better act fast. "Faith, I'm sorry I snapped at you. I'm dragged out from that drive."

Faith smiled as if to accept my apology but then turned back to Teri and continued. "Mom was a good person. She was a painter and a poet. She was just sick with alcoholism and drug addiction. And they didn't have good care for her in those days. I hope you know that. Mom took care of the four of us. Her husband, Robert McNamara, was not helpful at all." She giggled nervously, looked around at us, and added, "I still call Robert 'Daddy.'" Then she looked down at the table and fidgeted with her coffee cup.

Dammit, Faith! How do I unring this bell? My heart started racing and my hands clenched into fists. I held my breath and looked at Teri. Her face had softened, leaving a faint frown, enough to let me know I should've told her about Mom. She turned back to Faith and nodded as if to invite more.

"I didn't know that," she said.

So many options were racing through my mind. Say nothing? Let the conversation take its course, then suffer the long drive home, getting drilled about my past? No way. Tell her everything about Mom? About me? Those details would never leave her head. What would she think of me? No, too risky. What would my friend Lloyd do? Tell her a half-truth and change the subject? Exactly.

As easily as Faith could interrupt, she could be interrupted. "Faith, you made some good points about Mom. She did pretty good, as you pointed out. Thank you. I want another caramel roll." I turned to get one.

Then, as usual, Renee saved the situation. "Teri, I was hoping you'd take a look at what I'm doing wrong with my plants out back. I can raise kids, but I can't grow plants." She pointed the way to her backyard. Teri looked at me long enough to make me squirm, then followed Renee out the door.

I turned to Faith. "I haven't told Teri a lot about Mom yet. I'm going to, but when the time is right. Please don't dig into that anymore. It could cause a lot of confusion. Okay?"

"I'm sorry. I didn't know. But you and Renee need to see the good in Mom, too."

I held up my hand to interrupt her. "I know, Faith. Will you promise me now, though, that you won't say more about that during this visit?"

"Yeah, sure. I'm sorry, I was just—"

"That's okay. You meant no harm. I love you." Although she was tactless, she had a pure heart.

Renee and Teri came back into the kitchen. Renee said, "I need to write down all this good advice." She grabbed a small pad to start writing.

I waited till she was done writing. "Renee, now's a good time to show me your dying plants, too. I'm always amused at your efforts."

We took our cups out back and over to her garden. She pointed at the array of shriveled, droopy leaves and we both laughed.

"Do you ever wonder how you ever got here? This family? This safety? If it could disappear tomorrow?"

"Every day." She looked off in the distance.

"Do you ever tell anyone about Mom, what we grew up with?"

"Oh, God no. Not the details. I never will. You?"

"Oh God, no. Never."

We both stood there absorbing what we'd said, then walked back into the house.

The next day was relaxation and the joy of family: sleeping late, playing with the kids, and card games with the adults. We siblings never brought up our past again. I knew Teri would on our way back home, though. An hour into our drive, I glanced at her. "Are you okay?"

She knew I was asking about the visit and was quiet for a few seconds. "Yes. I like both of them a lot . . ." I knew more was coming. "I didn't know about your mother. That she was an alcoholic and a drug addict."

"Yeah, it sounds worse than it is. Lots of people have parents like that. You learn to live with it."

"I want you to know you can tell me anything. I want an honest and open relationship with you." She didn't have to say more. She knew something wasn't being said and she wanted to hear it.

It was just a matter of when.

"You wear a mask,
and your face grows to fit it."

– George Orwell

Part 2
Haunted by My Past

(1982-1985)

"Life can only be understood backwards;
but it must be lived forwards."

– Soren Kierkegaard

Carter McNamara

A Big Change Is Coming

It was five days before Christmas, 1981. I was driving around the chain of lakes in Minneapolis. Cedar Lake. Lake of the Isles. Lake Calhoun. Lake Harriet. Teri was in the passenger seat, hands resting on her pregnant belly. It seemed that we always had a serious talk whenever we drove around the lakes. I could feel one coming on now.

One difference between Teri and me was that I would feel an entire experience. Bright, crisp sunlight glistening on the snow like tiny diamonds. A fairy land of holiday decorations. All around: feelings of energy, joy, and gratitude. In our car: affection, safety, and companionship.

In contrast, Teri would notice the details. "Look at the little girl pulling that big sled onto the ice. Her brother tried to help, but the little girl pushed him away. She wants to do it herself. You go, girl! Oh, see the snowman? It's got a pocket and buttons. I wish I had the camera! I love a great snowman!"

Suddenly, she grabbed her stomach. I glanced at her. "You okay?"

She smiled. Nothing to worry about. She'd felt a strong kick from the baby. Three more weeks and we'd be parents.

As if on cue, she said, "We should talk about getting ready." She sounded like a teacher telling the class, "Now we're gonna color in our books!"

I took a sip from my dark roast coffee, piping hot even in winter. "We've been talking about it ever since we started the birthing classes. What more is there to talk about? How about just enjoying the ride?" Am I being over-confident about being a dad? How would I know? I could feel her eyes on me.

She said, "Let's talk about our lives. This will be a big change, but we're good at adapting. Look at how well we've handled all the stresses over the past six months. New city, new jobs, new condo, new car." She smiled. "New marriage. But we haven't had a good talk about how we feel about the big change that's coming. How do you feel about being a dad?"

Wow, she'd hit the bullseye on her first shot! She asked that question because she knew it'd get me hooked right away. Still looking at the road, I answered, "My best friend, Stevie, and I learned to ride bikes together. We must have been six years old. I hated training wheels and took them off right away. I learned fast by falling over a lot. Stevie's mother wouldn't let him take them off. It took him forever to learn. I'm tired of reading books about being a dad. I want the training wheels off. I want to start the real thing."

I could still feel her eyes on me.

"Okay, good, because it will be chaos. There'll be messes and you hate clutter. We'll make mistakes, but you're such a perfectionist. We'll need to share parenting, but you always want to do things yourself. Promise me you'll ask for help."

I thought about what she'd said. All of it was true. I glanced at her and then back to the road. Was I dealing with the baby by not dealing with it? Was I burying the entire topic? More to myself than her, I said, "Sure, I'll need to be realistic and patient about what we can do, especially about what I can do myself. It won't happen overnight, but I promise I will ask for help."

She let out a deep sigh. "What if we have another big disagreement like we had about you quitting your job?" She was actually wondering if I would drive away from our marriage again.

With my mother, I could do anything and she wouldn't notice. It was as if I wasn't even there. I grew sick of being ignored. But Teri noticed me and she hadn't forgotten when I drove away. I felt ashamed and appreciated at the same time.

I paused, not because I wasn't sure of my answer, but because I couldn't find the right words to say. I pulled over to the curb and looked at her. "Love, that night alone in the apartment, after I drove away, was the worst night of my life. I learned a lesson that sank deep into my soul. It wasn't just missing you. I remember the image of you standing in the doorway, watching me drive away. I loathed myself for doing that to you, to us." I could feel the familiar stinging in my eyes, but I would not cry.

I pulled onto the road again. I waited until the next stop sign to turn and say, "Teri, I'm so sorry for that night." She took my hand and squeezed.

"So now, how about you? How do you feel about the baby?" I should've waited to ask that because now she was staring out the window, engrossed in watching three kids lying on their backs in the snow, waving their arms up and down to make snow angels. I knew she would narrate their every action.

"See those three kids . . ."

After she stopped describing the scene, she said, "Well, you know by now that I don't mind some clutter." We laughed with affection at her many piles of it. "I know I'll make mistakes. Maybe now you'll help me be more responsible for those rather than you quietly blaming yourself. Also, I'll need your help sharing tasks because I take on too much, too. So you're ready to embrace a baby?"

I knew she meant more than hugging the baby.

"Thank you for starting this conversation. I'm ready now more than ever."

That was the only thing I'd said that wasn't true. Instead, I felt like I was on a giant rocket that would soon shoot me into space.

Fade to Black

It is April 1965. Soon, we can play outside without parkas. I'm daydreaming about visiting my niece, Darienne. I'm in the sixth grade and Mrs. Borgen is my teacher. I'm so excited I can't concentrate. Darienne is Renee's little girl. She's two and half years old. Darienne is the first person that I really feel good to be with since Renee had to go when she got married.

Whenever Darienne sees me, she comes to me right away and puts her fingers in my hair and doesn't let go. I'm tall for eleven, so when she holds my hair, I have to lean over to go wherever she goes.

She's beautiful. Lots of curly reddish hair. She was born with lots of medical problems, so she doesn't talk much yet. Her face is different from other little kids. It's kind of flat. Her eyes are different, too. They don't move to the sides like ours do.

Her feet are tipped to the outside, too. Someone called it being clubfooted, but I don't like that name. To make her feet better, the doctors put a steel bar between them and somehow locked each shoe so her feet would be turned inward a bit. She hates that and screams a lot. Renee and I talk to her and stroke her hair to calm her down, but that doesn't always work. She can't walk yet, especially with that bar between her feet. So she scoots around really fast in her walker. That's how she gets to me so fast. People say that I am really good with her. I feel special around her. Not like with anyone else.

Mrs. Borgen comes to my desk and tells me to go into the hall with her. She tells me to go home right away. I live right across the street from the school, so I can do that fast. I'm worried that Mom is drunk again and wants help. I hope that she isn't outside where people will see her.

I walk into the house. Mom is putting clothes in a suitcase. She's wearing that big dress with the small blue and white squares on it. On her front is an apron that she wears when she's cooking something. She has a cigarette in one hand and is packing clothes with the other. Her lips and thumbs are twitching a little like usual.

I am very happy because this means we are going to see Renee and Darienne right now. I ask Mom, "Are we going to see them now?"

Mom doesn't look at me. She says "yes" and keeps packing the clothes in the suitcase.

"How come we're leaving now? I thought we weren't going for two more weeks?"

"Darienne died." She said it like the boring way the man says the weather on the radio.

Now I am really scared. I feel like I'm falling into a big hole in the floor. I put my hand on the closet door and lean on it. It's made out of plywood and it's shaky. I hope it doesn't break. I don't know what to do next. It's hard to breathe. My chest really hurts.

"Is she really dead, Mom? Really?" Sometimes Mom says things that aren't true, especially when she drinks. But she doesn't look like she's drunk now.

"Mom! Mom, look at me!"

Mom keeps putting clothes into the suitcase that we use when we go on trips. It's dark brown and hard, with bumps and scratches all over it. It smells old, but Mom says it's a treasure.

"Get your clothes now. Faith is coming to get us."

"No!"

I run hard out the door and down to Cherry Creek. I push through the scratchy bushes down to the water and find my tiny cave. I crawl in and squeeze my fists to stop shaking. After running so long, it's even harder to breathe.

But I feel good because I know I am never going back to our house. I will stay here forever where everything is safe. Maybe Darienne will come here.

I remember when Robert McNamara died in our house. Mom didn't want me to go in the room and see him. My sisters said he wasn't my real dad, anyway. If Darienne is really dead, I should go see her. Maybe she's not dead, though. I hope not. I crawl out of my cave and walk home.

I get in the car with Mom. Faith is driving. No one talks on the way to Belfield. Both of them are smoking all the time. It really stinks in the back seat. I open the window, but they tell me to close it. I hate it.

Sometimes when I have a dream, I can tell that I'm dreaming. That's how the funeral is. Everyone wears black. It's like the TV show the "Twilight Zone" where nothing makes sense and everything is in black and white. Darienne is in a tiny white box, but I don't want to look at her. I just want to wake up instead.

All the adults are sniffling and talking together. Some people say that she died in her sleep. Does sleep kill people? Maybe it's only the little people. I hope not.

At the cemetery, no one is talking to me, so I walk up on a tiny slope on the edge of the crowd and look down at everything. People are standing together in a clump down there, wearing black and white. Then everything—the people, the sky, the dirt—seems black and white like that TV show. I am black and white now, too. I am sad, but I won't cry. Mom says big boys don't cry. I will make myself forget all about this. Forever.

Playing by Heart

The Monday after our drive around the lakes, Teri took the day off because she started having random contractions on Sunday evening, two weeks earlier than we'd expected. I came home from work early, feeling like a bomb was going to explode and there was nothing I could do to stop it.

Teri collected all the items to take to the hospital. As she put them in a bag, I noticed they were all hers. None of them were mine. This birth is all about her and not me.

By nine p.m., the timed contractions were finally close enough to go to the hospital. When we arrived, they immediately parked Teri in a wheelchair and began pushing her down the hallway of doors and overhead lights into what they called the birthing room. Rather than being rushed into an operating room, Teri had wanted the birth to be natural, to be in a bed with me by her side, holding her hand. The room was designed to look like a typical bedroom. Still, the furnishings felt like props in a play, creating a curious cross between a bedroom and a hospital room.

Around one a.m., after continued contractions, Teri was exhausted. The contractions suddenly stopped, so she fell asleep. I felt useless, as if I was going to be fired for doing such a bad job. I sat down in the recliner to relax. But when I tipped it back, it laid out almost flat. Not good. I'd be asleep in ten minutes. To keep myself sane, I started journaling about the birth, using the notebook I'd brought along for Teri.

As the day progressed, with Teri sleeping off and on, I captured the smallest of details to give myself something to do to feel useful. *Teri seems so tired. I'm holding her hand. I got some crushed ice and put it on her lips. She smiled.* On and on it went, both of us alone, Teri on her back in the hospital bed, me in the recliner scribbling in the notebook.

Nurses in uniform would stop in every once in a while. If Teri was awake, they'd say, "No, still not dilated enough" and they'd leave. No one spoke to me. I was invisible. It felt like being with my mother.

Every once in a while, Teri would open her eyes and smile as if to say, "We're doing this! The three of us!" I'd try to be useful by reminding her to breathe and be calm, although she appeared calmer than I was.

Finally, at seven-fifteen p.m. when contractions were two minutes apart, the room exploded. Nurses burst through the door with various pieces of equipment, all of them on rollers, with what seemed like hundreds of cords. Minutes later, all the pieces were connected. Still, all the chaos was reassuring. In those few hectic minutes, the room had transformed from a pseudo-bedroom into a hospital room full of beeping machines.

I climbed out of the recliner and dutifully went to Teri's side, ready to do my job. One of the nurses put her hand on my shoulder and gently moved me away as if this was none of my business. I felt even more invisible. In retaliation, I moved up beside Teri and put my hand on her shoulder.

A nurse reached down to the side of Teri's bed, turned something, and the bed rose under Teri's head. At the same time, another nurse rolled a contraption between Teri's legs and, with both hands, quickly lifted and spread Teri's legs onto stirrups. Teri's eyes widened, and she looked down to see this cold, gray device that would soon welcome our baby.

The doctor casually strolled in, covered in blue—the top, bottom, cap, and mask. He said something to a nurse and she rolled a stool to the foot of the bed while he snapped on his latex gloves. He looked down between Teri's legs and said, "Dilation's enough."

Teri said to him, "Tell me when I can start pushing." She seemed calm and ready to do her part, as if she hadn't done enough already.

"When I tell you, take two deep breaths and push." He was entirely reassuring. A few minutes later, he told her to push. "Here it comes."

I would not miss this. I left Teri's shoulder to watch our baby arrive. I saw the first inch of the baby's slimy pink head. It was slowly turning clockwise. A nurse tugged on my arm to move me away. I gently removed her hand and said, "Not now, thank you." Then I planted myself next to Teri. The nurse knew to leave me alone.

The room was pierced by the cry of our new baby—a girl! Right away, I noticed the birthmark on her left forearm. That was the marker I'd always look for to be sure that she was ours. I glanced at the clock. Eight-twenty-two p.m. on December 22, 1981.

The doctor masterfully guided the baby the rest of the way out. He carefully examined her as if making sure there were no flaws in the diamond ring for his wife—except this diamond ring was not happy. She was crying and flailing her tiny arms. He nodded as if to indicate the baby was fine so far, then handed her to a nurse who gently rocked her back and forth. She laid our baby on a small changing table, wiped her shriveled face, and swaddled her in a soft white blanket.

Then the nurse promptly headed for the door with our baby. She was already between the door and me, yet I got to it before she did. I held out my arms and she knew what I wanted, yet she didn't acknowledge me—the invisible man. I stood my ground.

I stepped closer. "This is gonna happen. I'm going to hold my baby." She glanced back at the doctor. He nodded, so the nurse handed our daughter to me and I held her for the first time. I know it's cliché to talk about how holding your baby for the first time changes you. It's a cliché for good reason. I was determined that our baby would always feel safe and seen. I was ready.

I gently handed the baby back to the nurse, who dutifully took her away to be tagged and weighed. Before going, she turned and asked, "What's the name I should put on the tag?"

Of course, Teri and I had talked about names. We'd mentioned names of relatives, friends, and acquaintances. I'd mentioned a niece I'd lost once, but then retreated from the idea. It seemed too painful. She'd shared names from magazines, including lists of the most popular names of the day, but none stood out.

Now I looked at Teri and she just smiled. That was all she could muster, considering what she'd been through.

She said, "You go first. What's your choice? I trust you." Then she added, "You're courageous."

I picked up the phone and worked with the operator to call Renee. When she answered, I immediately asked her the question. In the background, I heard her ask LeeRoy. Then she returned to the phone and said, "Yes."

I hung up the phone, walked over to Teri, kissed her on the forehead and said, "Let's name her 'Darienne.'"

Enough of This Mess

I'm ironing the white cape I'll wear for the spring choir tomorrow night. Our music teacher says I sing very good for a twelve-year-old. I've already ironed the black pants and shined my black shoes. I put them on and they looked good on me.

Then Mom yells from the bathroom, "Carter, I need your help with my enema again." She sounds like our neighbor when he yells at his dog.

Faith is in her tiny bedroom next to mine. "I'm busy. Ask Faith. She should do that."

"No." She never asks Faith to help. How come?

I ignore Mom and keep trying to finish my cape.

"Carter, come here now. I'm ready. Mommy needs your help." I wish she wouldn't say that word. I don't call her Mommy anymore. It seems like every few days she needs that enema. Let's get this over with or she'll just keep yelling.

I go into the small bathroom. It's just a toilet with a shower curtain hung around it. It's the only bathroom we have and it's in her bedroom. I hate that because sometimes when I poop in the night and she's drunk, she thinks I'm a thief and comes at me, and sometimes it pulls the curtain down.

She's sitting on the toilet waiting for me to get the enema bag ready. We don't have a hot water heater, so I warm up the water on the stove. I put it in the enema bag, attach the red rubber hose to it, and clamp the hose closed so the water won't drain out yet. I go back into the bathroom and hang the bag upside down from the curtain rod. The other end of the hose has a plastic piece that Mom puts into her butt. I'm glad no one knows I do this. It doesn't feel right.

She stands up from the toilet, takes the plastic piece and puts it in her butt. Then she gets down on her hands and knees. She says, "Okay. Let some water go in." I open the clamp a little. "A little more," she says. I open the clamp some more. Now she says, "That's too much."

We go back and forth like this with her telling me more water and too much water. Then she bangs her fist on the floor and yells really loud, "You don't listen to me. That's not enough."

That makes me really mad. I yell, "Goddammit! Here's all the water then."

The hose stiffens right away with all the water going through it and into her butt. She lets out a loud, "Oh," and falls forward onto her stomach.

Then there's a gushing sound like when a water balloon explodes and a trickling noise like water going down our rain gutters. I look down and my pants and shoes have warm water on them from Mom's butt. It smells like a rotten egg. The hose is still leaking water all over, so I grab it and close the clamp.

She pulls herself up, turns her bare butt around and sits on the toilet. She leans over with her elbows on her knees, raises her head, and says, "Now look what you've done. Get me back to bed now and clean up this mess you made."

I start to shake. I'm so angry that I want to kick her, hard. Instead, I make tight fists with my hands and yell, "Why can't you poop like other people? Why do I have to help you? Why not Faith? You say I'm mean. You're the one who pooped on the floor. You always blame other people for what you do. You can't even take care of yourself. I always have to clean up after you. I hate you."

Mom acts like she doesn't hear me, so I don't say anymore.

I help her get up, pull her slip back down over her bare butt, and guide her back to bed. She crawls up on it, rolls over, and lies on her back. She grabs her stomach and says, "My stomach hurts so much.

I'm in such pain." Just like yelling at a dog again, she barks, "Make me some soup." She always wants split pea soup and peeled oranges when she's drunk. Sometimes her hands shake so much that she needs help holding a spoon.

I go into the kitchen and open a can of soup like I've done many times before. I scrape out a glob, toss it into a saucepan, and start heating it on the stove. I start peeling an orange. I look out the kitchen door to the shed and remember when I almost froze her in there by mistake. I'd thought about leaving her there then, but I was scared that the cops might take me away, so I didn't.

I sure feel like doing that right now. I know there's rat poison in a container that Mom keeps under the sink. If I poisoned her, the cops might take me. There'd be no more choir. I'd miss my friends.

I sit down on a chair by the table and look at my pants and shoes. They're wet. I can smell the poop on them. I get really sad because they're meant for the choir that I love so much. Now they have Mom's poop on them. My heart hurts. Going to jail would not be this sad. Nothing would be.

I open up the cabinet under the sink and take out the small, round container that has Mom's writing on it: "Rat poison." I put it on the table. I pour the warm soup into a small bowl and bring it to the table.

I've watched Mom put a tiny pinch of it in a small bowl of corn to kill the rats. A couple of times, rats have died and we found them after they started stinking. Mom is bigger than a rat, so I stir a big teaspoon into her soup. I pick up the orange and the bowl and start bringing them to her, but then I go back to put in one more teaspoon, just to be sure.

I set them down on her bed stand and help her sit up against the headboard. I give her the bowl and spoon. I say, "I'm sorry I let so much water go into you. Here, eat this soup. It'll make you better."

She takes the bowl and spoon. Her hands shake like they always do when she drinks. She starts slowly slurping it into her mouth. I watch her. I won't even miss her.

I walk back into my room, take off the wet pants, toss them in the back yard, and put on different ones. I wipe off the shoes with paper towels. Then I walk around the block about ten times.

I go back into the house and into her bedroom. She's lying curled up on her side. Maybe she's dead. Then I hear her snoring like she does with her mouth open a little. It sounds like when crows say "caw," but softer. There's green stuff around the bed in front of her face. Smells like sour milk and peas. She'd puked it all out. Damn. That didn't work. It's my fault. I gave her too much, too fast. Oh, well . . .

At least now I can finish my cape.

"You're Doing Fine"

The thing I wanted most was to be a great dad. My biggest fear was not being one. It was early February 1982, six weeks since Darienne's birth. I was doing my best but still felt like I was on a high wire. If I screwed up, it would be a long fall. What good were all the dad books at three in the morning when I was juggling a screaming newborn with a filthy diaper and trying to heat up a bottle? Unless I'd memorized them or they were already open to the right page, they were useless to me now.

Teri's maternity leave was over and she was back at work full-time, so we took turns feeding the baby at night. It was a precious experience to rock her to sleep after feeding her from the bottle. Despite working fifty to sixty hours a week, I still slept much lighter than Teri, so I'd often hear Darienne first and would rise to feed her. Sometimes I would sneak in two turns in a row, just to be with her. The moonlight through the sliding glass doors basked us in a glow that mirrored how I felt when holding her. I relished the fragrance of baby powder and shampoo. I tickled her feet and watched them curl. I mocked her tiny wrinkled face. She looked like the actor Edward G Robinson. Other times, Winston Churchill.

I wanted so badly to assure Teri I could be a great parent, but she was already much better than me. She was constantly coaching me, but I felt it as criticism. "Her head can fall back and hurt her neck." Meaning, *Carter, you aren't holding her head up when you pick her up.* "If you make the diapers a bit tighter, they won't leak." Meaning, *you don't make the diapers tight enough.* "We don't need so much baby powder." Meaning, *you could use half of that and not be sneezing all the time.* "We need to make sure the temperature of the formula is not too hot." Meaning, *you still don't know how to make it yet, do you?* A few minutes later, "Don't make the hole in the nipple of the bottle so big. The formula comes out too fast and she chokes sometimes." Meaning, *maybe we should give up on you feeding the baby*. I tried hard to act cool and appreciative of her advice, but underneath, I wanted to storm out the door.

Teri was out shopping. Darienne was crying hard in her cradle. I wondered if her diaper rash had gotten worse, so I put her up on the bathroom counter and unpinned her diaper. As soon as I did, her cries became one long, loud moan. Then a large blob of soft, tan poop came bursting out. Sounded like someone blowing their nose. Poop was all over her blanket, butt, and thighs. Some on my shirt and pants, too. Brown drops on the carpet.

I had changed her diaper countless times before, but now, when her poop burst out everywhere, I was suddenly engulfed by the familiar signs: face burning hot, heart racing hard, hands in tight fists, holding my breath. My whole body was trembling like I was in a massage chair turned on high. I didn't trust myself with the baby. All my concentration now was on backing away from the counter. What was going on with me? Should I call our neighbor, Stu? Should I tell him what was going on? But what was going on? This was not what dads were supposed to do. Why can't I even change Mom's diaper now?

I realized I'd thought *Mom's diaper*. Then it all made sense. Same sights, sounds, and smells as when I'd done Mom's enemas.

Should I tell Teri? She'd be horrified. She'd ask about the enemas. What kind of dad would she think I was? She might keep me away from the baby. I have to remember Darienne is not my mother.

In our drive around the lakes, I'd promised her I would be patient with myself as a dad and that I'd ask for help when I needed it. I planned to talk to her about her giving me advice so often, but I wouldn't mention Mom's enemas.

Later that evening, I said, "Teri, you have so many suggestions about how I could be a better dad. I feel more like I'm in the way than being helpful. You are so much better at this than I am. I know I have a lot to learn, but I don't know if I'm learning it all." Then, in case I was scaring her, I quickly added, "The baby will always be safe around me."

"Carter, you shouldn't expect yourself to know everything. I took care of the baby during maternity leave while you were working. I learned a lot then. Plus, I babysat when I was a teenager. When I call Mom, I usually ask her for advice. Of course I know more than you do about the baby." She could've added that I didn't have a functioning mom or a dad. "I'm not worried about you because I know you're so committed to being a good dad. That makes you an amazing dad." She seemed to genuinely think I was doing a good job. She couldn't lie about that. She couldn't even tell a joke if it meant stretching the truth.

Suddenly, I felt like my boss had just promoted me and given me a big raise—not knowing I'd screwed up, big time.

"You Can't Go on Like This!"

I charged into the condo, not even looking at her or for one of her hugs.

"What's wrong, Carter? Are you okay?" She was standing in the kitchen. It was late March. Snow was melting. Cold and wet. Puddles, potholes, and slush everywhere. We were holding our breaths, waiting for spring.

I took a deep breath and said, "I just want to sit down for a minute," trying to sound reassuring. I'd gotten home from work late, as usual. It was seven in the evening and Teri had been home since five. She had already gotten our daughter from daycare, fed her, put her to sleep, and started our dinner. I could hear beef patties sizzling in the pan. My mouth was watering already.

Me? I was shaken. On the way home, I'd stopped at a green traffic light—a green one. I'd waited for it to turn red, so I could proceed. That's how spaced out I was lately. I hadn't told Teri that I'd caused the brown marks in the microwave when I microwaved a metal pan full of water.

I tossed my parka in the closet and dumped my satchel by the door. I hugged Teri and sat down at the table, wondering how much I should tell her. I'd promised to be more truthful, but she was already carrying the load for both of us. What was wrong with me? Did I have some sort of mental problem? Had I inherited something from my mother? Would Teri finally say to hell with this?

She brought over the plate of burgers and beans and poured the milk. She sat down and said, "Carter, talk to me. What's going on?" She didn't say it like she was asking a question. She sounded like she was pissed at me for ignoring her.

"On the way home, I spaced out. The traffic light was green, but somehow, I thought that meant stop. The cars behind me were honking. I didn't know why. I was waiting for the light to turn red, so I could go." I said it mechanically, as though I was reciting from a list. I looked over at her. "I was completely confused. I'm sorry. I'm just so tired all the time."

"I've been worried. The other morning, I saw you put two heaping tablespoons of instant coffee in a cup. Then you poured hardly any water on it. You didn't drink from it. Instead, you were chewing on it, out of the cup. Are you so tired that you're doing that to get through the day?" She wasn't done, though. "A few days ago, I came home with Darienne and you were in the hallway talking to Stu. You both got in the car, I suppose to run to the store, but you'd left the water faucet running full blast. It was like you'd turned it on and then just walked away. I didn't think much of it, but still, it worried me. Now, this sounds like there's more going on. We need to get help with this." She didn't add "or else you'll hurt the baby."

"I'm sorry. I'm a little scared. Lately, I feel . . ."

How would I tell her there was so much stress from every angle? New job. New marriage. New condo. New car. New baby. New dad. I couldn't sleep at night. I had nightmares. My boss called me a "space cadet" because I forgot our staff meeting again.

"Feel what?" She looked so concerned. Or afraid? "Carter, you need to see a doctor." She was already heading for the phone book.

"Teri, no! I just need some sleep. Maybe we can take turns having naps. It'll be good for you, too." I hoped she'd say "yes."

Instead of affirming the wisdom of my ideas, she said, "We're different people. This is a stressful situation. Different people handle stress differently." Oh, God. She'd dumped a rainfall of clichés on me. I wished she'd just stop. "You take half a day a week whenever you want. I'm doing what I want. I love being here, taking care of our daughter, taking care of you. This feeds me."

I felt like I was stuck in a rerun of a *Father Knows Best* that was badly cast. Instead, I wasn't a husband. I wasn't a leading man. I was a spaced-out neurotic trying to act like father of the year.

We'd agreed on naps, but how could I take a nap when I couldn't even get to sleep?

Knives in the Night

"Mom. Mom! Wake up. It's nighttime. You're in my room again. Put the knife down. Get out. There are no rats under my bed. Let's get you back to bed." I take the knife from her hand.

She's wearing the same torn pink nightgown, the one with one torn strap hanging down. She's drunk or stoned on meds or both. She moves in slow motion.

She mumbles again, "Rats eat our food. From the barn. Have to clean now." She thinks she's a little girl back on the farm.

I have to be gentle with her or she fights and yells at me about being cruel.

I slowly walk back to her room, hoping she'll follow me like the family dog. Instead, she lies down on the living room floor and snuggles into our green shag carpet. I just leave her there and go back to my room.

But how did she get into my room this time? I'd slid the plastic accordion door completely closed. The lock on it doesn't work, so I'd braced it closed with the gun rack I'd made with my friend, Gordon.

When the sun comes up, I'll check in on her again. Maybe she'll vomit and drown in it. I can only hope.

If not, she'll recover and if I tell her what she did during the night, she'll say I'm lying. She'll say, "Why are you so cruel to me?"

Now I won't get back to sleep and might not wake up for school again. I've already missed twenty days this school year and it's only April. I hope they pass me anyway, so I can get into the ninth grade.

I wish I could keep her out of my room. I never get used to it. She still wakes me up and scares the hell out of me.

"Wake Up! Wake Up!"

It's mid-April now. The snow is mostly melted. Temperatures are creeping into the '50s. Creatures can be seen sometimes if you look hard enough—ants, flies, and spiders. In a few weeks, lilacs will blossom with their sweet, heady scent. My favorite flowers.

I'd been trying to meet my promise to get more sleep, but guilt kept getting in the way. It's hard to be the perfect husband when you need time off, but your wife doesn't. Besides, even if I slept most of one day, I was still exhausted the next.

"Get out of my room, Mom! Put the knife down. Now!" I was standing by our bed, yelling at the doorway.

"Carter! Wake up! Wake up!" Teri grabbed my shoulders from behind and tried to shake me awake.

I turned and yelled, "Don't touch me! Don't touch me!" I laid back down and drifted into a silent sleep.

The next morning, a Saturday, I tried to wake up. I felt like I'd drunk several bottles of wine the night before. My mouth was dry and pasty, making small popping noises when I moved my tongue. When I tried to open my eyes, I swear I heard the sound of sandpaper on wood.

I ached to lie back down and sleep ten more hours. I rolled over on my side and pushed hard on the mattress, trying to sit up and get out of bed. My body was lifeless, like dead weight. Another night like this. When would they stop?

I dragged myself into the living room. Teri was sitting on the couch. She was staring out the French doors, shoulders down, forearms resting on the couch. Was it the baby? What was wrong?

I sat down and said, "Love, are you okay?" It came out like a whisper.

"No, I'm not okay. You stand there yelling at your mom in your room with a knife. You won't even let me touch you. You fight me off. Then you turn around and go right back to sleep as if nothing happened, and then you wake up and act like you don't even remember! What's going on, Carter? I don't understand!" She started crying while waiting for an instant explanation.

How would I answer her? I couldn't even fake this one. Hell, I thought I was still asleep. I just stared at her, but then it hit me.

"Were my eyes open when all of that happened?"

"What do you mean, 'were my eyes open?' You were looking right at me! Was someone attacking you? Was it your mother's ghost or what?" She stopped and took a long breath. "Honey, we've got to deal with this. We need help. You can't go on like this. I'm scared."

Now, she was talking about getting help—about therapy! I yearned for a strong cup of coffee—or two or three.

"Love, I think I know what happened. I can explain. That's not a nightmare. It's called a night terror. I used to have them in my early teens. Please. It's nothing to worry about. I'm okay. I am." I sounded as insincere as a used car salesman. "Teri, I think the stress of what we've been going through is what's causing the night terrors."

I reminded her of the many changes in our life over the past year. Still, there was no change in her face. Clearly, I was not convincing. I took a deep breath and began to explain that I was afraid our Darienne might die.

"Teri, remember I mentioned before that my niece, Darienne, died in her sleep when she was only two years old? Sometimes when I can't sleep, I check on our Darienne. That wakes me up even more." I didn't tell her that sometimes I lie by her cradle and cry. I was in no mood now to sob in front of Teri. We already had our hands full with this night terror crap.

Tears rolling down her cheeks, she reached out for me and I took her hand. "Look. I know they're scary, even terrifying, for you, but here's what to do. Just ignore me. I'll go back to bed and won't even remember it in the morning. They sound worse than they really are."

She wiped the tears from her face, but just stared at me. Had she heard me? I didn't think so, because then she said, "I think we need help."

No! "I know this is scary. Just do what I'm suggesting. We'll be fine."

"I need some time alone to just think about this and what we should do. I'm exhausted now. Carter, your body is telling you something. You can't ignore it any longer. We have to talk about this soon."

My heart was ramping up and I was feeling much hotter. I was losing this debate. This could go wrong in a big way if some therapist started analyzing these night terrors. I could just hear them: "Your mom was in your room at night? You need long-term therapy!"

"Okay, you're right. Let's take some time and settle down. I'm hungry. How about you?" I started to the kitchen to make a pot of strong coffee. Now was not a good time for her to see my coffee sludge routine again.

As the day wore on, I tried to think about how to avoid a therapist. I didn't need counseling. Instead, I needed a long talk with my body. It kept betraying me with these night terrors, reminding me that my mom had been in my room with a knife. Hell, she'd done that several times. It was no big deal.

We had a good day. I actually took a long nap and Teri caught up on her newspapers. That evening, she made one of my favorite dinners, fried potatoes, beans, and wieners, just like Mom had made when she was sober. The house smelled like cooking oil and fat from the wieners. Wonderful! It felt like being back to normal, like Teri had forgotten all about my ever needing help.

We sat down to eat. She'd been quiet most of the day. I sensed something was coming, but didn't know how to stop it. I started to pick up my fork when she put out her hand to stop me. "Before we start, I want to say something. I want you to just listen. I don't want you to respond. I just want you to think about what I'm saying."

Then she went through it all. She hadn't missed a thing. My absent-minded mistakes. The increasing nightmares. My overreacting to the smallest missteps. The blow-ups that seemed ready to start but then stopped. How I always blamed myself for everything that went wrong. My constantly reassuring her. I sat there, terrified that she had noticed all that about me. I felt as though a ten-pound weight had landed on my head.

"Carter, I love you. I want you to worry about taking care of yourself as much as you worry about taking care of us. And that's why I'm going to support you through therapy. Will you go to therapy?" She put her hand on mine.

As usual, my mind started racing. I'd have to buy some time. Yet, she'd thought about this all day long and had still said *therapy*. I worried I'd damage our relationship if I tried to talk her out of it. As scared as I was of therapy, I was more terrified about losing her.

"Yes, I will."

But that didn't mean I'd tell the therapist everything.

I'm Not Going There

The following Monday after work, we got Darienne from daycare. We fed her and put her down to sleep. Then we snacked on leftovers and chatted about our day. I told her that Lonny was still saying "hey" to me. She mentioned a monthly party at a co-worker's house. I flinched. That was not for an introvert like me.

With a mouth full of old rice, I said, "I found a therapist near here so it won't be a hassle to do it." I felt like a student with a report card showing all A's.

"So, success in therapy is how close their office is?"

I immediately felt defensive and was starting to explain, but then she started laughing. Oh good, she was teasing me. This was off to a great start.

"Carter, I'm sorry if it seems like I'd pushed you into this." She waited for me to reassure her that she hadn't. But yeah, she had. "I'm excited. I want to know more about what's bothering you." She nodded, like she was ready to start now.

"Teri, I'm glad you're excited about this. I am, too," I lied. "But let's keep our eyes on the reason I'm doing this: to get some sleep." I realized my mistake. "Of course, that's the second biggest reason. The first is, I'm doing it for us."

"But you don't seem all that excited."

It was time to set some limits on this. "Love, I just don't want you to expect too much and get disappointed. Therapists help you with what you want to work on now, not everything about your past. Also, it's not a quick fix. They don't just tell you what to do. They help you understand your thoughts and feelings. They help you to decide what to do about them."

"Yeah, I suppose. I don't expect things to be perfect after this, just better, especially for you, right?" Her brow furrowed and her voice got higher, like a child asking for a treat.

I felt like I was kicking a puppy. I smiled and said, "You said that better than I did. Now let's clear the table." At least this was over.

Teri and I started the ritual of putting food away in our tiny walk-through kitchen. It looked like a one-on-one basketball game, each player dribbling deftly around the other. The sounds of popping lids on containers, the tinkling of silverware in the dishwasher, and the thuds of closing the fridge door. Then I realized she'd stopped the game. She was standing there looking at me.

"Then how can I help you in your therapy?"

I leaned back against the counter and crossed my arms. "Good question. I think it's more of what not to do. Don't feel sorry for me." Mom had enough self-pity for all of us. "Just treat me normal, okay?"

"Why would I feel sorry for you?"

"Exactly," I said. "Don't try to cure me. It's not like I have a disease. I just need to get more sleep somehow."

"Okay. I agree."

So far, this was going well.

"A big thing you can do is not to always push me to talk about therapy. Sometimes people just need to think about what's been said with the therapist. I will tell you things when they become clear to me, okay?" That hadn't set well with her. Now she was looking at the carpet and not at me. I took both of her hands in mine. "I promise I will share everything that will help me deal with the night terrors."

"I know. It's just that Faith said your mother was an alcoholic and a drug addict. That's serious. We should talk about that."

Goddammit, Teri! "She was. But she's dead and now I have us."

"I'm sorry I'm making such a fuss. How do you feel about therapy?"

I paused. "I'm a little scared."

"Of what?"

"Well, anyone would be scared of something like this." They would be if therapy meant talking about a childhood like I'd had.

"I understand your feeling scared, but you're not alone. You're with me. We'll be fine as long as we share and support each other. Get used to it." She finished with a warm, soft smile.

I took that as a threat, not a comfort.

Promising and Pretending

My friends, Gordon and Danny, tease me that I don't have a dad. It hurts a lot when they do that. They go fishing with their dads and I get jealous. I go alone.

Now Mommy says for the first time that she's gonna go fishing with me! She promised. I told my friends. They don't believe me. I'll show them. I don't need a dad now.

I've been waiting a lot of days for Saturday to come. Now it's here. It's nice outside. I got the fishing rods together. One for her. One for me. I got my can of worms that I dug out of our backyard. We'll share my tackle box. It's all in the shed waiting for us. This will be so much fun.

Finally, Saturday gets here. I rush into Mommy's bedroom. "Mommy, are you ready to go?" She'll be excited to learn fishing from me. I fish better than anybody and I'm only nine.

Like always, she's sitting sideways on her bed, reading another paperback book. She's wearing the big white shirt and black pants that end at the top of her ankles. She's smoking a Kent. The house stinks.

She doesn't hear me. Doesn't look at me.

I frown and feel scared. What happened? Isn't she gonna come? She has to. "Mommy, are you ready to go?"

She twitches her left thumb a bit like she does sometimes when she knows someone is looking at her. "Go where?" She stares down at her book and doesn't look at me.

I step closer and say louder, "Go fishing. Like you promised." I try to sound happy. "I'll teach you how. Let's go."

She keeps looking down at her book. "I'm not feeling well. I've got nerves today."

Tears start coming into my eyes. My shoulders sag and my voice gets higher, "No, Mommy. You promised! Please, just get up and go. I'll do everything. You can just have fun." I hold my breath.

No answer. I step closer. Now my voice is even louder but lower. "Mommy, don't lie to me again. I've been waiting for days. I told my friends."

"You go. I'll bet you'll get a lot of fish." She still didn't look at me.

I step even closer and start yelling so loud that my throat hurts. I yell about her lying, stealing, drinking, and stinking. Tears run down my cheeks and my nose plugs with snot. I can't breathe. "I hate you so much! I want a different mother! I want a dad!"

Her right hand starts trembling and her nose and lips twitch a little, too. She keeps looking down at the book. Almost like she's bored, she says, "Don't be cruel to me, Carter. I told you I'm sick today. You go fishing. I'll go with you next time." That's a lie and she knows it. She thinks I'm so stupid that I'll believe her.

I turn and walk out the back door, through the shed, and into the backyard feeling like I ran into a wall really hard. I hurt all over. She says big boys don't cry. In the backyard, Mommy won't see me. I sit down on the grass and start to cry really hard. I bend over and hold my knees and rock back and forth. I cry with lots of tears and snot and gurgling.

Finally, I just stop. I walk back into the shed. I'm gonna break my fishing rods and throw my tackle box in the garbage. But then I know I will feel even sadder, so I don't. I pick them all up and hold them tight.

I take my fishing stuff down to the creek. I put a worm on the hook on the string of each of the two rods. I put a bobber on each string, too. Then I toss the hook and bobber of both rods into the water. I set each rod down and I sit on my tackle box.

I feel very lonely. I used to have a dad. Robert McNamara was his name. I don't remember much about him. He was a very old man. He was dying for a long time in a room in our house when I was four. Mommy never let me go in there. One time, I heard my sister say that Robert wasn't really my dad. Didn't matter. He was a stranger anyway, like he was just made up.

I know, I can make up a dad! He can use one of my rods. I'll call him Daddy. Then I won't feel so lonely. Good idea.

I look at his rod and I ask, "How come Mommy doesn't love me, Daddy? She breaks promises to me. She never even looks at me. She says I'm mean."

Daddy won't answer me 'cause he's not real. But I can make him real. I can talk for him.

"So what? You don't need her, anyway." That's what he says back to me.

When I think of Mommy, I feel so mad and so sad, like I lost a good friend forever. Like she's so far away and is never coming back. I don't want to think about that now.

"Am I a good fisherman?"

"You're the best," he says back to me.

"Daddy, from now on, I'll teach you all about fishing."

"Okay, son."

"I'm gonna be the world's best dad. Fish with my kids all the time. Play catch with a baseball. I won't steal their money. I won't lie to them. I will never, never break a promise to them."

I reel in his fishing line for him. "I won't tell other people about you, though. They'll think my brain is sick like Mommy's. Sometimes she talks to dead people."

"Okay, son."

I like fishing with my dad.

"Tell Me All About You"

A few days after I'd scheduled the appointment, the therapist's office mailed me an intake form. It directed me to answer all of its questions and promptly mail back the form. When I looked at the questions, the therapist fiasco suddenly seemed very real. The form encouraged me to answer the questions "with complete honesty" and assured me that my answers would be strictly confidential. Writing my answers felt like jumping off a cliff. There was no climbing back up.

Physical ailments? No. Physical abuse? No (for all of us kids, our wounds were internal). Sexual abuse? No. Suicidal thoughts? No. Medications? None. Drinking? Yes. How much, how often? Two glasses once or twice a week at dinner (any more than that reminds me of my mother). Goal(s) in therapy? Stop the night terrors (duh!).

I'd had my share of broken promises, so I was determined not to break mine with Teri. I'd share what pertained to the night terrors. I wouldn't share anything more than that, nothing about the "Big Ick"—the lying, stealing, pissing, pooping, screaming, stinking snake pit of my childhood. Whenever I thought of the Big Ick, I felt like I'd been dunked in a toilet that hadn't been flushed. No, this therapy would have nothing to do with that.

The building was not what I'd expected. Not a multi-level gridwork of concrete, glass, and steel. Instead, it was a one-story brick structure surrounded by green grasses and budding bushes. I walked in and immediately the place felt as far as possible from my expectations. The walls weren't lined with racks of trifold brochures, each trumpeting an ominous medical condition. The air didn't feel charged with pain, hope, and impatience to see a doctor. Instead, there were pictures of thoughtful, smiling adults and active, happy families. There was a faint smell of . . . what was it? Sandalwood?

Three walls were lined with rows of padded chairs holding small pillows of different colors. Five other clients were in the chairs, idly glancing through magazines.

I approached the receptionist's desk. She'd been studying me from the minute I'd walked in. What was she thinking about me? Suicidal or just looking for an address? Confident or just cocky?

"I'm scheduled with Astrid Nystrom at four p.m. I'm Carter McNamara."

She quickly looked at her appointment book and said cheerily, "Yes, we have you. And we got your completed intake form. Thank you! I'll let Astrid know you're here."

She stood up and walked around the corner. I heard a muffled conversation and then laughter. Were they laughing at me? What's was so funny? Were they mocking their clients? Was I being paranoid?

She came back, still smiling, and said, "You can go right in! Here, I'll show you now." That's a relief. I hated waiting for people in rooms where everyone was looking at you, wondering what mental disease you had.

We walked along a hallway lined with pictures of nature scenes. Ah, a picture of whitewater rapids. Signifies turmoil? Mountains. Challenge? Fields. Openness? Woods. Reflection? Lotus. Enlightenment? Nice.

Sandalwood was even more present but not overwhelming as I walked through Astrid's door. In front of me was an overstuffed couch spotted with multicolored pillows. A small table with tools to make tea. Quaint. A variety of plants in the corners, unlike a doctor's office. More like a visit to a dear friend.

She was at most five feet, four inches tall and weighed one hundred twenty pounds with rocks in her pockets. She had copper-colored hair. She was wearing a white blouse and . . . blue jeans? Fashionable jeans, but jeans just the same. That comforted me. She was authentic enough to wear what she wanted.

The first sound from her was a full-throated laugh. She said, "You stared at my jeans." Then in a teasing voice, she said, "My therapist wears jeans to work. Can you believe that?" She stood up and extended her hand to shake mine. Then she gestured toward a padded earth-toned chair across from hers for me to sit in.

What a relief. It was not the classic therapist's couch with her sitting behind me. She waited until I settled in, then in a dutiful voice started describing her professional background. I looked at each diploma on her wall as if I was taking in what they'd actually meant. BA in Psychology. Masters in Social Work from Washington University in St. Louis. Next to that, Licensed Clinical Social Worker.

After looking at the diplomas, I looked back at her. She was smiling at me. "Should I ask you to tell me what I just said?" I'd heard none of it. We both laughed. I was feeling relieved already. This might not be a gauntlet of "no-pain, no-gain" bullshit, after all.

She offered me a cup of hot water and a bowl of assorted tea packets. I picked chamomile in case I needed calming. She picked peppermint. Was that for reducing tension?

Back at her desk, she picked up some papers. "I've read your intake form. That was quite helpful. Thank you. It says your primary goal is to stop night terrors. Is that still the reason you're here?"

That's when I made my first mistake. "My wife said I should get therapy." That sentence is at the top of the list of things never to say to a therapist. I put up my hand to stop any reply. "That's a bad way to put it. We both think I need therapy, my wife—and me." Now there was a faint upturn on the corners of her mouth. She was quietly laughing at my gaff. "I'm here because . . ." I paused. Why was I there?

"Carter, that's okay. You'd be surprised at how many clients aren't sure why they're here. That's one of the first breakthroughs in therapy: to get clear on why you're here. You're already on the right track."

She's good. She's already reassuring me. I tried again. "I'm here because I've been having night terrors. They're terrifying my wife and interrupting my sleep."

"Explain what you mean by night terrors."

She wanted to be sure I knew there was a difference between night terrors and nightmares. "I remember my nightmares. I don't remember the night terrors. Even when someone tries to wake me up, I don't remember. If they touch me during a terror, I might yell at them. My eyes can be wide open, but I'm still asleep. My nightmares are usually later in the night. My night terrors usually happen earlier."

She said, "Night terrors are usually caused by stress or trauma."

I wanted to head off any talk of trauma, so I jumped right into the stresses: the move, job, condo, marriage, new baby.

"Yes, those stresses could be overwhelming. You've been through a lot recently. I'm curious, how is the stress showing up?"

She wanted more? Okay. I told her about my confusion with traffic lights, microwaving metal saucepans, and forgetting running water.

"Carter, the traffic lights concern me. Despite all that's going on in your life now, you're doing one of the most important things. This therapy can put everything in perspective." She sat forward. "There's a big misunderstanding about stress. You probably know, though, that different people are stressed by different things. The misunderstanding is that stress is caused by people having many stressors. But it's not. It's caused by how people manage those stressors. Some people can have a long list of things to do, and they manage it all just fine, so they have hardly any stress. Other people can have just one or two things, but they're feeling completely overwhelmed. The stress that people feel depends more on their inner situation than their outer one." Then her arrow hit the bullseye. "What's going on in your inner one, Carter?"

"That's for you to discover, right?" I laughed at my own joke. She didn't. "Everything I say with you is completely confidential, right?"

"Absolutely. Carter, here's where you decide if you actually want help or not. If you're ready and you want to change, for your sake and your family's, you'll talk."

"My dad died when I was four. I don't remember ever doing anything with him. He probably wasn't even my dad. Anyway, now I am a dad and I'm not sure what I'm doing. I had no role model. I'm nervous all day long. My wife has a lot of confidence in me, but I'm terrified." I hesitated, but she knew I wasn't done yet. "At night, I'm afraid my daughter might die." I explained the situation I'd told Teri about my niece, Darienne, and about checking her cradle at night. Unlike with Teri, though, I told Astrid that I'd laid there by the cradle and cried about my niece. I cried because I was a kid and she was the only person I'd connected with, but suddenly she was gone. There was the stinging in my eyes. It was too late to stop them. The tears were already streaming down my face. She handed me a box of tissues from the table and waited.

"Have you told your wife about crying by the cradle?"

I blew my nose. "Yes. I mean no. I told her about worrying that our Darienne might die because my niece died in her sleep. But I left it at that. I haven't told her about why I cry."

"Do you know why you didn't tell her about the crying?"

I leaned back and let out a loud sigh. "Because she'd make a big deal out of it." I lifted my arms in the air and let them fall on my lap to show my frustration. "She'd want to know more about what happened back then."

"Carter, do you know what it's like to feel vulnerable?"

Where'd that question come from?

"Yeah, it's feeling like you're not safe. Why?"

"In therapy and in healthy relationships, it's opening yourself up to a truth. It's letting a truth come out so you can grow. It takes wisdom. It takes courage. Now, tell me. Have you told anyone how you felt when Darienne died?"

I started shaking my head, "Oh, no. I'm not going there. I'm here to deal with night terrors. Let's get back to that."

"I wonder if the reason you're afraid your daughter might die, the reason you're not sleeping, the reason you're having night terrors, is because you haven't grieved your niece's death. Your body is reminding you of that. Your reaction now is about avoiding something quite painful." She paused. "What was your niece like?"

Here came more tears. "Oh, she was beautiful. She had a condition where her face and her eyes were different. She moved differently, but those differences made her ours, even more to love."

"How did you feel when you played with her?"

"I felt such joy. Pure joy. Like no one I'd ever been with ever."

She moved her chair closer. "How did you feel when she died?"

I wrapped my arms around myself and started rocking back and forth. "At first, I didn't want to believe it. When I saw the tiny white box she was in, it was like I'd flipped a switch. I turned it all off." I flicked my finger down like I'd flipped a switch. "I can do that. I can shut anything off, so it doesn't bother me."

"Anything? It doesn't bother you?"

I shook my head. "Oh, you'd be surprised."

"Did anyone talk to you then about her dying?"

"Who would? Renee was grieving like I can't imagine. As usual, Mom tried to make it all about her. Mac wasn't even there. Faith was dealing with her own pain. She deals with pain by going inside herself. She disappeared around Mom. I don't blame her. So I just shut down."

"Carter, grief never goes away. You learn to accept it. That's the way of learning from it over time, even honoring it. I'm hearing no one held you. You needed to be held when you grieved. You're holding yourself now."

I looked down and she was right.

"What would she want for you now?"

This was all too intense. I felt overwhelmed, exhausted. I looked down, feeling numb. "She'd want me to be healthy, to be happy."

She paused, letting what I'd said sink in. "You said your sister, Renee, raised you, but she moved away when she got married. Where was your mother?"

By then, I was feeling such release from talking about my niece and such trust in Astrid, that I answered with the truth, "Mom was a zombie. She was so doped up or drunk, we never had any kind of relationship. She rarely looked at me."

"What about friends and neighbors?"

Good question. "We made sure they didn't know about us. We didn't let them in the house. We were too ashamed."

"What about your mother's family?"

"She'd alienated them all. She accused one brother of murdering the other when there was no evidence of it. She accused her sister of attacking her when it was probably the other way around. Astrid, to this day, I don't have friends who ask me personal questions. That's because I don't allow it. I'm still back there, keeping people out of my house."

"Carter, look at me. What you've told me is you had no relationship with your mother. You were close to your sister, Renee, but she moved away when she got married. Your sister, Faith, survived by going inside herself. Your brother wasn't even in the picture. You were close to your niece, but she died suddenly. So you were left alone, much of it as a child, taking care of a zombie. No wonder you flicked a switch—and it was all gone." She paused and moved her chair even closer. "But it's not." She pointed at my chest. "It's there in your body. Grief, fear, anger, and confusion. In the next session, I'd like to understand more about what you grew up with, if you're willing. That might have a lot more to do with your stress than all that current stuff you told me about. Is that okay with you?"

All I could manage was an "okay." I doubt it sounded convincing to her because it hadn't to me.

"Great work today, Carter. It's a privilege to watch your courage. I assure you, if you keep it up, the stresses and night terrors won't be the problems they are now. You're giving a gift to yourself and your family."

"That's fifty minutes already? It felt like we were just getting started." I felt cheated.

She laughed and said, "I've had clients say it's the shortest and longest experience of their lives."

We got up and stood long enough to get blood back to our legs. I felt like I'd stepped into a warm shower on a cold, winter day.

She walked me to Julie's desk to schedule another appointment. Along the way, she handed me a sheet titled "Tips for Managing Stress" and suggested that I discuss it with Teri. She smiled and was gone. I told Julie that I'd have to call her back when I had my calendar so I could schedule the appointment.

I got in the car and glanced at the tips. Avoid coffee after four p.m. Not gonna happen. Turn off the TV after six p.m. Not that either. Go to sleep at the same time every night. Tell that to Darienne. Avoid naps during the day. No problem. I rarely take naps. Sleep and wake at consistent times. Take ginkgo biloba or valerian root. So much for this list.

I pulled into a park near our condo and wrote down notes from the session. I had to write them down right away or I'd never remember them. It all seemed like a dream to me. I wondered why I'd shared so much, so soon. The dam broke when she got me talking—feeling—about my niece. She was right about everything she said in the session.

Back home, Teri was at the bathroom counter with Darienne tackling another case of diaper rash. "Hand me the ointment. Now the baby powder. There, now we'll leave her without a diaper to dry her little crotch."

I took five steps back.

"Teri, I had an amazing session with Astrid today. Lots of tips about managing stress." I showed her the sheet of tips. "There's a lot we can learn here." I sounded like a child back from the zoo.

Holding the powder in one hand and ointment in the other, she looked at me. "That's wonderful, Carter. That's what I was hoping to hear. Share with me when you're ready. I trust you."

Over the next three days, before my next session, I didn't share more of it. I didn't feel afraid, I just wanted those intense feelings, the joy of that discovery, to be my own. It all felt so real.

That Explains Everything

On the way to this second appointment, I wondered what it does to brain cells to be immersed in computer code then suddenly doused in sharing feelings? I felt comfortable working with computers, but ended up feeling that way with Astrid, too. Would I get psychological whiplash with more therapy?

"Hello Julie, I'm Carter . . ."

She finished my name. "McNamara. Good to see you back!"

It was good to see her again, too. She walked me back, past the pictures of the nature scenes. Strange how a good experience can change how you see the same pictures. Last time, I saw them with skepticism and suspicion. This time, with comfort and trust. Last time, I felt more like the rapids. This time, more like the fields. Would Astrid be wearing jeans again?

I walked into Astrid's office. No, she was wearing formal office wear. Olive green slacks and a blue jacket with a tan blouse. Why the change? Would this be a more formal session? I hoped not.

I didn't need to worry. She looked up at me and smiled. "You won't mind if I take off these heels? I was on a panel discussion. I miss my jeans." Good. Now it felt like welcoming a friend.

She motioned me to the couch. Not the chair? Then I noticed the box of tissues and a small blanket. Were those there before? Was she planning an emotional session this time?

She poured two cups of tea. Peppermint for her again. Chamomile for me. She'd remembered. She sat down on her chair.

"Welcome back. Before we start, do you have any questions? Anything you want to bring up? Again, all of this is confidential."

"No, just that I'm grateful to you for letting me ramble on about my niece. I still feel self-conscious about that. I'm not used to people listening to me, but then I seldom give them a chance."

"I hope, as we go on in therapy, that you won't feel that way. It's not rambling to be sharing your heart and soul. It's honoring yourself and those listening to you. It's our stories that make us real, especially to our partners. You might think about that." Then she got right down to it.

"How'd it go talking to Teri about our last session?"

"Yes. Well, I shared the tips about stress and stuff. She agreed it'd be great to work on them." I hoped that little report was enough. She waited for more. Was this her way of reminding me this was about honesty?

I confessed. "I didn't talk to her about grieving for my niece or about Mom, the zombie. It's hard to explain, but I want my private stuff to be private. I feel like it's mine. Okay?"

She moved her chair closer. Here we go. "I understand. I do, but your growth depends on how much you share with her, with your loved ones. Sharing your pain helps you face it, to not be so afraid you'll be ambushed by it in your night terrors. The more you face it, the more you accept that it happened. That doesn't mean always feeling that pain again. It means not exhausting yourself in burying it. Remember how good you felt talking about your niece?"

Everything she'd said made so much sense, but it was like telling me, "If you climb Mount Everest, you'll feel so good." Yeah, but I'd have to climb it first. Still, I sat there nodding my head.

"Sharing your pain and your stories lets your loved ones know you trust them enough to be yourself. It means being real. It lets them trust you enough to help them grow, to be real, too."

I felt like an obese person being told all the ways I could cut calories. Sure, those would work. That's not the problem. The problem was getting myself to do all those things.

"Why do you suppose you haven't shared about your niece or your mother?"

I just sat there, shaking my head. She didn't rescue me. She waited.

"Carter, I wonder . . ."

I raised my hand to stop her. "No. I want to answer that . . . somehow. It's like there are so many reasons." I threw up my hands. "I don't know where to start."

She waited.

"How do I put that mess into words? Unless you were there, you could never understand. I don't understand, so what's the use? If I talk about it, I have to relive it. I can't. If I talk about it, it becomes real. It's here. It's here anyway. I know I sound confused, but . . . worst of all, they'd pity me." I said the word "pity" like I'd bitten into a dead rat. I sat back exhausted, not remembering what I'd said. My mouth felt like I'd been chewing cotton balls.

She poured me a glass of water. I grabbed it and chugged the whole glass. "Astrid, I understand why you suggest that I share my feelings. I do. I'm so glad you're here for me. I know you said last time that you wanted to understand more about my childhood, how it affected me. But I tell you, I'm not ready to go there." I shook my head. "I'm not." I looked at the door and ached to flee back to my den at Cherry Creek.

"There are other ways to understand your childhood. It doesn't have to always be bad stuff. Tell me some good things that happened."

"I don't know if this makes sense, but it hurts even more to think about the good times. Most times I'd get my hopes up, they'd get crushed. For a little kid, that's devastating. The times that were good—that were sweet—reminded me of what I could never expect again, anyway. Getting my hopes up just meant a long way to fall."

She paused for me to reset myself. "Carter, this therapy is yours. Our work should come from you, from what you're ready to talk about. My job is to share with you what I'm hearing, what I'm seeing, to advise you and to support you to do something about it. But it's up to you where we go with that. That's fine. That doesn't mean we're stuck. It just means we take a different road for now. I'll show you the map. We take the journey together. Okay?"

Thank God I was comfortable crying around her, because that's what I did. I let the tears flow in a gentle stream.

She paused, then rolled her chair back to her desk. She opened a drawer and pulled out a sheet of paper. "I have an idea. I'd like to pose some questions to you, not about your past, but about where you are now. Are you up for something like that?"

"Sure," I said, glad that I hadn't stalled out the entire session.

"I apologize in advance if these questions seem like they're one after another, like I'm reading from a list. That's because I am. You can say as much as you like. And like before, anything you say is confidential." Then she rolled over to me. "Okay, one more thing. I need your open and honest answers. No hanging back. This is for you . . . and your family, okay?"

"Yes." I said that louder than usual, trying to convince myself.

"Okay, let's start. Are you most comfortable with people or alone?"

That was easy. "Alone."

"Do you often feel like you're a phony, not telling people the truth about yourself?"

That was also easy. "Yes."

"Do you try to control things around you, so there won't be any surprises?"

I laughed because the answer was so obvious.

"I'll take that as a 'yes.' Do you often feel unsafe, like you must always be on guard?"

I paused, not because I didn't know the answer, but because the questions all seemed so familiar. I'd been asking them to myself for years. "Yes."

"Do you feel more nervous than most people most of the time?"

By now, I was feeling nervous about my answers. Would I get committed to an institution? She sensed my hesitation.

"Carter, no one's going to judge you on your answers because they won't know about them. They stay in this room."

"Yes."

"Do you feel that you have as much fun as most people do?"

"No." I left all that behind when my life became a war zone.

"Do you think you remember as much about your childhood as most people do?"

"No." I wished I didn't remember all the Big Ick scenes. They keep replaying in my mind.

"Have you, or do you still, use drugs or alcohol to excess, such that your use damages your health and perhaps those of your loved ones?"

"No, but I did six years ago and was in treatment for it. Since then, I don't use either one to excess anymore." But I worry I will unless I get my mom's ghost out of my life.

"A related question, do you work excessive hours and obsess over your work to the extent that you or others are concerned?"

I paused. "Yes, I do."

"Those two questions were about addiction. The first one about drugs and alcohol, the second about being a workaholic. That might be your biggest refuge from your pain, but your biggest threat to a healthy life. You need to be careful. Last question. Do you often guess at what is normal because being normal is so important to you?"

That question was like asking me if I was a male or not. Of course, I measure everything I do against whether it's normal or not. "Yes."

She scooted her chair back to her desk, picked up two small packets of papers, and rolled back to me again. She didn't show the packets to me yet.

"Carter, all of your answers strongly suggest you have many of the typical symptoms of an adult who grew up with at least one highly dysfunctional parent—in your case an alcoholic and drug addict. You didn't have a healthy parent to manage the dysfunctional one. And too many times as a child, you were alone with that dysfunction. That finding is a gift to you and Teri. You don't need to carry all those private concerns that you've worked so hard to hide. There is help. I'll show you now." Then she picked up the two packets from her lap. "I have some articles I'm hoping you and Teri will read. Here are two packets, one for you and one for

Teri. They're about a condition called 'adult children of alcoholics' or ACoA."

I looked down at one of them. "So is this my diagnosis?"

"No, but it's your situation. Some people call it a syndrome. Many adults who grow up as children of alcoholics have the same traits. The questions I asked are about many of those traits. The articles will suggest why you have those traits and what you can do about them. They will clarify that it's not your fault." She paused. "That it's . . . not . . . your . . . fault."

Tears started rolling down my cheeks, coming in waves. My chest started heaving. I couldn't get my breath. I clung to the arm of the couch. *Don't let me throw up.*

Astrid got up and put her hand on my shoulder. I quit crying at once. She didn't know I couldn't be touched when I'm not feeling safe. She quickly took her hand away. "I'm sorry. Are you okay?"

I nodded.

"Okay. Let's do this. The next time we meet, I'd like to hear what you think about the articles, if you think they describe what you experienced."

Then she grabbed a tablet and jotted a few things down. She handed me a list of what she called "assignments." She encouraged me to talk with Teri about them. The list included reading the first article together and discussing our impressions. She wanted to know, does the syndrome seem like my situation and how has it affected me? Affected Teri?

I shook my head. "I prefer not to involve Teri in this yet. Let's wait until I'm farther in the therapy."

"Carter, your recovery depends on involving her. Just like the family you grew up in, your situation affects your entire family and will affect it even more if you don't work on recovery. Your wife can be a support to you—perhaps the best support. What are you concerned about? Tell the truth. I'm not judging you."

"I'm afraid she'll leave me if she finds out that I'm . . . not normal."

"ACoAs have many fears. I think the biggest of them all is fear of abandonment. The irony is that you're more likely to keep Teri if you work on your recovery than if you don't."

She asked me to make an appointment for the three of us—and soon.

"Carter, I can't stress how important it is that you follow-up with me. There will be a time when you'll feel more comfortable sharing who you are, what you've gone through, and what you've learned from it. That will happen with more therapy. I'm privileged and honored to be part of your quest."

As before, I drove to the park and took notes. I couldn't help myself. I started reading the first article, then more. I must have been there for an hour. They were fascinating. It was like reading about myself from the inside out.

I couldn't wait to tell Teri and to give her packet to her. I drove home feeling giddy, totally alive—and for once, my mind was completely quiet. It had surrendered and was just going along for the ride.

Everything was going to be just fine now.

Promises, Promises

Late November 1968. I just turned fifteen. Renee knocks on my bedroom door, "Carter, Mom's on the phone and wants to talk to you." Oh, no. I feel like someone dumped slime on my head. Why is she calling me? She seldom even looks at me.

Two weeks ago, I was living in Watford City, my hometown. Mom had been so drunk and drugged that someone had noticed her and called the sheriff. How anyone had noticed, I don't know. I'd kept her in our house like always. The sheriff contacted the social worker, Mrs. Hayward, and both suddenly showed up to take her to the state hospital for "the cure." Meanwhile, Renee and LeeRoy took me into their home in Belfield until Mom gets out.

I've been here for two weeks and I love it. Different town and different school. Different home and different home life. Hot water, bathtub, and shower. Clothes washer and dryer. The house is clean and bright. I feel like I climbed out of a cesspool and stepped into a shower. I love it here. I can see why Faith moved out of Watford and into an apartment in Dickinson a year ago. But I have to remember I could get jerked away from Renee's in a day if Mom moves me back. I'm used to her disruptions.

I pick up the phone. "Hello." Here comes the phony drivel.

"Carter, I've missed you so much, my son. It's so good to hear your voice." I don't trust her. Haven't for years. What does she really want?

"I was in the state hospital and they were so good to me. Renee told lies to the sheriff who put me here but the hospital knew better and they let me out early." What? Renee told lies? Bullshit. Last time I looked, Mom had been passed out for two days. House stunk of wine and split pea soup.

"I'm coming to bring you back to Watford where you belong. A child should live with his mother. Where you want to be." No, I don't want to be there. Why is she so eager to get me back with her? Just to take care of her? She hardly noticed it when I did before.

"No, Mom, I don't want to be . . ."

She continued like she hadn't heard a word I'd said. "I'm so sorry she made you go through this and be torn you away from your only home where you want to be, living with me." That home was the Big Ick. I'm never going back.

"Mom! Mom, I don't want to be . . ."

She ignores me again, like she always does. "It'll be soon, Carter. Don't you worry. First, I'm coming there to help Renee with her new baby." I know that's not true. Renee doesn't want a thing to do with Mom. Neither do I. Why is she coming here?

"Mom, listen to me, I don't . . ."

She ignores me again. I'm feeling a blow-up coming, big time— but I'm safe, away from her. Calm down.

"Then we'll get you back home, with you living with me, where you want to be. You tell Renee that's what you want—to live with me." There's no use trying to talk to her. She just ignores me, but why is she pushing so hard for me to live with her? I won't be her nurse anymore. It won't happen.

"Son, I know sometimes I accidentally took too much medicine." Too much wine is too much medicine? *"No one knows the pain I've had, the cruelty, but I'm fine now. I won't ever be sick again."* I've heard this crap for years, so I hold the phone away from my ear until she might finally listen to me.

One more try. "Mom, stop. Listen to me."

She ignores me again. "I'm sure you remember all the good times we've had. Times we played checkers." And she let me win. *"Times we fished together."* She never fished with me.

"Mom, those are all lies and you . . ."

Blah, blah, blah.

"So, Carter, you tell Renee now that you want to come back home. Now put Renee back on the phone. Mommy loves you so much. We'll be back together soon, like you want it to be. The hospital taught me how to deal with all the pain I've had in my life." I hate her self-pity so much that I want to scream and smash something.

"Mom, I'm never going to live . . ." I don't bother to finish my sentence. What's the use? I feel like I've been yelling into the toilet.

About now, here comes her promises. *"So Carter, no more wine. No more pills. I'm cured now. I promise with all my heart and soul. You know Mommy loves you more than love itself. My love knows no bounds and . . ."* She thinks I'm so stupid that she can play me like a doll. I tried to pretend the Big Ick never existed. Now, it's back. I'm so angry, my hand is trembling when I set the phone down to get Renee.

On the way to the kitchen to get her, I hear her say to LeeRoy, *"Mom wants Carter back, probably just so she can keep getting the welfare money. She won't get that unless he lives with her."*

Cured!

I was thrilled to get home and tell Teri about my session with Astrid. After learning about ACoA, I didn't feel alone anymore. I felt validated, like I was real, almost like I'd been cured. Teri will be so thrilled for me. Maybe we'd get back to being normal now.

When I walked in, she was on the couch sorting baby clothes. Right away, she got up and hugged me. "Are you okay? I thought the session was over an hour ago. Where have you been?" She'd been worried about me surviving the session?

I closed my eyes and wrapped my arms around her. I held her back, so I could look straight into her eyes. "The session with Astrid today was a big breakthrough. Afterward, I went to the park and made notes so I wouldn't forget. I'm sorry I'm late. Let's feed Darienne and put her to bed so we can talk."

"That's all done, Carter. She's already sleeping."

We sat close together on the couch and I started. I described what Astrid had said about stress being caused by how you feel about what you're doing, not by how much you have to do. I explained how those feelings might not have anything to do with what you're doing. They might have more to do with something that happened a long time ago.

Teri frowned and said, "What?"

"Love, if someone saw a bloody car crash, they might not want to talk about it. If they ate a hamburger long afterwards, they might feel stressed if it's dripping with ketchup." Then I brought it closer to home. "If I saw a new neighbor who was six feet, five inches tall with a bald head like Lonny's, then I'd feel stressed." We laughed at the thought of it.

I went on. "The old feelings don't go away because those people haven't talked about them, haven't faced them. Today's session was about that. Do you know what I mean?"

"I understand now. But what things caused you a lot of stress before that you should be talking about now?"

I felt like the cops had barged in and I was holding the smoking gun. "Good question. I'll get to that." Sort of.

"You'll remember that Faith mentioned our mom was an alcoholic and drug addict. I said then that you get used to it—and you do. It's just sometimes there'd be a lot of yelling and we'd get into big arguments. Lots of noise. It could get really hectic. I'd get mad sometimes and stay alone in my room. That's what many people in that situation do. It was stressful, sure, but it sounds worse than it was." Oh, if that were only true.

"Then why did you need therapy for night terrors?"

Now I felt like I was on the witness stand and the prosecutor was probing me with questions.

"I'll explain. She said research shows a lot of people who grew up with a parent like mine often have similar feelings about it. Therapists say they have adult children of alcoholics syndrome or ACoA. It sounds worse than it is."

"Do you have that ACoA syndrome?"

"No. I mean, yes, but it's common and there are tips about what you can do about it. She gave me some great articles. I brought them home for you, too."

"How did she know you've got that syndrome?"

I hated that word. It made me sound like I was contagious.

"She went through a list of feelings or traits, asking me if I had each one. After I'd answered all the questions, she said I had the syndrome. She said the night terrors are from the stresses you and I have had lately and from my old feelings about stress coming back. That's all."

"I'm so happy that the session was such a breakthrough. Tell me what those feelings are. What do we do about each of them?"

I'd been giddy with relief when I came in the door, but now I was pissed. She wanted me to dig into my therapy. I'd told her not to do that and she had agreed.

"Love, let's do this one step at a time. I'll mention the traits to you now. Down the road, we'll get to why I have them, okay? Remember, the traits and what to do about them are in the articles. Let's just focus on that for now, okay?"

She didn't respond. She crossed her ankles and let out a big sigh.

"First, you're gonna hear a list that sounds like problems with me. They're not. They're just traits."

"Okay," she blurted out.

I'd better move on. I looked at my notes. "These are traits many ACoAs have. Anyway, they get irritable because they carry a lot of anger at their parent." I didn't mention they can have terrifying blow-ups, too. "They like to be alone, because they were trying to get away from the parent." I didn't mention crawling into a hole in the ground just to be alone. "They don't feel safe because their parent was yelling and smashing things around them." Or, they'd been attacked by their parent when trying to clean the sheets.

I looked at her to see if this was making sense. Now she's nodding again. Great. I can stay this vague and she'll be satisfied.

"They're nervous around others because they never know when the parent will explode." Or come into your room at night with a knife. "They avoid conflicts with others, especially by remaining silent or appeasing others." Or by lying with half-truths. "They work hard to be in control by managing every situation around them. Often, they had to be the parent in the household." I couldn't add any more to that one. Teri doesn't need to know that her husband feels like a phony and isn't normal.

"Carter, everything you said from your list is you. I couldn't have put them into words, but they are all you."

"What do you mean 'they are all me'?" Ten minutes ago, I felt normal. Now I felt like a freak again.

She shrugged her shoulders. "It was something I'd sensed. It wasn't a big deal. It was just you." She'd sensed all of that and was still with me? I felt surprised and relieved. "This has been wonderful, so good for us." She took my hand and squeezed it. "What do we do next?"

"She gave us some assignments. First, you and I are to read the articles about ACoA together and talk about them. We'd talk about whether they describe my situation and what effects the situation had on me." I didn't add that we're supposed to make an appointment with her afterward.

Teri rubbed her hands together. She was primed to start right away.

"Love, I'm hungry. It's been a long day. I need a break now." I got up, playfully kissed her on the nose and headed into the bedroom to change clothes and get back to being normal.

***

The work with Astrid helped form a firm foundation for the next three years of stability. From early 1982 to May 1985, Teri and I followed most of Astrid's many tips for dealing with stress. We'd cut back on coffee, scheduled more sleep and relaxed about parenting. We accepted that our baby would not die if we didn't feed her on time. I had one more night terror and then they stopped.

During that interval, in January 1983, our second child, Ian, was born. Taking care of one kid was like playing a musical instrument. Two was like conducting an orchestra. We sold the tiny condo and bought a house where the kids could eventually have their own bedrooms and Teri could grow flowers.

Also, during that interval, in September 1983, I was promoted to lead engineer, ironically because of my ACoA traits: always feeling responsible for everything around me and being on top of details. The ACoA articles helped me accept that my feelings about myself and my traumatic childhood were, well, normal. Those same traits got me promoted again, in May 1985, this time to supervisor. Even though it meant working more hours, it was more satisfaction because I was working with people rather than computer printouts.

In October of that year, Teri followed a cherished boss to join another company using even more exciting technologies.

Meanwhile, I didn't schedule any follow-up sessions with Astrid. Why should I? It seemed after those two sessions, everything would be just fine. I'd been cured.

"To know that you do not know is the best.
To think you know when you do not is a disease.
Recognizing this disease as a disease is to be free of it."

– Lao Tzu

Part 3
What Kind of Dad
Am I?

(1985-1988)

"Every arrogant person considers himself perfect.
This is the chief harm of arrogance. It interferes with
a person's main task in life: becoming a better person."

– Leo Tolstoy

Carter McNamara

Broken Promises

Early December 1968. It's only been two weeks since Mom got out of the state hospital after that sickening phone call where she'd promised no more pills, no more wine. She's been staying with Renee and LeeRoy, getting ready to move her and me back to Watford or maybe to live with my brother Mac in Williston. That won't happen. I'll run away first.

I'm walking back to Renee's from my new friend Kenny's house in Belfield. I turn the corner to Renee's house, hoping she'll have fresh caramel rolls. Instead, I see an ambulance in her driveway. The medical people are rolling a gurney out of her house. I panic that it might be Renee. As I get closer, I can see that it's Mom in the bed. I go inside and Renee is standing there, holding her daughter, LaRae, and watching the ambulance pull out of the driveway.

"Renee, what happened?"

She looks down, shakes her head and presses her lips together. She looks so disgusted. "Mom had been acting drugged again. We knew she wasn't drinking. There was no smell, no bottles. I looked all over and couldn't find any pills. Where she got them, I don't know."

She didn't have to convince me. I'd spent years as a kid feeling under her mattress, under her bed, looking in her closet, trying to find the wine. The bottles I found were always empty. We figured some man was bringing them when I was in school. When our hometown pharmacies wouldn't give her pills anymore, she'd get them somehow from pharmacies in other towns. She could hide her pills anywhere, so I just quit looking for them.

"Anyway, she didn't come out of her room this morning, so LeeRoy looked in on her and she was blue from lack of oxygen, so we

called the ambulance. They said it looked like she'd overdosed. They found an empty pill bottle underneath her. We looked all over and didn't find any more. Maybe she'd taken them all. We don't know what kind they were. I doubt she was trying to commit suicide. She doesn't have the courage to do that. At least she's out of here."

I shake my head. "Two weeks ago, she promised 'no more wine, no more pills. I'm cured.'" We both snicker at the thought. We'd heard those promises so many times.

"I'm going to call the state hospital and give them a piece of my mind. This time, they better keep her a lot longer than two weeks."

I feel like I've won the sweepstakes. Now I can stay in Belfield even longer.

Cat's in the Cradle

September 14, 1986. My birthday. Fall is the season for slowing down, for reflecting on the busyness of summer. Instead, I'd steeped myself in the chaos of sixty-hour work weeks. I loved it. I was getting awards for my work and promoted faster than most. Astrid had warned me that ACoAs often became addicted to alcohol, drugs, or work. That wasn't happening to me because things were still okay at home.

Teri had scheduled a romantic dinner, our first in six months. Considering how awfully busy I was, that was like trying to stop a hurricane to take a picture.

She made a seven p.m. reservation at our favorite restaurant, the Nicollet Island Inn, in Minneapolis. For this North Dakota boy, the Inn served the best steaks in town. For Teri, their salads were crisp and colorful. Most importantly, the Inn was quiet, so we didn't need to yell to be heard.

Although it was a Saturday, I worked until seven p.m. We were installing a two-million-dollar computer system that my department had worked hard to buy. Once the system was installed, it'd take weeks to fine-tune it. That meant longer weeks of work.

For this special night, I'd brought along my favorite attire: light blue shirt, dark blue jacket, and khaki pants. I changed into the clothes and headed out.

I knew she would arrive early to be sure we'd get our favorite table by the window that looks out on the Mississippi. We first ate there five years ago when we'd moved to the city, ready to start our careers and our lives together.

At twenty after seven, I scurried in, hoping Teri would not make an issue of my being late again. She stood up to hug me. Maybe I was off the hook. She was wearing a knee-length, strawberry-red dress. Her thick, brunette hair draped down her back and a string of white pearls adorned her neck. She stood three inches higher in her dark heels. She meant for me to see her—and I did.

"I'm sorry I'm late. The contractor didn't have all the parts and had to get them at the warehouse. Security wouldn't let them back in . . ." I'd shared so many excuses for being late that I didn't need to say the rest.

The waiter politely approached us with menus and water, then announced the specials. I thanked him, then ordered decaf coffee and passed on the wine. Teri did the same. The waiter brought the cups and we toasted each other with our coffees.

"Happy birthday! Thank you for making time tonight. I wanted to talk to you."

I tilted my head slightly and lowered a brow. "This won't be one of those apologetic dinners where the wife confesses she's in love with an older man?" I remembered Astrid telling me the biggest fear of ACoAs is abandonment. She was right. My heart was beating hard.

She put her hands on mine. "No, of course not. I love you and want to spend the rest of my life with you. But your management job has been sixty hours a week since you started it. Of course, my hours have been irregular since I started my new job, too." She sat back and rested her hands on her lap. "I feel like we've been in constant commotion—always asking which of us will do what, where, and when."

She didn't add that I'd been more irritable and impatient lately. She didn't add that I was rarely at home. I hadn't told her about my nightmares. Would they become night terrors, too? I'd been trying hard to follow advice from the ACoA articles. Don't expect perfection. Don't judge yourself. Feelings are okay—it's what you do with them that counts. Talk to someone. Breathe. Take a walk.

I offered a meek, "Maybe it will settle out." Maybe I belonged in the 1950s when wives worked in the home and husbands worked when they were needed at the office.

"I hope so. Ian's acting up at daycare. Darienne's detaching. I miss you."

"What do you think we should do?"

"I've been thinking, what about us joining a health club? We both could use the exercise. We could bring the kids along, too. Or, how about planning a week-long family vacation next summer? The good parks get filled up early, so let's schedule it now." Sure, it wouldn't hurt to schedule it. We could always reschedule it later if I was needed at work. Best to not say that out loud.

"Absolutely, Teri. Let's do both. Let's start a reservation tomorrow."

She lifted her cup for another toast. "For now, I want this to be a romantic dinner, a chance to reconnect."

I felt reassured she was still with me. It was like stepping into a warm embrace after a long, frigid walk. "Okay. Let's do that."

I ordered my steak and Teri ordered her salad. Through much of the meal, we held hands when we could.

We drove home in our separate cars. On the way, I felt haunted that I hadn't noticed what was happening with my family. I wished I would've remembered what was most important in my life: my wife and my kids. Maybe I would've remembered if I'd followed through on the therapy—the follow-up sessions I never scheduled with Astrid.

Instead, I acted like I was suddenly cured. All that seemed too familiar. Then I remembered what Mom had promised two weeks before she got drunk again: "I'm cured."

I felt like such a phony.

"You Hurt Me"

I hate taking a crap at night. Our toilet is in Mom's room and there's no door. It's just a foggy plastic shower curtain hanging on a rod around a toilet. Sometimes when she's drunk, she thinks I'm somebody else. She staggers to the curtain, grabs it, and tries to pull it back to see who's in there. When she sees it's me, she mumbles, "Get out of my room. Do that in your room." She says the words like she's trying to sing a song, but her mouth is full of cotton.

I never get used to it. I always feel like I'm being attacked. Usually, I just tell her who I am and she goes back to bed. This is one of those times when she doesn't. She keeps mumbling and grabbing the curtain, not realizing it's me. I'm sitting on the toilet with my underwear around my ankles, trying hard to keep the curtain closed. I'm thirteen and big for my age, but she's standing up and can reach the rod.

I can go back to my bedroom, not knowing if she'll just follow me. Or, I can get her back to her bed where she'll probably just pass out again. Then I can finish pooping.

I'll try get her back to bed. I pull up my underwear, open the curtain, and grab her by the arms. Her upper arms are soft and puffy and easiest to grab onto. I get a handful in both hands.

This time, though, she tries to swing her arms around and get loose. I squeeze her arms even harder and start pushing her backwards to her bed. She starts crying and saying, "You're hurting me. You're hurting me." I try to ignore her, like I do most of the time with her.

Finally, I push her backward onto her bed. She lands on her back and rolls away from me, like she's mad at me. Her voice quivers and she says, "You hurt me. You hurt me." I cover her up and go back to my bedroom.

In the morning, I decide I'm done with that. No more attacks. I have a door in my room that goes to the outside. It's been nailed shut since I can remember. It's summer now, so I'm gonna open that damn door so I can crap outside.

I use a hammer to pry off the little lathe boards Mom nailed around the closed door. I have to sit on my butt and push hard with my legs before the door finally pops opens. It feels really good to have the air come in. It smells like the grass our neighbor mows all the time. Now I can piss and crap outside under our trees if I have to. There are lots of trees in our backyard.

I don't see her for a couple of days. When she's done being drunk, she stays in her bedroom for a few days. She likes it really dark in there. Sometimes, I hear her in the kitchen making split pea soup and peeling oranges for herself.

The next time I see her, she is sober enough to make coffee in the kitchen. She's wearing a summer dress without sleeves. I come in just long enough to grab the loaf of bread and peanut butter and get the heck out of there.

Before I can leave, Mom says, "My arms hurt so bad. Look." She says it in that whispering way she always does when she starts getting sober. Her mouth is always dry and makes small clicking sounds when she talks.

I see three or four small, round, bluish-purple spots on her upper arms. They each have a faint yellow ring around the outside. Right away, I know they're from when I grabbed her a lot harder than usual. This time, I really did hurt her. She doesn't ask me where they came from. I would've lied to her, anyway.

I go back to my room and sit on my bed. I keep seeing those spots. I didn't know I actually hurt her. My eyes start to sting and I know I'm gonna cry. That's okay. She won't hear me, anyway.

I am cruel, like Mom always says.

The Mark

It was evening, Friday, December 11, 1987. I'd worked all day to keep the computers going for the twelve hundred people in our building. I managed the people who supervised the people who did the real work. All that meant was that I just stayed out of their way. I was the boss at work. Teri was the boss at home. When I got home, I reported to Teri to help with the remaining housework.

Afterward, I walked up to her. "Dinner is done. Baths are done. Kids are playing in their room. Now what?" I was standing in the middle of the living room, waiting for instructions, feeling like a puppet on a string. She looked as vacant as I felt, eyes unfocused, arms at her sides.

"Let's look at the lists." She sounded like a man going to the gas chamber.

"No." I said it in a monotone, yet it was a primal scream to just stop. I felt like I was at the edge of a cliff, looking down.

"Are you okay?"

Now that I had her attention, what should I say? Where would I start? I felt like the match was too close to the fuse. She took my hand and led me to the couch. "What's going on?"

"I feel like I'm ready to explode. The goddamned lists. Christmas lists. Darienne's birthday on the 22nd. Ian's on January 18th. Our different work schedules. People bitching at work. I'll be okay if I just vent for a while. I'm fine."

I wasn't sure she'd even heard me because the kids were yelling so loud. Then we heard a "thud, thud, thud," like someone running across our roof. I turned to Teri. "What the hell was that?"

"They're just playing. Whatever. Go on."

"This management job. In over a year, I'm already frustrated. I have little input into the decisions that really affect my department. They're made by people who don't even know what we do. It takes months to approve the resources that I need right now. I'm just moving paper around and wearing a tie."

"What do you want to do, Carter? You know I'll support you. I wonder if . . ."

Boom! Thud, thud, thud.

It was from their bedroom. I rushed in to see what happened. They were both still naked from their baths. Darienne was on the bottom bunk and Ian was standing on the ladder to his top bunk. Books were spilled all over the floor.

I gasped. "What happened?"

They didn't answer. Both of them were looking at me, laughing.

In a gruff voice, I asked again, "What's going on?" Darienne quit laughing, but Ian was laughing louder.

I gave up and stacked the books back on the shelf. "Be quiet and go to sleep." Darienne rolled over toward the wall and Ian jumped onto his bed. I turned out the lights and went back to Teri.

"You were asking me something about 'what if?'"

"I was wondering if . . ."

Boom! Thud, thud, thud.

I rushed into their room again. The light was back on. Books were back on the floor. Ian was on the ladder again, laughing again, but this time, looking directly at me. Was he challenging me?

I snarled and spanked his behind, hard. He quit laughing. He didn't cry. He just stood there on the ladder, staring at me—his eyes big and round.

I was enraged. I pulled back my hand to spank him again, this time even harder. Then I saw the mark of my fingers on his butt from where I'd just spanked him. I cried out and rushed from the room.

Teri met me in the hall. She grabbed my arm and asked, "What happened?"

I froze in my tracks. "He was just a little boy! He was just a little boy!"

"Who was just a little boy?"

I put my hand on my head and frowned. Who "was" just a little boy?

She stepped around me and into their bedroom. I sat down on the couch with my head in my hands. I felt sick about what I'd done. I heard her ask them what happened and then faint sounds of Darienne trying to explain. Teri talked for a few minutes, probably trying to reassure them.

She came back out and repeated her question. "What happened?"

I looked up at her. "I'm so sorry I hurt him. He didn't deserve that. He's just a little boy." I started crying again.

"I saw the red marks on his butt. You spanked him too hard. Carter, when I was a kid, I got spanked by my parents, sometimes with a wooden spoon. You've been a model for me in parenting, in treating our kids like humans, not just children." She sat down, put her hand on my chin and turned my face toward her. "So, what's going on?"

By now, I'd moved from fear and panic to self-loathing and disgust. "That mark. I can't get it out of my head. I will never spank them again. I can't be that kind of dad. Were there bruises on his arms, too?"

"No. There weren't any. Why would there be?"

I didn't remember grabbing him. Why would there be bruises on his arms?

"How were you disciplined when you were a kid? Does that have anything to do with why you're upset now?"

"No. I was very rarely spanked when I was a kid." Actually, I don't remember Mom ever spanking me.

She sat there, squeezing my shoulder, waiting for me to say more. How could I explain it to her? I remembered when Astrid asked why I didn't talk about my childhood. I'd answered that I didn't know where to start. I couldn't explain it. People wouldn't understand. They would pity me. I hadn't said that they'd judge me—judge me for the hurt that I'd caused.

The next morning, I asked Ian if I could hug him. He let me, but he did it like I'd ordered him to. He opened his arms and didn't squeeze. He held his head back as if hugging me because he had to.

That afternoon, I took two chairs from the dining room table and put them across from each other in the family room. I found Ian in his room, playing with his Legos. I asked him to come in with me, then invited him to sit on a chair. He sat there, looking so small, wearing his white cable-knit sweater and brown corduroy pants. He started doing what he always did when he was nervous: he rocked back and forth.

I sat down across from him, clasped my hands and said, "Ian, thank you for coming in here with me. I love you." I paused, trying to find the right words. "I hurt you when I spanked you. I'm so sorry I did that. Did I scare you?"

He nodded, rocking back and forth, still wide-eyed, holding his head back.

"Ian, I will never spank you or Darienne ever again." I let the tears start. He did, too. "Never. I promise. You're a good boy." I got up, kneeled in front of him and hugged him. This time, he hugged me back. Then he headed back to his Legos. Teri had been standing by the door. She came over and hugged me. "How does it feel to apologize to him?"

"Good." I hugged her back and walked over to the window to look up at the sky.

When I bruised Mom, I should have apologized to her, too.

Hear Me!

"Mom! Mrs. Leiseth said I have a great voice. She said I can carry a tune. I'm practicing a solo in the Christmas song all by myself. She says you'll be so proud of me. Can you come?"

"Maybe, son."

"You haven't ever heard me at my concerts. Lots of other parents come and talk to their kids after the concerts. Can you come to at least one? This time you'll hear me sing by myself, okay? Mom? Mom! Did you hear what I said?"

"Yes, son, you have a very good voice."

"Mom, I asked if you'll come to the concert. Will you?"

"I don't know, son. I've had a bad case of the nerves lately."

"Mom, we live right across from the school. You can go right back home if you get sick. I don't know if she'll ever let me sing by myself again. Please?"

"I said I'd try."

"You're not gonna come, are you? Don't lie to me!"

"Don't be cruel to me. You know so many people have been so cruel to me. That's why I get so sick sometimes."

"Mom, you're not really gonna come to the concert, are you? Just say so. What are you a mother for, then? Why did I end up with you? You only think of yourself! I will always show up when I'm a dad! I won't be like you!"

Mom is crying again. I don't care.

The Little Buddha

Ian was the emotional compass in our home. He would get upset when he sensed conflict, and lately there had been too much conflict between Teri and me. We'd been working overtime and both of us were exhausted. I was sure Ian sensed my irritability when I was struggling with my internal demons.

When Darienne was upset, she'd retreat to her room and escape into her books. If Teri and I were arguing, she'd avoid us until we'd settled down. When Ian was upset, he'd sit on a chair, stare at the floor, and rock back and forth. Sometimes he'd try to intervene to distract us by showing us something he'd made. Usually, Teri and I would realize what he was up to and we'd stop.

Playing with our kids was a great gift to me because it reassured me they still felt safe around me. I was having fun and being a good dad. Teri often said that I played with them more than she did, while she was busy acting like the only parent.

Ian often played alone, particularly when assembling something. On many of those occasions, I would lie on my belly just off to the side, so I could be with him but not get in his way.

Usually, he'd be sitting on his butt on the floor, legs bent at the knees and crossed at the ankles like a tiny Buddha, but with his back slightly bent and his head down to study whatever he was doing. He'd rock slightly back and forth as he worked.

Sometimes I would ask if I could help. Sometimes he would shake his head, but he'd still let me talk to him. Usually, I'd say four to five sentences. Then he might respond with one or two but he'd never stop what he was doing.

On those rare occasions when he'd let me help, it'd usually be with some straightforward, orderly task that had little risk of interfering with what he was doing. On one occasion, we were planning to assemble a small plastic model of a 1966 Mustang

125

Pony. It was baby blue with a white roof, a replica of my first car. The model was a present from my family for my 35th birthday.

Early January 1988, we were both on the hardwood floor of our living room. I was wearing denim coveralls. He was wearing a white pull-over sweatshirt with Goofy, his favorite cartoon character, on the front, and black sweatpants, even though it was warm in the house. He hated anything tight against his skin. His long brown hair hung down past his ears, the way he liked it.

He was doing his Buddha thing. I was sitting on my butt with my legs out straight. If I tried to sit like the Buddha, I'd dislocate both knees.

I started by pouring out the model parts from the box. I picked up two small wheels, intending to start by connecting one to each end of an axle.

"Ian, I need the axle for the front tires. It'll be a gray stick that's about two inches long. You have it?"

"Yes." That's all he said. What was he waiting for?

"Well, then. Ian, can I have it?"

"Yes." Once again, that's all he said. What in the world was he waiting for?

"Can I have it now?" I realized he was playing with my mind—and he was only five years old. This didn't look good for my future as a parent.

"Yes." Then he handed it to me. I saw he was trying to hide a smile.

I took the axle from him and pushed a small wheel onto each end.

He laughed out loud.

"What's so funny?"

He pointed the tiny index finger of his right hand at the axle with the two tires on it—the axle that I was feeling so good about. He broke out giggling, holding his arms around his stomach, rocking back and forth even faster now.

The little bugger was laughing at me, not with me. Okay, now I was getting a little irritated. "Ian, what's so funny?"

By this time, he was giggling so hard that he just tipped over sideways onto the floor.

Then I realized I had attached the two wheels, each with its designer hubcap, to be facing in toward each other. I quickly pulled off each wheel and switched it to be facing outward so the world would see the designer hubcaps. I looked at Ian, hoping for some sign of approval.

He sat back up, did the Buddha thing again and nodded his head to show his approval. His hazel eyes were twinkling. Yeah, he was approving, all right. Meanwhile, he had his right hand over his mouth to stop himself from giggling out loud again.

A few minutes later, there I was, lying on my belly, stacking similar-looking pieces of the model together. Every so often, he'd smile, ask me for a particular piece, and then quickly connect it to another while we assembled the car—together.

"Did your dad play with you?"

"I didn't have a dad. Remember, son?"

"That must have been sad for you."

"That was very sad, son. But I'm so glad I get to be your dad."

This kid was amazing—and I get to watch him grow up.

The Tipping Point

I'm lying on my bed in my room, trying to focus on a schoolbook about earth science. I'm in the eighth grade and I love this class. It's all about nature, the world that's my real home, not this hell-hole that I yearn to escape from.

"Carter! Carter! Get in here!"

She chops up the syllables in her words like each one has to be pushed out of her mouth. She talks like her tongue sticks to the roof of her mouth. What'll it be this time? She can't get to the toilet? Needs another enema? Can't reach her wine bottle? Lost her pills? Maybe she'll just fall asleep again.

"Carter! I know you heard me! Get in here!"

She's lying on her right side on her bed. She's wearing the same torn pink nightgown that she always has on. Somehow, she's managed to raise her head, propping it up with her right arm bent at the elbow. Her thin, straggly hair is matted down on her head, probably stuck there from vomit or sweat.

I used to try to clean her up during a binge, but that was useless. It was like cleaning a filthy bird cage with the birds still in it. Total chaos—screeching, scratching, and fluttering about, and soon the filth's right back the way it was.

She reaches out her left arm to me, holding a small piece of paper in her trembling hand. She tries to hold her arm still, but it waves around like she's writing her name in the air.

"Here. Take this note to Larson Drug. Not Lundeen Drug. Momma is too sick to do that now. She's got the flu. You better run. Larson Drug. Not Lundeen Drug."

Standing as far from her as possible, I pluck the note from her hand, already knowing what's on it. Sure enough, in writing like she'd scratched it out with a stick pin, she'd written "Spill doorden All gone Refill Bad nerves McNamara." Bullshit. She didn't spill the pills. They went down her throat. She's lying.

"Mom, I can barely read this. What's d-o-o-r-d-e-n?"

"You know. Don't pretend! It's my door-ah-den. Don't be cruel!" She reaches for the pill bottle and meekly tosses it at me. It lands on the floor and I pick it up. The label says "Doriden" on it. The monthly refill date is two weeks away and already she's taken the entire bottle. The drug store won't refill this without the doctor's orders. If I tell her that, she'll stagger downtown herself, and the world will find out what goes on in our house.

No use asking my sister Faith to do this. She'll just disappear. My brother Mac doesn't have a phone, so I can't call him in Williston. My sister Renee lives seventy miles away.

So I lied. "Sure, Mom. I'll leave right now."

"Larson Drug, not Lundeen Drug!" Her head bobs up and down with each syllable. Then her head collapses back onto the snake pit I call her bed.

The last time she tried Lundeen Drug, they called the doctor on her. Larson Drug will simply tell me they won't refill it until it's due. Why waste my time? She'll pass out now for a few more hours. I'll put a chair in front of each door and hear her if she tries to get out.

I go back to my room, crumple up her note and get back to my school book.

Can't Tell Frank

It was Wednesday, January 13, 1988. I'd stopped at my secretary's desk to glance through some memos she handed to me. I was standing on the other side of the bay wall where my employee, Frank, was sitting with his bay mate, Nick.

I dreaded hearing Frank's voice because I knew that I'd be laying him off on Friday. Executives had handed down an edict to lay off ten percent of our workforce. We were to notify the doomed employees at three-thirty p.m. on Friday, so they'd be escorted out the door, never to return. Frank was a kind and thoughtful engineer everyone liked. But he worked on a technology that was rapidly getting out of date, so his job wouldn't be needed.

I could hear Frank's conversation with Nick. "So tonight, I'm shopping with my wife. I thought Christmas had bled us dry of money. But now she wants to buy new carpet throughout the house, so we'll look pretty for the reunion this summer. Tomorrow, we buy braces for our daughter so her teeth will be pretty then, too. No problem, though. We don't have to pay for it. We'll just charge it." They laughed at his irony.

I rushed into my boss's office. I'd stop Frank from spending money he wouldn't have.

Louis was a company man. He focused on plans, policies, and procedures. But he had a very human side, too. Unlike many other managers, he knew the names of all seventy of his employees and spoke to each of them by name. If an employee had a personal crisis, he'd be the first to offer help. I was counting on his human side now.

"Louis, thanks for meeting with me so soon. This should only take a few minutes."

He had a nervous twitch that I worked hard not to see. Right before he spoke, he'd make a short, snorting sound. It sounded like a crow. It also made his nose twitch, so I'd look just to the right of it, so I wouldn't laugh.

Caw, twitch. "Sure, Carter. Sit down."

I told him about what I'd heard from Frank. "I'm going to tell him about the layoff now. I just wanted you to know that. I know HR said not to tell anyone yet, but this is a special situation. Thanks." I knew he'd approve of this special situation, so I turned to go.

Loud caw noise. "No. No you're not. I'm sorry about Frank's situation, but we can't tell anyone until Friday at three-thirty p.m. You'll have to wait."

"He's buying a carpet and braces. That's thousands of dollars. Christmas already bled him dry. We can stop that. You have my word. I won't tell any of the other employees."

"But we don't know if Frank will tell them. We can't control that. If he told one person, they could tell ten. HR would be down our throats. We're not risking that."

"I'll get Frank to promise not to tell. You know Frank. He's a great guy. He'll understand. Please. What am I supposed to do around him for the next two days? Act like I don't know anything about layoffs?" I hated the sound of my voice when I was begging.

"What if another manager comes in and wants to tell one of his employees, too? Do I let him because I let you? Then it would be even more likely that HR would find out. Carter, you've got a great career here. You're on a fast track. It might feel good to save Frank the money, but in the long run, you'd be hurting your career. You know the right thing to do, don't you." He wasn't asking, he was affirming that I'm the kind of person who would do what the company said. Was I?

I walked out of his office feeling like I'd hit a brick wall. Was I a company man now, too? Where was my human side? It would take two minutes to tell Frank and I know he wouldn't tell anyone else. What should I do?

My secretary came up to me. "Your four o'clock starts in five minutes. Better hurry."

"Is Frank in his bay?'

"Yeah, but you know him. He leaves right at four o'clock. Should I get him?" When I paused too long, she repeated, "Should I get him?"

Which was more important? Saving his money or saving my career?

"No. Never mind."

Off the Track

Late January 1988. Five degrees above zero. Feels as cold outside as I feel inside.

I'd just gotten back from a convenience store where I'd grabbed a quick lunch. I was too troubled to socialize in the company cafeteria. I bought a sandwich wrapped in plastic and a plastic bottle of juice both stuffed in a plastic bag. Plastic—the synthetic stuff. A perfect description for me in my role: a fake manager.

I closed my office door, sat down at my desk, and loosened my tie. Over the past few months, it felt more like a noose. I picked up the phone and dialed Teri. It rang so long, I thought it'd go to her secretary. Damn. I needed to talk to her.

"Hello, this is Teri." She sounded frazzled. She was getting ready for another business trip again. She'd been traveling so much lately.

"Hey, how's it going? Ready for the trip?"

"Yeah, but I'm ready for a break from airports, taxis, hotels, and restaurants. How about you?"

"Do you have a few minutes? I need to talk." My voice sounded soft and low. This call had to be very private.

"Yeah, Carter. What's going on?" She always said my name when she was very serious and focused. Good.

"You remember Paul, my network engineer?"

"Sure. He's the one who's always stuck with working overtime." She laughed at that caricature of him of him working so hard. I didn't.

"That's him. He just finished the network expansion and today we tested it. Three hundred employees moved here from the other building and now all of them are on the high-speed network—today. That's a big deal. No bugs. No problems."

"You don't sound happy about it."

"Two weeks ago, I put in for a bonus for him. Today, my boss's boss turned it down. Said we didn't have the money in the budget but could give him some stretch goals, so he could work harder to maybe earn a promotion instead. We say our values are to honor and respect our employees. That's a lie. I'm so fed up with this bullshit." I felt like a giant mirror was standing right there in front of me, confronting me with myself. "Teri? I . . ." I was so glad I'd closed the door to my office. I was tearing up now.

"Carter, no one else is around me right now. I've got the time. What's going on?"

"I haven't been honest with you. I didn't want you to worry, but I've been feeling like this job just isn't for me. I feel like such a phony. I should've told you this before." I rested my head in my hand. I ended up looking down at my calendar. It was full for the next two months.

"Love, what are you saying?"

"This job used to matter so much to me, but a lot of that was just my ego. I felt so validated having a job with such status." I remembered how ACoA articles said we seek validation. Yeah, that was me.

"What's changed?"

"I keep seeing myself sitting on the floor, watching Ian put a car model together, instead of sitting here, putting budgets together." Then my voice got sadder, softer. "I also remember spanking him, that mark on his butt. Back then, I felt like a race car, speeding down the track, right into a wall. Hell, I still do."

"I feel like you've already come to some kind of decision and you just need to hear yourself say it." She'd said those last few words in a higher voice, like she was really asking me a question.

"Teri, I know we've got a house and car to pay for, college funds to start, all that new furniture in the house."

"Love, you're really talking to yourself, aren't you? You're thinking out loud about a decision. That's okay. I want to hear this. I love you."

"I love you, too." I took a deep breath. "I want to quit my job. Teri, I have to quit my job." There. I felt like I'd been parched, wandering in the desert for days, then stuck my head in a cool, flowing stream.

"I know, Carter."

"You knew? Why didn't you tell me?" I started laughing at myself, thinking that she knew my life's decisions well before I did.

"For the past few months, it seemed like you'd drift off in your mind. I was going to talk to you about it, but I've been so involved in my own work."

"Yeah, my mind has been off somewhere. I kept thinking about this job and what happened with Ian and I realized I'm turning into somebody that I don't want to be."

"Carter, I knew you were never meant for the corporate track."

"Whew! I'm quitting! God, it feels good to say that out loud. I need to tell Louis. Last time I talked to him, he told me I'm on a fast track in management. He'll be pissed. I need to update my resume. Do some interviews and . . ."

"And take some time off," she added. "Build something with the kids." We both laughed. "I love you, Carter."

"I love you, too, Teri."

"Hey, before you go, I just wanted to tell you. You are such a great dad."

"Thank you."

I hung up and sat there, staring at my packed calendar.

He Dropped the Ball

I got my new Rawlings baseball glove yesterday. It's for right-handed outfielders, so it's longer and thinner than Gordon's fat catcher's mitt.

It's beautiful! It's brown and smells like leather. Kinda like Mom's little bottles of vanilla or the sticky sap out of our trees. I love it. I bet this is the best glove of any fifth grader.

But it's real stiff. I have to break it in so it gets soft. The store told me to put water on it and move the fingers on the glove around. I did that for a long time last night. They said to throw a ball real hard into the pocket so it gets rounder inside. I did that, too.

I'm in the backyard throwing the ball real high and catching it over and over. My brother, Mac, stops his car in front of our house. I don't see him very much, but he's still my brother. I run up to him to show him my glove. He might want to play catch with me.

"Look at my new glove! Feel how soft it is."

He takes the glove from me and pounds his fist in it once and smiles. He knows something about baseball gloves.

I say, "C'mon, let's play catch in the back yard. I won't throw hard."

I turn to run back there, but he doesn't follow me. I turn to him. "C'mon, just for a while." I turn back again and this time he's coming with me. My heart starts to beat fast. I don't get to do things with him very much because he is so busy. I'm getting so excited to show him how good I can catch.

In the backyard, I first throw the ball to him very soft because he doesn't have a glove. I'll let him use mine in a little bit. He caught the ball real good.

Then I run farther away so I can show him how good I catch. "Throw the ball as hard as you can and I'll catch it." I crouch down like catchers do.

Mac throws it real hard. It goes way over my head and way behind me. That was a terrible throw. He can't throw very well. I turn to run back to get the ball. I pick it up and turn around, but Mac is gone. I stand there and wait for a long time.

Then I hear him yelling with Mom in the front yard. He doesn't remember I'm in the backyard, so I run to the front yard to get him, but he's driving away in his car. He doesn't come back.

I feel really sad. Danny's dad plays catch with him all day long. I'm really mad at Mac now. I go to the backyard and throw the ball in the air again.

You Were Respected

It was May 22, 1988. I was in the kitchen wiping pots and pans. Amidst the clatter, Teri said something to me from the living room. I must have misheard. What I'd heard could not be true. I headed into the living room to investigate.

"Carter, Mac died." Teri was standing there, holding the phone, staring at me. She emphasized the word "died" like she needed to believe herself.

I stared back. "What do you mean 'he died'?"

"That was Renee on the phone. LeeRoy found him dead this morning." Mac had been living with them the past few months while being treated for lung cancer, but I didn't think it was that bad.

Teri asked, "Should we go to Renee's?"

I felt like I was not part of this conversation, like I was hearing dialogue from a movie. I sat across from Teri, clasped my hands and stared at the floor.

Mac was my blood brother and also my brother in arms. We had been in a horrific war together—a war all four of us had survived but none of us had won. I couldn't describe that to Teri. I knew I should say something to her, if only to get my mind back.

"I don't know what to say. He was a good guy. He . . ." My voice trailed off. What else could I say? I felt defensive. Mac was fifteen years older than me. We didn't have much of a relationship. "There's such a huge age difference between us. He was rarely around." He'd be the first to barge out the door when Mom started a rage. I tried to remember anything about him. Then I started chuckling and shaking my head.

"Remember, I told you his favorite food was beans and wieners? With minced ham and mayo? On white bread? He'd wash it down with cans of Budweiser? Remember when we visited him, the first thing he did was make that for us. We declined the beer, remember?" I burst out laughing. Soon, I was squeezing my sides and giggling so hard, I couldn't catch my breath. That turned into a small stream of tears. God, it felt good to cry for him.

"Yeah, I remember the minced ham. It was awful." Now she was laughing, too. She got tissues for both of us to blow our noses.

"You two hardly ever talked. What do you remember?"

"He talked Mom into buying me a bike for Christmas. It was beautiful. Red frame, chrome fenders, and twenty-four-inch wheels. They'd kept it hidden behind the old mattress in the shed. I cried when they showed it to me. Then, I had to stare at it for four months until the snow thawed." That was the most personal thing that had ever happened between us. There was that other time, when I'd tried to get him to play catch with me. He walked away from me and I was mad at him for a long time. As I got older, I realized who he was probably yelling at and why.

"Renee said Mom could never tell him to do anything. He'd just get mad and walk out. Renee and I could never figure out how he'd made it through the Army where they're telling you what to do all the time." I scratched my head. "One time, she met a man who was in basic training with Mac. He said there's a thing in the Army called KP. It means kitchen police and every soldier hates it because basically it's just peeling potatoes. So, sergeants use it as a means of punishment." Now, I was laughing so hard, I could barely push out the words. "He said the guys rarely saw Mac because most of his time he was in the kitchen doing KP."

Three days later, I was on the road to the funeral home. Teri stayed home with the kids. My friend, Bob, wanted to come along. He was staying with us while he attended school to learn sign language. He'd met Mac and liked him. Besides, I could use the company. He was six feet tall and weighed one hundred forty pounds when wet. He was constantly practicing sign language, his long bony fingers jerking through the air. They looked like stick men fighting each other.

He said, "Remember when Mac was in treatment for alcoholism and we used his car? Remember when he checked out early from treatment and he couldn't find us and his car because we'd taken it fishing? You could tell he was furious, but he never said a word." Bob laughed his unique laugh—a loud, sharp cackle followed by a long wheeze. "Actually, he never said a word, at all. I don't even remember what he looked like."

I smiled at the memory of Mac's image. "He was about five feet nine. I was taller than him even when I was in high school. He had thin auburn hair tinged with gray. His hairstyle was the nineteen-fifties rebel look. He'd grease it, then comb the top to one side and the sides straight back. He walked with his head forward, but his back and shoulders slouched. He was a bit duck-footed. When he walked, it looked like his head, body, and feet didn't quite match." Both of us started laughing. I was so glad he'd come along.

At the funeral home, I kept thinking this might be the most attention Mac had ever gotten. But he'd worked so hard just to be alone. While we waited for the minister, some thin, tinny, religious music started playing. It sounded like an old transistor radio about fifty feet away. It would've provoked a barrage of cursing from Mac. He would've stormed out the door. I glanced over at Renee to gauge her reaction. She was doing the same thing with me. Immediately, we both broke into giggles. We tried to squash the giggling behind pressed lips, but that made us sound like we were playing the kazoo.

The other mourners misunderstood and looked at us with sympathy: heads tilted, bottom lips protruding. They thought Renee and I were crying. Of course, that made both of us laugh even harder. Mac would've loved it.

After the service, we piled into our respective cars to follow the hearse to the cemetery about forty miles away. As our funeral procession slowly approached the major highway on the edge of town, a group of six men was waiting for the hearse. They were dressed in their military uniforms. When we came to a stop, they stood at attention and sharply saluted him—right there, where everyone driving by would see the respect that Mac had earned as a veteran. Then they backed away to let the hearse proceed.

I said to myself, "See, Mac. People see you and they respect you. I love you, my brother."

***

There's a famous fable about boiling a frog. If you drop a frog in boiling water, it will jump out. If you put the frog in warm water and slowly heat it, the frog will boil to death. It wouldn't notice the incremental change. That described the interval from May 1988 to December 1989. We hadn't noticed the changes that were slowly heating up our relationship.

In May 1988, I quit the technology company and started at the University of Minnesota in a job with less responsibility that happily meant more time at home. Suddenly, I went from the exhausting sixty-hour work weeks down to a relaxing forty. In contrast, Teri's workload steadily increased. She led bigger teams with greater challenges and was traveling more often. That all added up to more conflicts and stresses in our lives.

The distance between us was more than geographic. We had different schedules, work, and groups of friends. Ultimately, the distance between us became emotional as well. We were more like partnering parents than parenting partners.

Our mornings consisted of getting the kids out of bed, hurrying them through their breakfasts, and dropping them off at school. Then we'd each step into the merry-go-round of work. Afterward, we'd get the kids from school, share a dinner, read them books, put them to bed, and finally, go to bed ourselves. The next day we'd get up and do it again.

Meanwhile, my frustrations and fears of abandonment continued to grow. I no longer spanked the kids. Instead, my anger was funneled into the verbal outbursts that I'd honed so well as a child.

"The ultimate ignorance is the rejection
of something you know nothing about
yet refuse to investigate."

– Dr. Wayne Dyer

Carter, Renee, Mac (Dion), and Faith McNamara
(left to right), ~1955

Carter McNamara, ~5 years old

Elvina Granlie McNamara, ~1955

Carter and Teri McNamara, July 24, 1981

Carter & Darienne McNamara, ~1996

Carter & Ian McNamara, ~1997

Roger Krumel, Laverne Malott, & Carter McNamara, 2010

Faith Bellon, Carter McNamara, Renee Lowenstein, 2014

Renee Lowenstein, 2018

Carter & Teri McNamara, July 24, 2006

Carter McNamara

Part 4
Attacked by My Past

(1988-1993)

"No beast is more savage than man
when possessed with power
answerable to his rage."

– Plutarch

Carter McNamara

"I'll Visit Sometimes"

I love summer in our backyard. We have more trees than any other house. No other seven-year-old can climb as high as I can. If I crawl underneath them, no one sees me.

I'm playing under the trees and my sister, Renee, tells me to come into the house. I always do what she says because she's so good to me. I like her more than my mommy. She holds me and squeezes my hand and stuff. Mommy never does that.

I crawl out from the trees and go into the house. She asks me to go to the front room with her. She sits on the big green chair. It has tiny brown holes in the arms where cigarettes burned it. She asks me to sit on the floor in front of her. Will we play a game?

She says, "Remember my friend, LeeRoy? You met him here."

"I remember him." I don't want to say anymore because I don't like him. He's mean. I don't want to hurt her feelings.

"Did you like him?"

I don't want to say anything so I look down at the floor.

"Didn't you like him?"

I shake my head and say, "No. He said I was fat."

She laughs and says, "He was just teasing you. I wanted to tell you that I am going to marry LeeRoy." Her eyes get big and she's smiling. She says it like she's happy.

"So will he be living here, too?"

She laughs again. "No. He and I will move to a different house."

"So you won't live here with me anymore?" My heart starts beating faster. My voice gets higher. I better not cry.

"No, but I'll visit sometimes—sometimes a lot."

"*You can't leave me. Who will hold me?*" *My voice gets higher and I try not to cry.*

"*I will always be in your life. I will visit a lot.*" *She reaches out and squeezes my shoulder.*

I start crying really hard, so I run out the back door and squat down under the trees. I wrap my arms around my knees and rock back and forth.

At least I have our trees and Cherry Creek.

"I Met Someone"

December 1989, the dinner table was cleaned and the kids were asleep. Teri and I were on the couch reading, each with a glass of wine. This was the best part of the day for me, when we could just let ourselves relax. We could hear the wind howling outside. The street light lit up the snowflakes blowing past our bay window. It was ten degrees above zero out there. A perfect seventy-two in here.

Tonight she seemed more fidgety than usual—lots of short sighs, moving around to get comfortable, and picking at her finger nails. Finally she sat still, looking out the window.

"Carter, when I was in Seattle, I met someone." She said it in a monotone voice as if she'd given up trying to find the right tone to ever say something like that.

What did she even mean? I looked at her, waiting for her to say more; more words, so I'd know I'd simply misheard her. She didn't say anymore.

I felt like when Mom told me that my niece had died, like I was falling into a huge, dark hole. I started to tremble. I felt cold. My ears started ringing and I struggled to breathe. I sat straight up, ready to bolt from the couch.

Finally, she turned to me and said, "Nothing happened."

"Then why did you tell me?" I sounded like the detective standing over the suspect.

"Because I realized something that I wanted to tell you, something very important."

"What's going on, Teri?" My brain was shrieking, Don't scare her! She'll freeze! My gut was demanding, *How dare you do this to me*? My heart was pleading, *Please don't leave me!*

"I was drawn to him because he looked like you and he sounded like you. He was funny and kind. He listened to me. He was like . . ." She trailed off. I knew what she didn't want to say. Goddamn it! I was going to make her say it.

"Like what, Teri?"

She said, "Like before our lives got so crazy, Carter. We've been drifting apart ever since you started that management job and ever since I started mine." She put her head in her hands and started crying.

I just sat there, frowning and shaking my head. I had so many reactions. Anger that she would betray me. Fear that she would leave me. Confusion about what I should do.

She reached for the box of tissues on the end table and blew her nose. She let out a long, deep sigh. Not looking at me again, she said, "I want us to go to therapy." She didn't look at me because she knew how I'd react.

"You and me together? What would we work on?" To hell with therapy together. She's the one who strayed, not me. "Tell me more about this guy. What's his name? What did you really do with him? Tell me the truth, Teri."

She turned to me. "Carter, we talked. One time, after drinks. Another time, after class. You know how when you're talking to someone you might never see again, you feel safe to say things you wouldn't otherwise. You might share your dreams and fears. You say things you've wanted to say to someone just to hear yourself say them. I haven't felt that way for a long time with you." She blew her nose again. "I'm going to therapy. I hope you'll go with me. We've been in this craziness for far too long. Talking and trying just isn't working. We need help."

Would I go to yet another round of therapy? This time with Teri? Not so fast. But how else could I get the truth out of her? Maybe a therapist could, since I couldn't. I was terrified, like I was dancing on the edge of a cliff. If I did go, who knows what would come out of it and in front of Teri? But if I didn't go, I could lose her.

"Carter, come to the first session with me. Hear what the therapist says. That can't hurt." Yeah, the fall from the cliff could be a big thrill—until I hit the bottom.

I remembered the terror I felt a few minutes ago when I thought I lost her. If therapy would keep us together, fine. "Yes, I'll go to therapy with you."

"Thank you. I love you. I don't want to lose you."

I went into the kitchen and poured another glass of wine.

Out of the Crosshairs

Two days later, we were already in the first session with Sandra, the therapist Teri had found. A client had rescheduled which had created an opening. This was going too fast for me. Over the past two days, I'd panic and ask her a question, trying to understand what had happened and why. She'd answer, "Let's wait until therapy." At my worst, I'd pout and give her the silent treatment. At my best, I'd go for long walks.

I wanted to interrogate her even further to find out the truth—any kind of truth that would explain all of this without causing any more pain. I wanted to turn the clock back to the way things were, to being normal again.

Sandra specialized in family and marriage counseling. She was taller than Astrid with a softer voice. She smiled and laughed more, but her office had the same look and feel. The overstuffed couch with multicolored pillows. The small table with tools to make tea. The variety of plants in the corners.

"Welcome, Teri and Carter."

Why did she say Teri's name first?

"Your appointment was so close to when you'd called that there wasn't time for an intake form. So I need your patience while I ask some questions today just to understand your situation and what you'd like to accomplish in therapy."

I was pleased that she looked at both Teri and me while she talked. Maybe I wasn't being stereotyped as the abusive husband in all this. With my anger issues and Teri's concerns about our marriage, I could've been.

She started by explaining that the sessions are completely confidential and that progress depends on how open and honest we were. I remembered it all from my intake with Astrid. After asking for details about our ages, work, and children, she finally got to what we were paying her for.

"I'd like to hear from each of you about what you hope to accomplish in therapy. Often, it's best to start with a vision of what you hope for, rather than what you've been struggling with. Teri, why don't you start?"

She's first again?

Teri must have thought about this because she had a powerful answer. "I want an open and honest relationship, like you said about these sessions. I want to feel like we can say anything to each other and not worry about the other person getting mad. I want more time with each other. I want more trust and communication. I know I love Carter very much and I believe he loves me that way, too. I don't think our struggle is his fault or mine. We just got lost somewhere along the way." Teri looked at me.

Sandra said, "Carter?"

Wow, how do I follow that—all that honesty?

"I don't mean to sound like I'm not trying, but Teri described it far better than I could. I want us together a lot more, too. I want to be a good husband and father." I stared directly at Teri. "I want to know that we're always committed to each other." For good measure, I added, "I want Teri to be happy."

"My compliments to you both. I don't hear either of you blaming the other. You realize that struggles in a marriage are usually not one partner's fault. The challenges are in the relationship itself. Carter, tell me what that challenge is for you now—why you're here."

Bullshit. Teri's the one who caused all this, not me. I turned to Teri. "Teri, you described it so well at home the other day. If I try, I'll just get us all confused. Why don't you tell us about Seattle?" Yes, you explain what you did to us. Good luck.

Then Teri summarized what had happened and how our lives had changed since 1985. She explained about Seattle and why she'd asked me to do therapy with her. She said all of that with such honesty, clarity, and composure that I was sure the therapist would find Teri more credible than me.

"Teri, thank you for the great explanation. Carter, do you want to add anything?"

I shook my head, but I knew I'd better say something. I said, "No." This wasn't going well at all.

"Teri, tell me why you'd like your relationship to be more open and honest. It's not that way now?"

Teri didn't answer. She just turned and looked at me.

"I noticed when I asked you that question, you looked at Carter but didn't answer." Sandra shared that observation so naturally, without a hint of accusation. Thank you.

Teri started to cry softly. "I struggle sometimes just to say things. I freeze up and lose track of my own truth. I'm afraid of what will happen if I say what I really feel." She looked down and then, after a pause, looked up at me. "And Carter, it happens with you a lot, especially when I think you might get mad." She said that like she was pleading, like she was apologizing to me.

"Teri, do you want to say more about why you sometimes struggle with what to say to Carter? Say that to Carter." Sandra nodded toward me.

Teri turned to me. Was there a target on my head? I wasn't the villain here.

"It's when I'm afraid it will make you distant or angry, if I ever ask about your childhood." She said that like an accusation. "When you get mad at me, sometimes you say I'm like your mother. I know you hate your mother." She started crying again.

There were ten minutes left. I knew because I'd learned to watch the clock during a session. Sandra looked at me and smiled, then looked back at Teri.

"I think you're both very wise—and courageous—to be here now. I know a lot of partners who wished they had started their work earlier. I'd love to help with you both. Teri, I think you and I should do that together. Perhaps we can talk about how Carter can join us later. This isn't leaving him out." Sandra turned to me.

"Carter, I'd like to recommend another therapist who would work with you. I could brief him on what transpired from this session. How do each of you feel about that?"

Teri answered, "Yes, I agree it would be best if we start separately." This time, she didn't look at me. She knew what she wanted.

"I agree," I said. "You can put me in touch with someone and tell them about this session. Whatever." I had to work hard not to show my relief.

The next day, a Saturday, I got a call from Rich, the therapist. He explained that Sandra had recommended him and he wanted to introduce himself. He added that Sandra had suggested my work with him should focus on my relationship with my mother.

"Rich, I appreciate your calling. I was already in therapy in 1982 about my childhood. I was diagnosed then as being an adult child of an alcoholic. I got a lot of help. I don't need any more work in that area. Thanks for calling, though." I hung up.

Teri said, "I only heard part of that call, Carter. Was that the therapist?"

"Yes. He's never met me and already he diagnosed me as having a big problem with my mother. That really pissed me off. You and I had agreed we were working on our marriage. I told him, 'No thank you.'"

She tilted her head back and pressed her lips. That was a sure sign that she didn't agree with me. She was right. I had a lame excuse. I felt like a drunk who'd walked into the wrong house and was trying to convince the owner that I lived there.

To hell with therapy. Been there. Done that.

Ready, Fire, Aim!

Five months later, it was May. Plants and animals were waking from their slumber. I was waiting for the lilacs, my favorite flower. Ian wanted baseball. Darienne wanted camping. Teri wanted yard sales.

She had settled into her therapy in her weekly meetings with Sandra. It was entirely private, as it needed to be. Still, I was haunted by the thought that one day she might walk in and say, "Carter, I've decided to leave you. You're not normal." So far, that hadn't happened. I must be doing okay.

Teri and I were at the kitchen table, engrossed in our spring ritual: drafting our list of what to improve in our home. As usual, our list was growing much longer than we'd expected. Finally, I put down my pen and looked at her. "I've been thinking about my job at the university."

She mumbled, "Do you think we should replace the screen door? It doesn't always lock." Without waiting for my answer, she wrote down "replace screen door."

"Teri, did you hear me?" I hated being ignored. "I've been thinking about my job at the university."

She paused, put down her pen and gave me her "are you serious?" look. Lowered eyebrows, wrinkled nose, and raised upper lip.

Oh, she thought I wanted to quit my job. I laughed at the irony. "No, I'm not saying I want to quit. I was thinking about the culture where I work. It's entirely different from my last job. There, your performance was measured by whether you had met your goals or not. Here, there are no goals. Your performance is measured by how well you get along. Your boss might harp at you because you had pissed somebody off, even if that person was just having a bad day." Frustrating, but my ACoA people-pleasing trait sure came in handy in this job.

"Sounds like a soap opera to me. I don't envy you."

"Yeah, and it's boring. I like the feeling of getting something done." Another ACoA trait: the feeling of being in control. "Another thing. They seem to know very little about good management. In my last job, they had plans, policies, and procedures. Here, there are no plans. It's what your boss wants done for the day." I shook my head. "It doesn't have to be that way. I could teach them a lot, but that's not my role."

"Carter, what are you getting at?"

Good question.

I moved the list away from me and looked at her. "I've thought a lot about this. I didn't enjoy those years at the company when my job was engineering, the technical stuff. I enjoyed it later on, when my job was management. I was really good at that. I took this more technical job at the University now, so I could be with you and the kids more."

"I know, Carter. The kids love having you around more. I know you're not as happy as when you were managing. When you're not happy, it shows. Your mind is off somewhere else. You're here, but you're not. What are you thinking?"

"I want to get an MBA." Oops. I should've said that with more finesse. I should've led up to it.

She looked like I'd ask her to buy me a Mercedes. She let out a deep sigh. "You saw our list for our house." She moved the list closer to me. "We've got so many bills and there's going to be more as the kids get older. You . . ."

I felt my face flush, so I interrupted her. "It might help if you actually listened to me." I put my hand up to show I was re-starting myself. "I'm sorry. You'd be right if I was going to quit my job. Or if an MBA meant being gone a lot. Or if it would cost us a lot of money. But none of that would happen. The university pays the tuition. I'd be in class one weekend a month and I'd keep my job full-time."

Whenever she was thinking hard about something I had said, she would stare at me, right between my eyes. Yet, it always felt as if she wasn't really seeing me at all. It felt that way now.

"Teri? What are you thinking?"

"I was remembering how disappointed I was when you didn't work with Rich, even if that meant first focusing on your mother. The other day, in my therapy, I was thinking about how it always seems like you're on some kind of quest, always looking for something. I didn't know if it was about something in the future or in the past."

"I know. I should've discussed it with you before I said no to him. I didn't want to repeat the therapy that I did in the past. I wanted to work more on my future. I would start the MBA in September."

"Carter, my therapy is helping me get more clear about myself and about us. I'm learning about assertiveness. This feels fast, but if you really need the MBA for your growth and your sanity, I won't stand in your way. But if it causes more distance in our relationship, I'm going to speak up clearly and right away."

"I understand. That would be best for both of us. Thank you."

I was surprised by myself. What was I feeling? Relief to do the MBA? Sure. Yet haunted when she mentioned her therapy? Sure. Intimidated by her being more assertive? Yes, a bit, but also reassured that if and when things got worse in our relationship, she'd speak up sooner about it—because it was clear that I hadn't been paying attention.

"Tell Him Who His Father Is!"

"Mom, who's Roger Buell? Renee and Faith say he's my dad. Is that true? Mom!"

She raises her head from her book a little and softly mumbles, "Go play." What does that have to do with the question I asked?

She's in her usual statue position in her bedroom even though Renee has come to visit. Sitting on the side of the bed, left leg crossed over the right. Looking down to her left. She's smoking a Kent and the whole house stinks, as usual. Her lips and thumbs twitch once in a while, like always.

I step toward her. How can I ever make her see me? I repeat the same question again, louder.

Now she raises her head a little more, but still looking at the book, and asks me, "Where did you hear that name?" But her voice is a little louder now.

"Mom, I heard Renee and Faith in the kitchen just now say, 'Mom should tell Carter that Robert McNamara is not his real dad, that Roger Buell is.' Then I asked them who he was, but they were just quiet. They won't tell me. Who is he, Mom?"

She mumbles even louder now, "Oh, he's just a friend." She still doesn't look at me.

Now I'm getting really mad. I step closer again. "Mom, don't lie to me again! Who is Roger Buell? How come they say he's my dad? I wanna know who my real dad is. Now!"

She doesn't say anything. Then I stomp my foot really hard on the floor. If I stay here, I'll yell at her really loud for a long time. I hate it when I do that. I hate everything right now. I run outside and throw rocks at the brick wall of the school house across the street. I

165

can throw really far. I throw until my arm won't move like I want it to. It's too tired.

Then I go back into the house through the back door. I hear Mom in the front room yelling at my sisters, "Don't mention Roger Buell again!" One of my sisters says, "But he should know who his real dad is!"

"I'll tell him when he's older. He doesn't need to know now."

I know she won't tell me when I'm older. I know she's lying. We all know. I'll never really know who my real dad is.

The Gatekeepers

In late September 1990, our family was watching the movie *Field of Dreams*. I was sitting on the couch next to Teri, as I often did. Darienne was sitting on her throne, otherwise known as our tan-striped wingback recliner. Ian was on the floor, sitting in his standard Buddha position. All of us were munching popcorn.

Near the end of the movie, Ray Kinsella, the protagonist, is playing catch with his dad. When Ray was fourteen, he and his father had a huge argument and the two never reconciled before his dad died. So in the scene, Ray's actually playing catch with the ghost of his dad.

I was sitting there thinking of every cliché about a child without a dad. Boat without a working rudder. Car without a rearview mirror. Child with a make-believe dad?

After the movie, Ian turned to me. "Who is your dad?"

"We're not sure, actually. Sometimes kids don't know who their ancestors are. What did you think of the movie, Ian?" I was the master of deflections.

"It was okay. So is my grandpa alive?" He was the dogged digger of facts.

"We don't know because we don't know who he is for sure." Take that comeback, young man!

I turned to Teri to help finesse this question. Instead, she said, "I wonder what it would take to find out."

Ian stood up. "Oh, could we? I'd like to meet him. Maybe he lives here and we could visit?" I didn't answer. I was still glaring at Teri.

I turned to Ian. "I never knew who my father was. My sisters said it was a man named Roger Buell." I should've known better than to give Ian a name.

"Is Roger Buell still alive?" Ian asked. This wasn't going well.

"No, he died before I was born." That should do it.

"Did he have any brothers and sisters?" he asked.

"I don't know," I replied, turning to Teri again. Will you say something to stop this? She just smiled at me.

"I wish I could meet them," Ian said. I didn't answer him. I wanted to stop this conversation.

"Daddy? Listen to me." He found my Achilles' heel: a child being ignored.

"Okay. I'll see what I can do."

I wasn't even convinced Roger Buell was my father. My mother had lied so often that we rarely took her seriously. Anyway, she'd taken her truth to the grave fourteen years ago.

Later, Teri and I were standing in the kitchen, picking out any edible pieces of popcorn.

"By the way, thanks for abandoning me back there."

She knew what I meant.

She set down the bowl. "Carter, he deserves to know who his grandfather is. I hardly knew mine and it felt like a hole all my life. So, yeah. I abandoned you—abandoned you to telling the truth to your son." Ouch.

"Teri, I would never call up some new family member and say, 'I'm Elvina McNamara's son, you know, the alcoholic and drug addict?' They'd either hang up on me or give me a lecture about the evils of drink."

"Yeah, maybe." She knew that wasn't a good excuse. She knew that I knew as well.

Among Mom's things was a small box of mementos. It included the program from Roger Buell's funeral. It was dated January 31, 1953—almost eight months before I was born. I recognized some of the names of the pallbearers, among them, LeRoy Veeder. LeRoy would be the first cousin of Roger Buell.

What the hell? If I could focus my family's attention on finding my father's family, maybe that would divert them from asking about my childhood. So I called the library in Watford City and the librarian gave me LeRoy's phone number. I dialed it before I could change my mind.

"Hello," he answered.

I had not planned what to say, so I just started talking. "My name is Carter McNamara. I grew up in Watford. My mother was Elvina McNamara. You might have known her?" I paused, steeling myself in case he hung up on me.

"Yes." He said it so softly that it felt like it came with a scrapbook full of memories.

I explained she had passed away several years ago. Among her things, she had the program for Roger Buell's funeral and a portrait of him. I'd noticed that LeRoy was a pallbearer.

I waited. Silence. "Do you remember that?" Long pause. Hello?

I heard him sigh. "I do remember. Roger was a good friend of mine. We all were so sad when he died." Wow! Roger Buell had actually existed.

"Well, LeRoy. I've got a quick story to tell. Could I get a few minutes from you?"

"Okay."

I described what my sisters had said and my mother's response. I told him that my son had asked to know his ancestors. I clarified that I was not looking for any handouts, that I was doing fine. I used the ruse that I was merely wanting to know if Roger had any hereditary diseases I should know about. Then there was another long pause.

"Well, he's got a sister, Laverne, living in Hot Springs, South Dakota. I know she's got some heart problems. Her name isn't Buell anymore. It's Malott now. She's got two boys and a girl. Chuck lives in Denver. I think the other one's in Colorado, too. I don't know about the girl. Laverne had a sister, Thelma, who died a while back."

Bingo! A contact: Chuck Malott in Denver, Colorado.

"Maybe I could reach out to one of them?"

"Carter, I think you should let sleeping dogs lie." He didn't say that like a warning, more like a father giving wise advice to a son.

169

"Thank you, LeRoy. I assure you, I'm not looking to hurt or use anyone."

"You sound like a good man."

I'd never met LeRoy, but that comment brought tears to my eyes. I couldn't remember ever being affirmed by a grown man before.

I updated Teri about my conversation. She was almost as excited as I was, but she sensed my hesitation. "What do you want to do, Carter?"

"I suppose I could call Chuck in Denver. I want to be sure any phone call to Laverne—from the son of her dead brother—won't somehow threaten her health. She's got a heart problem."

I called a library in Denver and got Chuck's number. If I waited, I might talk myself out of calling, so I dialed him. I was not a big believer in mystical beings or powers of influence. Philosophers would claim I'm an empiricist: I believe only in what I can verify with my senses. Yet, the first time I heard Chuck's voice, I sensed he was a cheerful, sincere, and caring man. I told him who I was and how I'd come upon Roger Buell's name.

"Yeah, he was my uncle," he said in his quick, sharp, and happy voice.

"Chuck, I've been told since I was a kid that Roger Buell was my father. I'm trying to find out if that's true." I quickly added my usual disclaimer that I was not out to take advantage of anyone. Then, just to be safe, I added that I was especially looking for information about any hereditary diseases. "So, I'm wondering, might I talk to your mother? I know she's got a heart ailment. I don't want to be troubling her."

"She's doing okay now, but she and Roger were quite close, so . . . I'll talk to her about it and get back to you." We said our goodbyes.

I told Teri, "Chuck was very receptive and understanding, considering the nature of the call—a stranger calls out of the blue and implies he might be a blood relative. It was like he and I had already spent years together, going to the same events, sharing the same feelings, asking the same questions. Wow."

"I'm so glad, Carter. The call could've gone the other way. This is a big breakthrough for you. How do you feel about it?"

I laughed. "If someone had told me that I'd be getting in touch with the family that might be my father's, I would've told them that doesn't happen in my sphere of life. Yet, here I am."

A few weeks later, the phone rang. It was Chuck. Yes, I could talk to Laverne. He explained how he'd told her about how a man had called and said he might be Roger's son. He said she didn't seem reluctant to talk to me. Instead, she seemed excited. He gave me his mother's number with a voice that sounded like a parent giving a child a pep talk before an upcoming race.

I hung up the phone and immediately briefed Teri on the call. "Now what do I do?"

She understood this was one of the most important calls I would ever make. Unlike me, she was moved more by her heart than her head. "Call her."

The confidence Teri inspired in me too quickly turned to fear. I realized that once Laverne answered my call, I'd be taking a big risk. A family I didn't know yet might reject me before I even had a chance to meet them. It was also the first step toward having any kind of father in my life, if only the family of my father. What kind of world would open up for me?

Finally, in early December, I'd had enough of going back and forth in my mind, letting those fears get the better of me. Fear not only of rejection, but of suddenly having more people in my life. What would they want and expect from me? Would it be magical or just normal? I grabbed the phone and dialed.

"Hello?" Her voice was like Chuck's, but a bit slower.

"Hello, Laverne. This is Carter McNamara. Thank you for—"

She interrupted me. "Oh, I'm so glad you called. Chuck told me about you. I said I'd be glad to talk to you. Tell me more about you and your family."

So I described Teri and each of the kids, their ages and personalities. I snuck in that we're doing fine and have everything we need. She interrupted me several times to say she wasn't hearing me very well. I started talking louder, like she was in the next room.

"Your family sounds wonderful. When can we meet each other? I understand you're in Minnesota. I'm in Hot Springs, South Dakota. I don't travel very much anymore. Might you come to visit, maybe after the holidays? Meanwhile, I'll send you some pictures. Can you send me some, too?"

"Of course." Long pause, like we didn't know what to do. We each didn't want to hang up, but we each had so much to process.

"Goodbye Laverne."

"Goodbye, Carter."

I sat there feeling overwhelmed. She had welcomed me, a stranger, almost as if I was indeed Roger's son. This had become so real, so fast. Too real, too fast? I needed to talk to Teri. I walked into the front room and found her on the couch sipping a cup of tea.

"Love, I'm feeling overwhelmed. I never thought I'd have a father—a dad. Maybe Roger Buell isn't my dad. Maybe he is. I feel like I've been shot out of a cannon. It's all going by so fast and I don't know how I will land."

She held out her arms for me to sit down next to her.

"Slow down, Carter. What are you feeling?"

"My heart feels grateful. That call couldn't have gone any better, but for every good thing I can think of, I can think of something bad, too." I laughed at myself. "My ACoA traits are kicking in like crazy. I want to control everything. Yet, I want to appear normal, not phony. I want to meet my father's family. Yet, I want to isolate." I started giggling so hard, I couldn't get my breath. I sat down on the couch, doubled over, as my giggles turned to sobs. My body was telling me how I really felt. Teri moved next to me and held me while my body did what it needed to do. Finally, the sobs subsided and I could blow my nose. I looked at her.

"That was my heart. My head tells me to go slow, keep perspective, and keep sharing all of this with you. Thank you." I put my hand around her neck and pulled her forehead close to touch mine. "I love you."

Truth Without Judgment

I was nervous about meeting Laverne. What should I expect? A barrage of questions about me? My background? My expectations? Or just hugs and a "welcome to the family"? I invited Renee, my safety blanket, along just in case.

In early February 1991, Renee and I began the drive south to Hot Springs. There were three of us in the car: Renee in the passenger seat, me driving, and my self-doubts—the incessant rattle in the back seat. Renee didn't work hard to reassure me. She respected me more than that. While I drove, she talked about Teri, my kids, her kids, subtly reminding me that I already had a family in case this new one didn't work out. I listened, trying to quiet my mind and my imagination.

I glanced at her. "Let's not say anything about Mom. I don't want Laverne feeling sorry for me, okay?"

"Oh, God no. I won't say anything," she said in a low voice, looking at her lap. Then she turned to look out her window. We each slid into our own private abyss, mired in our own thoughts and feelings.

After several miles, I glanced at her again. She looked smaller, more vulnerable. I remembered her telling me that Mom would make her sleep at the foot of Mom's bed, then kick her to get her some food. If she didn't get up right away, Mom would kick her again, saying, "You piece of shit. Get up!"

"I'm sorry I brought up Mom. I should've known better."

"Oh, no. That's fine." That was Renee, smoothing out everyone's feelings.

We pulled into the rendezvous spot we'd agree on, a large parking lot by a church. Laverne had mentioned on the phone that she had a tiny blue car. We'd arrived at the right time and place because there, in the corner of the lot, was the tiny blue car. I parked about ten car spaces away, as if to give us some space to get used to the situation. I turned off the ignition and immediately noticed a tiny, fair-haired lady already on her way to our car. She was walking in an excited march, arms and legs moving in quick unison. She had a wide smile on her tiny face.

She was slight and about five feet tall, with short, curly, blonde hair over a small, round face. Her eyes, nose, and mouth were gathered closely together. Where had I seen those features before? I realized I saw them every time I looked in the mirror. I got out of the car and she spread her arms as if to catch a giant basketball. It was one of the warmest hugs I'd ever felt.

She stood back and looked me up and down, then leaned in more closely to examine my face. She stood back and proclaimed, "You're not a Buell." My heart dropped. "You're a Veeder."

I remembered that Ella Veeder was Roger Buell's mom. I welcomed the news that I looked like part of the family.

"This is my older sister, Renee. She raised me." That truth deserved to be said, despite the questions it might bring.

She invited us to follow her back to her home. As we walked behind her, Renee said, "She's so excited. She's so cute. You two look alike, you know."

She parked her car next to her blue mobile home. She led us through her door, took our coats and sat us down. There were pictures of all sizes and shapes on her coffee table, end tables, and kitchen counter. She rubbed her hands together in excitement.

"I've got so much to show you, so much to tell you about. I don't know where to start. I need to take a deep breath and just calm myself down." She laughed self-consciously at her own excitement.

We spent several hours sharing lots of questions and answers, telling stories, looking at pictures, and just feeling like family—accepted and supported with deep affection and loyalty.

"What did you mean that I looked like a Veeder?"

"Oh, I'll show you a picture and you'll think you're looking in the mirror. Come here." She got up and led us back through a narrow hallway with numerous pictures hung on both sides. She stopped and pointed to a man in one of them and said, "That's Sid Veeder, your great uncle. That's an old picture, but just look at that."

Renee leaned closer to the picture and said, "Carter, that's ..." She trailed off and stood there, shaking her head at the similarity.

On the way back to the living room, Laverne said, "Renee, Carter said you helped to raise him. He must have been such a cute child." My heart started to race.

"Oh, he was. He was always asking questions. He was outside the house more than the inside." That was for sure. We all sat back down in the living room.

"Carter, in our phone call in December, you mentioned Robert McNamara was your legal father and that he died when you were young. Your mother must have had her hands full with four children." Laverne was wondering why Renee raised me as a child.

"Mom had a . . . disability. That's why Renee helped me so much." I didn't want to lie to her and I suspected she already knew about Mom. She had often visited her mother who lived a few blocks away from our house when I was a child.

Laverne kept pulling out more pictures like Christ breaking bread for the masses. "This is one of Roger with his buddies." Then she paused and looked at each of us. "Roger was a drinker." She emphasized his name, like she was adding it to an unwritten list with Mom—a list of those struggling with alcohol. I glanced at Renee. She looked at me, smiled and nodded that Laverne was tactfully reassuring us.

Laverne looked down at one of his pictures. "He and I were very close. We were so sad when he died in the car wreck. He might have been drinking." She shook her head and looked at me. "He died in January and you were born that September." She turned back to his picture. "Alcohol is a poison, you know. I am an alcoholic, too. I've been sober for decades now."

"Yes, it is, Laverne," Renee said. She was thanking Laverne for being so understanding.

Laverne showed us a picture of her three children—two boys, Chuck and Todd, and her daughter, Patricia. "It was so tough for my children with my drinking. I try to make it up to them somehow, you know." She kept looking at the picture.

I wondered if Renee had noticed the contrast between Laverne and our mother. Mom had denied her addiction. Laverne had attacked it head-on. I sat back, let out a deep sigh and glanced at Renee again. She nodded again, apparently thinking the same thing I was.

I said, "I spoke to Chuck on the phone, you know. He was very thoughtful and sensitive about a delicate situation. He should be a social worker or a diplomat." We all laughed.

Laverne said, "Roger was in the Army in Italy near the end of the war. Did you know that? I have all of his letters he sent home." She handed me a thick packet of papers. "Here, I made copies for you. Also, I'd like you to have these pictures for your family. I know we'll be seeing more of each other a lot over the coming years." I felt so touched that she had already gone through such effort.

After we'd exchanged hugs and were on our way out the door, I had to ask. I turned to her. "Laverne, what makes you think I'm really Roger's son?"

She stepped over to me and took both my hands in hers. "I just know you are."

As we drove away, I said to Renee, "We're two blocks away and she's still standing there in the road waving at us."

"So, Carter. How do you feel about having a new family?"

"You know how, when you lose something important—whether it's your car keys or a precious picture—you think you'll never find it? Then, when you do, it's such a surprise that it feels like a gift from the universe? Well, that's how this feels."

"That's a good description." She paused and smiled at me. "I really like Laverne. Good for you."

"You know, when your parent doesn't treat you like a human being, you grow up feeling like an empty jar, closed tight, vacant and boring. To try to be normal, you paste normal images on yourself hoping that's what other people will see. Still, nothing gets in. Meeting Laverne was like taking off the lid and putting something beautiful in there for a while."

The Black Hills were far to our left, running parallel to our road for a while. They looked like dark shadows reminding me of the shadows in my life.

"There were times when I felt a psychological whiplash. I wanted more information, but felt overwhelmed with it. I wanted to meet more family, but wanted my own close nest. I wanted to tell her about me, but not have her feeling sorry for me. I felt jealous of their family, but proud of myself. I felt like I was clinging to a giant pendulum swinging back and forth."

We both chuckled.

"It might take a while to take all this in."

"You're right."

For me—the lone wolf—my pack keeps growing bigger.

Another Brick in the Rubble

I really like Mr. Sanford. He laughs a lot. He looks at me when I raise my hand to answer questions. He's teaching science and I love science. He's the best teacher in the eighth grade. I like how he thinks really hard before he answers a question. I used to think that he maybe doesn't hear. But he does. He just wants to give the best answer.

I like the room where we have class, too. I can see outside to the playground. It's right across the street from our house. Sometimes it feels good to know that I'm so close to home. If I ever got sick, I could be there really fast.

I look out the window and there are kids standing around a small part of the playground by the street. I keep looking—and then I see her.

She got out of the house! How did she do that? I'd put a heavy tub of sand in front of the shed door in the back. That was to stop her from getting out the back. There's no way she could move that. I'd put a big cement block against the outside of the front door. Did she move that? I can't see it from here.

She's stumbling along the curb toward downtown. Her feet go sideways a lot when she walks and her head rolls around like she does when she's very drunk. When she drinks and takes drugs together, she turns into a zombie. She's been out of it for a few days now. She's wearing that old pink nightgown with the torn strap. She doesn't have her glasses on. She never does when she's out of it like this. Her hair is all straggly around her head. But where is she going? Maybe she'll turn around and go home on her own. I'll just sit here and wait. I don't want the kids to see me with her.

But now some kids are laughing at her. I raise my hand and Mr. Sanford looks at me and calls on me right away. Did he see me staring out the window? I hope not. Will he see Mom? I don't wait for Mr. Sanford to hear what I was going to say. I just get up, grab my papers, and run out of the room.

I rush outside and catch up to her. I've got to get her back to the house before the cops or somebody comes. I can get her back to the house. I've done that before, but she never got this far out before. I was always at home then and heard her.

Next time, I'm gonna put two cement blocks against the front door. Now everyone will know that my home is really weird, that I'm not normal. I wish I could turn the clock back now, but that's impossible.

The Rage

September 1991. I was in the kitchen making dinner. My mind was on fire. It always was after my MBA class. We were studying how teams and people have similar life cycles in how they grow and change. It often takes a big crisis to make them change in a big way. My families' big crisis was four years ago when I'd spanked Ian. That had caused a radical change for me. I hadn't spanked the kids since. I hoped we'd always be a stable team.

It was my turn to stay home and take care of Ian. It was the second day of his stomach flu. Classic symptoms: fever, headache, cramps, and my two favorites: vomiting and diarrhea. The doctor said Ian should rest and drink plenty of fluids. An eight-year-old boy? Rest? Has he ever raised children?

Teri and Darienne would be home soon, so I headed into the kitchen to start macaroni and cheese for dinner. Ian's favorite, so maybe he could keep it down. Teri always insisted on vegetables, so today we'd have peas on the side. Darienne loved oranges, so today they'd be dessert.

They both came through the door. Darienne greeted me and headed to her room to read, her daily ritual. Teri hung up her coat and headed to the bedroom to change out of her business attire. She came out wearing a T-shirt and jeans.

I wanted to connect with her. Since Teri began therapy, she seemed so far away sometimes.

"Hey, how was your group therapy?" Too late, I realized that was the wrong question.

"I'm not ready to talk about it now, Carter." She said it like I was trying to get away with something. After a therapy session, she was always in her own private world. It had been two years since she'd told me she'd met someone in Seattle, and still I felt petrified that she'd leave me. Now, if I tried to angle for a reassuring tidbit, she'd say, "My therapy is private for me. I'll share it when I'm ready."

I set the plates, glasses, and silverware on the kitchen table. I wasn't in the mood for the family's dining room ritual. I missed my wife.

I whispered to her, "Let's get a babysitter. C'mon! Just the two of us. Please."

She didn't look at me. She just shook her head and stepped around me to sit at the table. I gave up. I'd get Darienne and Ian. It'd be an evening just like all the rest.

Suddenly, there was a loud bang. I rushed into Ian's bedroom. The kids were playing catch with a football.

"Stop that. It's time to eat."

Now we were all at the table, doing our family act.

"Darienne, how was school?" I asked.

She replied in a monotone. "Fine."

"Ian, how are you feeling now?"

Even more monotone. "Fine."

"Teri? How was school?" She didn't laugh at my joke. She looked down at her plate, lost in her own thoughts.

In a baby-talk, mocking voice, I said, "No. We don't have to talk. Everything's fine." She didn't respond to my sarcasm. That really pissed me off!

After dinner, Darienne and Ian knew what was coming, so they headed back to his room to play. If I was going to connect with Teri, I needed to keep my head. I tried to remember some tips about dealing with stress. My memory was blank. I needed a strategy. I poured us a glass of white wine.

"I'm sorry. I know I'm being an ass. I'll give you some room." I grabbed my glass and a bowl of peas to snack on and headed for the couch. Teri picked up her glass and an orange and sat near me on the couch. Now maybe we could connect. I'd give her time and we'd see.

She sighed, but didn't look at me. "I'm sorry. I've just got to figure out some stuff. I'll be ready later, but I'm just not ready yet."

She took a sip of her wine and picked up a magazine from the coffee table. I jumped on her comment about therapy as permission to talk about it.

"Why can't you tell me anything about your therapy? I get it, that it's private. But I'm your husband. Your partner. I'd like to help. I tell you about myself. I . . ."

She turned to me, eyes wide, mouth open. "Bullshit. You don't tell me about you. You expect me to tell you about my therapy, but you've been carrying secrets around since I've known you. You think I don't notice? I've just chosen to put up with it. Lately, I'm not so sure." She looked back down at her magazine. I felt exposed, like back when I'd looked out the window of the school and saw my mom.

Ian yelled that he'd thrown up again. Still feeling on duty, I went to clean it up. I found him in the bathroom standing in a puddle of puke. He looked sheepish, but didn't move to do anything about it. That felt all too familiar.

After I cleaned up the mess, I walked slowly back to the couch, buying time to respond to Teri's attack. She was just sitting there peeling that goddamned orange. It was spurting juice all over the table in front of the couch. The room reeked of orange juice.

Soon both kids started yelling louder and louder. I turned to yell back at them to settle down but was too exhausted to take them on again. I picked up the bowl of peas. They reeked of split pea soup. I picked up my glass of wine to take a drink. It smelled citrusy, like lemons.

Then time stopped.

Suddenly, I was in front of Ian's bedroom door, shaking so hard I could barely stand. I was staring at the knob on his door and yelling. "Clean up your own puke! You don't even look at me! You lie and you steal! Why can't you be a good mother? Like Danny's!"

Everything was in slow motion, including the words coming out of my mouth. My head felt like a red-hot jack hammer. What was that smell? Vomit. The color? Red. The taste? Like licking a tin can. I could hear Teri's voice as if from a dream a thousand years ago.

"Carter, stop! You can't do this anymore! You're scaring us!"

I realized she was screaming at me. She was protecting the kids—from me. What was I doing? How did I get here? I turned and ran out of the house.

I ended up at the park a block away and collapsed on the park bench. My feelings had left me and I was hoping they would not come back. But they did. I sobbed so forcefully, my breath came in convulsions and gasps. Tears streamed between my fingers and down my wrists. I felt like I was twelve years old and Mom was in the next room calling out for me. It all felt so familiar.

Finally, my body had wrenched itself into total exhaustion. I sat there, elbows on my lap, trying to hold my head up, hoping that thoughts would somehow return. I needed to know what had happened. I realized, more than clarity, I needed reassurance; that they were okay, that they hadn't left me.

On the way to the house, I felt a force pulling me back. I was the Big Ick now. To save my family, I needed to stay away from them, to take it with me. And yet, my feet kept moving toward the house, toward the kind of person I wanted to become: someone who fought my demons, rather than denying them.

I opened the front door. The three of them were sitting on the couch. Teri had an arm around each of my children, protecting them from me. I didn't come in any farther than the door. I didn't want to scare them.

She held up her hand. "Stop, Carter. Just stop. Tomorrow, you call Astrid. You go back to therapy. You follow through with it this time. Something's really wrong here. That will never happen again. It can't."

Or else?

I wasn't just afraid. I was utterly terrified. There was no turning back the clock. I was lost. Everything was lost.

I didn't wait to call Astrid. I still had her number. On her answering machine, I struggled to describe my situation—short choppy sentences between short, sharp breaths of air, all the while repeating, "Help!" Teri heard all of that. I didn't care.

After leaving the message, I rushed out the door again. I couldn't face them. I shouldn't be around them. They're terrified of me! What the fuck had just happened? I walked around the block over and over again. Each time I passed the house, I'd look in to see what was going on. Was she packing to leave? Should I just leave instead?

Finally, the bedroom and living room lights went out. Still, I walked and walked. I had nowhere else to go.

I slowly and quietly slipped back into the house. It no longer felt like my home. It felt like the scene of a crime. It had been the scene of a crime.

I just stood there in the living room. Then Teri came out of our bedroom. I didn't dare walk toward her. I thought she might scream.

I whispered, "I love you. I'm so sorry. I don't know what happened. I've got to change—something. I'll sleep on the couch." She didn't answer. She just stood there, her arms hanging at her sides. I stepped around her to go into the bathroom, softly touching her shoulder as I passed, giving her a safe distance.

All Is Lost

The next morning, Julie left a message that Astrid could see me at five p.m. I immediately told Teri, hoping to reassure her that I knew this was a crisis.

I tried to bury myself in work but faked it all day long. Finally, I told my secretary I was needed in one of the other office buildings. I grabbed enough paperwork to make it look like I'd be very busy and left for the day. I drove around town, aimlessly stopping in parks and taking long walks. All I could think about were Teri and the kids. I had to do whatever it took to get them back.

At a quarter to five, I headed to Astrid's office. It had been nine years since I'd last seen her. She was in a different building now, and I was in a different place now, too.

Julie welcomed me and led me back to Astrid's office. Right away, it felt the same. There was still the subtle, woody scent of sandalwood. Her chair faced an over-stuffed tan couch with pillows of different sizes on it—all of them in earth tones. There was a small table holding a pitcher of water and some glasses. A small teapot sat next to a small bowl holding packets of tea.

She looked different, too. Tinges of gray sparkled in her hair just above her ears. Would she hug me? I wanted that hug, but I knew it wouldn't be professional for her to do so. She was my therapist and I was her client. It didn't matter; I was just so relieved to be there.

She looked up from her chair and smiled. I smiled back. It felt like a warm embrace from an old friend. She stood and looked at me long enough for me to feel seen. Then she looked at the couch and motioned toward it. I sat down and picked up one of the pillows—one with a tie and tassels on the edges—and held it against my chest.

She sat back down and rolled her chair over to me. "So what's going on, Carter?"

I was in such a panic, I didn't know what to say. I started apologizing for not having done the ACoA assignments. She interrupted me. "Carter, don't blame yourself for not doing them. I suspect you're blaming yourself enough already. I'm not here to judge you. Tell me why you're here. You look exhausted. You look . . ." She paused. "You're trembling. What's going on?"

"I don't know where to start." I genuinely didn't. I felt terrified that I might have lost my family and guilty that it was all my fault.

She'd read my mind. "Start with what you're feeling, Carter."

"I'm feeling terrible, terrible about myself. Who I am. What I've done to people and . . ." I felt lost. My mind was spinning. Now I was staring at the teapot. It was beautiful. Handmade. It was dark blue with darker blue shadows of trees. A small forest at night. I wanted to escape into that forest like the dream I kept having about a wolf that refuses to look at its image in the water.

"What have you done to people? Start with now, then yesterday, then the day before."

I looked at her. "I've got to get them back," was all I could say. The thought of losing them felt like falling, alone, down a deep, dark, ice-cold hole from which there could be no escape.

"I want you to take a couple of deep breaths. Let's get you a drink of water. Then sip it while I share something very important, okay?"

She poured me a glass and handed it to me. She sat back down, this time leaning back with her hands crossed over her stomach. She lowered her head, looking at me with a furrowed brow.

"Carter, before we can talk about getting your family back, we need to start with you. This is only about you now—you and your memories of that moment. I need to know what happened. I need you to go there with me. Close your eyes if you have to. Sip your water and do the best you can. Start with the details and we'll get to your feelings." She scooted her chair back to her desk, picked up a small tablet, and moved back to me again.

I took a long breathe, leaned back, and stared at the ceiling. I described making the macaroni and cheese. Asking Teri about therapy. She wouldn't tell me. Trying to get her to go out with me. She wouldn't. I described the farce called "dinner." Afterward, we both sat on the couch. The kids were in Ian's room playing. Suddenly, I was standing outside Ian's bedroom and yelling at them. Then I was sitting in the neighborhood park crying, not knowing how I'd gotten there, knowing that I'd done something terribly wrong but not knowing what it was. I described walking back home and Teri's demanding that I see Astrid. So I called her and rushed out of the house.

I looked back down at Astrid. She'd been taking notes while I'd been talking. She set the tablet down and sat forward again. I had never felt so listened to, so heard before, so seen. I felt like a real person.

"What were each of you drinking?"

"Wine. We were on our first glass. Two's our limit. I was so pissed at Teri."

"What made you so mad?"

I opened my arms and jutted my chin out. "I just wanted her to share something, anything, about her therapy. She's talking to her therapist about us. I'm sure she is, but she won't tell me anything about it. She could be leaving me, for all I know." I sat back, feeling defeated.

"Okay, then what happened back there on the couch? What would you have been talking about?"

I paused, took some sips from my water, and stared at the ceiling again. I remembered the feeling of us on the couch. I looked at Astrid and shook my head. "It feels like it wasn't anything good." I paused, remembering more. "She was mad at me. She rarely tells me when she is, but she was now. Something about me keeping secrets. I said something and she said it was bullshit. I remember feeling terrified and wanting to explain. That's when Ian threw up." I looked at the floor. Now, more smells were coming back to me.

"That's good, Carter. Keep going. What are you smelling? Hearing? Feeling?"

"I cleaned up his puke." I looked at her. "I'm really good at doing that. Remember the ACoA stuff?" I chuckled, hoping to break the mood, to lighten the pressure. She stayed focused.

"Yes, I remember it well."

"Anyway, I came back to the couch where Teri kept peeling that goddamned orange. It was spraying all over. I sat down and started eating my peas. Then I looked down at the floor. The smells were coming back to me. The peas, like split pea soup. The wine, the vomit . . ."

"What is it, Carter? Just keep talking. You're doing fine."

"I was mad, so goddamned angry." I wrapped my arms around myself and started rocking.

"That's okay. Keep going." She stood up and put a small blanket on my lap. What's this for?

"Yeah, all that is happening . . ." I just sat there.

"What were you tasting, Carter?"

"The peas. They were awful. They tasted like metal. Like tin. I hoped we hadn't poisoned the kids."

"What colors were you seeing?"

"Red."

"Take a few sips of the water, Carter. Take a few breaths. Cover yourself up. You're doing fine. This is very helpful." Then she waited.

By now I was fed up with this questioning. "Astrid, how is this helpful? How is all this going to help me get my family back?" Maybe this wasn't such a good idea after all.

"Carter, to get your family back, you have to get yourself back first. That's what we're doing here. I'm helping you to do that, but you have to want it. What happened next?"

I sat there, frowning. What did happen next?

"Carter." She was talking almost in a whisper. "What were you feeling back then? What were you seeing?"

"I'm real hot. I'm sweating. I'm shaking all over. I'm staring at the doorknob and I'm yelling. Everything is like it's in slow motion."

Then it was quiet for a while. I kept staring at the cups on her little table. They were handmade dark blue with dark blue trees on the side, just like the teapot. What if I just ran out the door right now? Get Teri to forget all of this and skip the therapy? Or, just leave the whole situation—the marriage, the family, the job, and Minnesota?

"Carter? Carter?" She waited until she had my attention again. "I think I know what happened to you. Has it ever happened before?"

I looked at her and shook my head. "No, never with Teri."

"Has it happened like that with anyone else?"

I tried hard to remember.

"I don't remember," was all I could say.

"Carter, you've done a lot of work here today. I've got a good idea of where we can go from here. We need to schedule you again soon. You might remember in our last meeting about the ACoA, I said that it's not enough just to know what's going on. You have to do something about it. Otherwise, things could even get worse. That's the situation you're in now—things have gotten worse and you need to do something now. Do you understand?"

I nodded. "Absolutely, Astrid. I believe you. It can't be like it was last time. I can't lose my family."

"Carter, you might get your family back again . . ." She waited for that to sink in. "But you'll never keep them unless you deal with your demons. Do you know that?"

I felt like I stepped into an ice-cold shower—smacked in the face with the cold, hard truth. "I know." I'd fought hard to hide my past, especially from myself. That fight had become who I was, every thought, feeling, and action. It was time to lay down my armor.

"Let's talk about what to do when you get back home, what you will say to Teri and the kids." She scooted closer to me. "Listen carefully. The more you focus on getting them back, the more likely you'll lose them. Remember the trauma you felt as a child? They're feeling that trauma right now. Imagine back then if your mother had come at you in a rage. How would you feel afterward, if she had acted as if nothing had happened? You'd feel confused, distrusting, and defensive."

"Believe me, I understand."

"Here's what I suggest you do when you get home. This is important." She picked up her tablet and began to write as she talked. "First, be calm. Just breathe. Quietly ask Teri if you can talk to her for a few minutes. Don't touch her. Don't go into any detail yet. Don't say anything to the kids right away. When you two are alone, then say you've met with Astrid. That she thinks she knows what's going on. That she wants to work with you for a while. That you'll be seeing her regularly. Say the therapy has to be different this time, that it will be different. That you don't want to be the person who was raging at your family. Then repeat that Astrid knows what's going on. Then, just be quiet while Teri takes all that in."

She tore the page from the tablet and handed it to me. "Here, I've written all that down. I've even numbered the steps to take and in what order." I looked at the list and swallowed hard.

"Okay," I said. "Then what?"

"Then ask her what she would like to do to feel safe, and then just listen to what she says. Do only what she says. No more. Don't keep talking. That's awfully important." This was the best advice I could've gotten. It told me to lay down my biggest weapon: my mouth. Teri needed to feel safe—to be heard, to feel heard. I needed to be still—for the both of us.

"What about the kids? I've got to say something to the kids. I just want to get back to being a dad again." Here come the tears.

"Carter, the best thing you can do is to ask Teri what you should do. She'll know. Will you do everything I just suggested?"

I nodded. That was all I could manage.

"I need you to say it out loud to me and to yourself. Will you do exactly what I said?"

"Yes, Astrid. I promise." I nodded again, this time to affirm the answer to myself.

"Good. Let's give all this a rest. You've done great work today. I'd like to see you again as soon as I can. Let's see what Julie has in the schedule." She got up and started toward the door. "Meantime, I want you to write in a journal. Write about some good times that you had as a child. Write all the details. What you saw, smelled, tasted, and touched. Then write about how you felt as a kid in those times. Then write how you feel now as an adult about those times. If you panic, call my office. Julie will get it and forward it to me. Okay?"

"Yes," I said. Now I felt more assured, like the student who finally understood the teacher's directions.

Astrid got up and walked me back to Julie's desk and asked her to schedule me for another appointment as soon as possible. Julie looked at her computer and gave me a date only a few days away. I grabbed it.

Like I had done back in 1982 when I was first seeing Astrid, I pulled into the park near our home and wrote down what I remembered. Just like before, this session had seemed like hours, but had lasted less than one.

Back home, the kids had finished their dinner and were already in Darienne's bedroom. Teri was sitting on that same couch where the rage had started with all of those smells and sensations. Except now, the room smelled more like lavender and flowers.

I quietly squeezed my coat into the closet. My heart was pounding and my mouth was dry, so I went into the kitchen to get a glass of water. I drank the entire glass, then went into the living room to do the speech that Astrid had taught me. I kept my distance from Teri so she'd feel safe.

"Love, I'd like to talk to you for a few minutes when you think that would be okay." I turned to go back into the kitchen.

"We can do that now."

I turned back to her, still standing at a distance. "Thank you." I had memorized what Astrid told me to say and I said it all to Teri, almost word for word. It had sounded mechanical and insincere, but my tears made it real.

"Thank you, Carter. I'm so glad Astrid might know what's going on. That was very scary for all of us." Her lower lip started trembling and her eyes teared up, but she didn't cry.

"I'd like to say good night to them tonight, if you think that's okay. I'll say whatever you think is best."

"Let me think about it. It sounds like they're playing now. We should just let them have fun."

She started heading toward the kitchen, then turned back to me. "Carter, who's Danny?"

"What? I don't know a Danny. What are you talking about?"

"Never mind."

She went into the kitchen and started cleaning up from dinner. I followed her and served up leftovers for myself, though I couldn't imagine eating. This time, it wasn't macaroni and cheese. Afterward, I sat on the couch to start journaling about the good times, like Astrid had told me to do. I wanted to write about the past few days, but I couldn't. No memories came to mind. No feelings rose in my body. It was simply telling me "enough." An hour later, Teri approached me.

"You should talk to them before they go to sleep. I think we should just explain that you had a very bad day. That you are very sorry that you got so angry. That you should not have been screaming. That you will never do that again." She emphasized the words *never do that again.*

I put down my empty journal. "I will do that. Thank you."

That's exactly what I said to them, with Teri standing by my side. Then each of them, one by one, let me hug them.

I Missed the Target

I'm shooting baskets with David on the school grounds across the street from our house. It's Saturday so no one's on the grounds with us. David is one of the popular kids, so I'm feeling special to be with him. I'm hoping people will see me with him. He tells me that I'm pretty good at making baskets. I'm tall for thirteen so I get a lot of rebounds, too. He stops and leans forward with his hands on his knees. He takes some deep breaths.

"Are you okay, David? Want to rest?"

"No, let's keep playing." He straightens up and I pass the ball to him. He shoots toward the basket, but barely hits the rim.

"I better sit down." He goes over and sits on the curb. He wraps his arms around himself like he's cold. It's summer and it's hot outside. What's going on?

"I'm cold and I might throw up. I need sugar. I'm diabetic." He turns to me. "Can I get a slice of bread with some sugar on it right away?"

"Sure. You stay right here." I set the ball down by him and run across the street and through the front door. I start making the sugar and bread to rush back to him, but there's no bread. I can't find another bag of it. I'm scared because he needs it bad. Will he die?

"Carter, your mom is on the floor in that room. Her butt is showing." His voice sounds shaky like he's been in the cold.

I'm standing in the kitchen and I turn to my right and see David. He's standing in the living room pointing into Mom's bedroom. There isn't a door between the two rooms so he sees right inside.

I forgot and left the front door open! I rush to David and see Mom curled up on the floor in her bedroom. Her nightgown is pulled up and her butt is showing. Now he'll know what happens in our house and he'll tell everybody. I just wanted him to be my friend. I should've closed the door. It's all my fault. I rush into Mom's bedroom and pull her nightgown over her butt. Then I grab a blanket from her bed and cover her up. I walk back to David. Now he's sitting on the living room floor with his arms around himself again, watching me.

"I need sugar bad. Just a spoonful. That's all I need."

I rush into the kitchen and pour a big spoonful. I put my hand under it so it won't spill and rush back to him. He grabs it and his hand is shaking. He puts the sugar in his mouth right away and starts chewing it. Gross.

I stand between him and the entrance to Mom's room so he doesn't look in there. I want to get him out of our house right away, but he just sits there blinking and looking around.

"Let me help you get up, so we can go outside." I start to help him up, but he pushes me away. We start to walk across the street again. I have an idea about what to tell him.

"Mom is sick. She likes sleeping on the floor when she's sick. I bet her dress came up when she rolled over. I know. That's gross." I want to feel like his friend again.

"I should get home and tell Mom I'm okay." He turns and starts to leave.

"David, please don't tell anyone about my mom. It's embarrassing. I'm sorry."

He doesn't turn back to me. "No. I won't tell anyone." I don't think he's telling the truth.

I'm so mad at her, I want her dead. Now, I know what to do.

I go into my room and get the twenty-two rifle from under my mattress. I stole it from a farm a couple of miles from town. I make sure there's still a bullet in the chamber and I sit down next to Mom. She's sleeping with her mouth open. I tip her head down and put the barrel inside her mouth. I get ready to run in case the gun goes off. I put her thumb on the trigger and I bolt out the front door. I leave the front door open so someone might find her. They'll think she killed herself.

I keep running until I'm at Cherry Creek. I feel kinda scared, but I'm glad that this mess will be over. I'll just stay away until someone finds her. But no one hardly ever comes to our house. I hope somebody does today.

I wait for what must be a couple of hours. Then I walk really slow back to our house. I sneak in to see what happened. The rifle is on the floor. She's on top of the bed, sleeping. It's like the time I tried to poison her, but that didn't work either. What's wrong with me?

I pick up the rifle and put it under my mattress again.

Next time, I'll shoot her myself.

Freeze, Flight, or Fight?

The night after my session with Astrid, I didn't fall asleep right away. I laid there, thinking about what had happened. Was it a blackout of some kind? Why didn't I see it coming? If I can't control my body, then what can I do? I can't promise it won't happen again. I felt about myself the same way I felt about Mom. So am I the "Big Ick" now? Should I just go and take it with me?

I got up early. I wanted to be gone when they got up. I didn't want to scare them. Just seeing them would magnify my guilt. I left a note for Teri, explaining why I was gone. I didn't know how to sign it. It felt hollow just to write "I love you."

Maybe that was the best solution, leave and take it with me, like the bomb squad taking away the bomb—but then I'd be leaving my kids without a father.

There seemed no way out of this. Renee used to tell me that I had an Old Soul alongside of me, a wise voice that guided me in difficult situations. What would my Old Soul say now? I thought maybe I'd hear that voice if I talked to Renee, so at lunch, I called her.

"Um, hello?"

God, it was so good to hear her voice!

"Hey, this is Carter. Your brother?"

"Yes, I know." She chuckled.

"What are you up to?" I already knew the answer. She'd be tending to the house, de-cluttering. She hated clutter as much as I did. She'd be thinking about what to make for dinner for LeeRoy and Rhonda, her youngest child.

"Oh, nothing. I was lying around reading a book about the history of North Dakota. It's a pretty interesting state, this state we grew up in. Did you know that?" My sister was great at small talk when it's needed to warm up to something more important. "And how are you, dear brother?"

I loved hearing her say that word!

"Oh, I'm a young professional living in the suburbs with two kids, two cars and . . . oh, I just realized we don't have a dog. Just a second, I'm gonna write that down."

"Did you ever think you'd be in that situation? Sounds kinda normal, doesn't it?" She stretched out the word "normal" to sound sarcastic, exactly as I wanted to hear it.

Is this when I should explain that I'd blown up "normal" and now I was the "Big Ick"?

"Yeah, Sis, it does. I never thought I'd be in this situation. Turns out being normal is every bit as difficult as being abnormal." She and I knew about being abnormal.

"Are you okay?"

I was so glad that she asked.

I summarized the entire situation. "There's still times when I remember where I came from, how much of that still sticks, and how much might be damaging those around me—and I think about what I should do about it." There. Now she knew. No one else would've, but she would.

"You know, Carter, I wonder what it would've been like if Mom had said, 'Children, I'm sorry for hurting you and I want to make it better, and I need to start by getting some help for myself because I'm very sick.'" She paused for us to ponder what that would've been like. For me, it would've been like a ray of sunshine, banishing the darkness in our lives. "So, dear brother, what is your Old Soul telling you?"

"It's telling me that when we hurt others, we need to take care of ourselves and our family, so we don't do it again. That simple, huh?"

"I see the Old Soul is still around. It always will be. You just have to listen."

I smiled. Yeah, she and I shared the same soul.

She asked again, "Are you okay?"

"Yeah. I'm okay. Thanks for always being my compass. I love you." I let the stinging in my eyes turn to tears. I knew what I had to do.

"It's Not Your Fault"

Before the upcoming session, Teri and I did the household routine that I had resented just days ago but now genuinely loved. It lent structure, clarity, and distance from the blow-up a couple of days before. It seemed the same except for the part that was different: Teri and I did the familiar routine as strangers. Darienne read her books and Ian played with Legos. Both were safe in their own worlds, away from the fear and terror that had exploded into their lives. Meanwhile, I walked on eggshells and did little talking. As Astrid suggested, I journaled about everything good as a child. Playing checkers with Mom. The way she sang while cleaning house. When she made my meals at lunchtime. That's all I could remember.

Before I went to the second session, I changed out of my office attire and put on my blue denim coveralls. They felt more like me: a North Dakota kid, just doing the work that needed to be done.

Julie welcomed me again and offered me coffee. I laughed and said I was high-strung enough already, thank you. She laughed and led me back to Astrid's office.

Astrid stood up and said, "Hello," then pointed me to my spot on her couch. On the way, I grabbed her small gray pillow and sat down. I was ready. That's when she noticed my attire.

"Are those coveralls?" She smiled.

"Yup. Ready to haul some hay." I loved how this was going so far.

"You did a lot of work the last time we met. How was it at home?"

I told her how Teri and I had followed her instructions. I described how the routine felt like a security blanket. I mentioned I'd journaled every day, but struggled to remember much of the good.

"Still, Carter, that's good for you. So, how are you today?" She asked like we'd merely refocused the camera.

The question shifted my mood from satisfaction to concern. I sat forward. "Today, I'm hoping you could help me understand what happened. I feel like my body ambushed me again, like the night terrors back in 1982. Let's stop this merry-go-round."

"I've got a good explanation, but we have a lot of work to do today." She grabbed a tiny tablet from her desk. "I wanted to summarize what you referred to as the blow-up. I'll need your patience as we do that. Carter, last time, you said you and Teri were on the couch together after the dinner you called a 'farce.' You were angry that Teri was hiding information about her therapy from you. The kids were extremely loud. You'd just finished cleaning up Ian's vomit. Right?"

"Yes." Where was she going with this? How was this moving us forward?

She went on with her list, verifying each item as she went along. What I felt, saw, tasted, and smelled.

"That all seemed so familiar to me, so I pulled out my notes from back in 1982. Do you remember what your mother used to eat when she was binging? The split pea soup and oranges? Remember what you smelled? Vomit and wine?" She looked up at me.

I sat back. I felt like I'd been slammed in the chest, pushing me backward down a dark, dank pit of despair, dread, and decay. My head was spinning. My ears were roaring. My hands hurt from squeezing them together. I was the Big Ick.

"Those sights, sounds, and smells? They're triggers and they caused a strong reaction in your body and your brain. Those two remembered your childhood and thought you were under attack. So they fought back . . . hard. You had no control over them. You were probably in a blackout." She paused, letting that sink it. "Those triggers and your reaction to them tell me you have what's called Post Traumatic Stress Disorder, or PTSD."

"You forgot. I've never been in the military."

"No, but PTSD can occur in victims of domestic abuse. Their experiences . . ."

I sat forward again. "I'm not a victim, so let's not start making a victim out of me. Teri and the kids are the victims here." Right now, if they billed me for this session, I'd mark "Return to Sender."

She pulled her chair closer and leaned forward. "Carter, you're at a crossroads. Sure, you can keep trying to hide from your past. You've done it for years. You might get your family back that way, but not for long. They're onto you. They know something's going on. Teri called you on your bullshit right before your rage. That was one of the PTSD triggers—you felt attacked. If you want to keep your family, you need to face your fears." She paused. "What really happened back then when you were a child? All of it."

So it began. I had to work up to it, though. First, I told Astrid about Mom's stealing and lying—the worst, not telling me who my father was. Then, the broken promises: not fishing with me, not quitting drinking, not going to my concerts. Then, her attacking me on the toilet, her raging at Faith, at all of us. Then, the knives in my room at night. Then, the enemas and her shit on my clothes. Astrid took notes in her tiny tablet. She set down her tablet.

"I can sense if someone has been traumatized just by the way they talk. They talk in monotone, like they're bored with the whole story. They're not—they just refuse to get into it, so they list a bunch of facts, like a travelogue. That was your voice just now. Also, they have what veterans call the thousand-yard stare. It's the blank look you have on your face right now, like you're looking right through me. How do you feel now?"

"Like I dutifully filled out a form." I took a deep breath and looked around, trying to break the trance I'd put myself in. "Astrid, remember I told you I struggled to think of any good? Any sensations of awe and innocence are only in my earliest memories. Then anger, fear, and disgust drifted in like a dark doom. It settled over me, forever changing how I see and feel about the world around me. I call all of it the 'Big Ick.' It's not just over me. It's over my siblings, too. Each of them has their own story, no less than mine."

"Carter, our therapy can . . ."

I put up my hand to stop her. "That's not all, though. It wasn't just her." I looked down and felt the gloom of my own guilt. I confessed to Astrid about my bruising Mom, trying to poison her and setting her up to kill herself with a gun. I told her of my most hurtful acts: my regular rages at her. When I finished talking, I was still staring at the floor, feeling again like I was the Big Ick, after all.

"Carter, no one can blame you for any of that, including you. People in trauma can choose to fight, take flight, or just freeze. You chose to fight. You did what you needed to do to survive. You had a normal reaction to an abnormal situation. You didn't ask for any of that. You were a victim of it." She stressed the word "victim," but she didn't have to. I was convinced.

"It really helps to hear that it was a normal reaction, that I'm not abnormal."

She rolled closer. "Carter, you weren't in the military, but you were in a war. Your war ended in 1968, but your trauma didn't. Carter, it wasn't whether it was a life-threatening war or not. It was whether a ten-year-old boy thought it was. You were in many battles, fighting for your survival—the survival of your soul. And when you looked behind you, there were no soldiers there to back you up. You were alone. And . . . you were just a kid."

In my mind, I could see this little kid sitting on the couch, rocking back and forth, waiting for his mommy to wake up and play with him. He was just a little kid wanting to feel loved, to feel safe. Instead, he was stuck in a fucking horror show. No kid deserved that.

I leaned over, put my hands on my face, and started sobbing, the kind meant to wrench out all the poison, leaving me clean, fresh, and innocent. My body fought itself, convulsing and needing to breathe. My heart sizzled with fear, betrayal, and rage. All the while, Astrid sat there, handing me tissues and reminding me again and again, "It's not your fault."

I felt like someone had taken me by the hand and led me out of the dark shadows and into the bright sunlight. What she had said made complete sense to me. Nothing else had. Soon, my sobs settled into a series of soft whimpers. Finally, I just sat there, staring at the floor, feeling like I'd floated back from a distance of five decades.

"Your mother was horribly sick. She had an illness, a mental illness. You learned that your mom valued her booze more than she valued you. There is no more painful betrayal than betrayal from a caregiver. One of the things you need to do in your therapy is to accept her illness. I doubt she grew up wanting to abuse her children. Someday, you'll need to understand that . . . and even to forgive her. So, how do you feel now?"

I sat there, considering. "I think I feel good?" It came out more like a question.

She laughed. "So you 'think' that you 'feel'?"

I caught the irony. It felt good to chuckle.

"Let's talk about recovery from PTSD. It has various phases, all integrated together. You might write them down." She handed me a pen and some paper.

"First is to appreciate the wisdom . . . the courage . . . that you have to even face what you went through. My guess is you had three things going for you. Your sister, Renee, gave you something you might struggle with all your life: unconditional love. You also have Teri, whom I've never met, but who I sense is a very wise woman, maybe more than you realize. Then, you have what Renee refers to as an 'Old Soul'. There's a deep wisdom in you that we'll be listening to. Am I forgetting anyone?"

I laughed. "While I never had a dad, I had a make-believe one." I told her about fishing with my dad and how "he" would share advice with me. "He was wiser than I realized."

She laughed.

"Use those resources to stay safe and stable during your recovery." She paused.

"The second phase then, is to go back to your childhood, but this time as the wise and courageous adult that you are now. Get in touch with what that child felt during those years, during those painful experiences. You got a good start today. You can go back with Teri, but only to the extent that you invite her in . . . and that she's willing."

"Third, get in touch with how you feel now about those childhood feelings and experiences. You'll need to understand your mother as a person who had a severe illness. Not someone who was, as you once called her, a zombie. Then, you'll remember all the good things about her and about yourself. Then, hopefully, you can forgive her."

She added, "This time, rather than just reading articles . . ." She winked at me, remembered my negligence in not following through with the ACoA therapy. "I'd like to get you into a support group for people with PTSD. A colleague of mine runs the groups and I'll see if I can get you in. Keep journaling, but I also invite you to write a letter to your mother. Write what she did that hurt you. Also, write what you probably felt back then. Then, write what you feel now. End the letter with what you remember that was good." She waited while I jotted that down on my paper.

We'd reached the end of the session. She smiled, stood up, and walked us out to Julie's desk. On the way, she turned back to me. "And, Carter. Try to have some fun."

Connecting in Heartview

February 1975, I'm in the Heartview Alcoholism Treatment Clinic. Two weeks ago, I'd committed myself because I'd been high during the last half of 1973 and most of 1974. Pot, speed, acid, and alcohol. I'd been flunking out of college in Fargo, too spaced-out to follow a schedule, much less any lectures. I was too ashamed to go home to Belfield. I didn't want Renee to see me like that. I felt lost and alone. A friend had committed herself to the clinic and said it didn't need any money upfront. Good. I didn't have any. She said it was warm and comfortable. So I packed my few belongings, walked to the Interstate and put out my thumb. I got a ride there, walked in the door, and was admitted the same day.

Two weeks later, I'm in Art's office. He's my counselor. He moves and speaks very slowly, the same way he puffs his cigarettes.

I ask him, "Art, what's my diagnosis? I know it's there in my folder right in front of you."

He pauses for a few long seconds. "Usually, we don't show it because it can cause patients to obsess over it. It's mainly to help the clinical staff." He indulges in a puff. I know I'll obsess over it, but I want to see it, anyway.

"I'm paying for the diagnosis. I'd like to see it."

An eternity later, he opens the folder on his desk and scans it. His head lowers down the page like he's falling asleep. Finally, he says, "Acute undifferentiated schizophrenia, likely attachment disorder, and addictive personality." I have some idea of what two of those mean.

"What's an attachment disorder?"

He pauses like time has stopped. The syllables crawl off his tongue. "Imagine a child raised in a cave with wolves. That would be you. You might suffer from a lack of personal connections."

No shit. They'd earned their money. That diagnosis was spot-on.

Two weeks later, four weeks after committing myself, I'm in my Family Week, an important part of my treatment. It's for family members to tell the patient how the addiction had affected the family and for the patient to atone.

I'd invited Renee and Faith to come. I wanted to apologize to them for my counting on alcohol and drugs like our mother had. They'd understand what that meant.

Art had told me to invite my mother, too. I told him that was hopeless, but I wrote her an invitation just the same. Sure enough, a week later, he got a letter from her, explaining that she was sick, but that she loved Carter more than the world itself, more than all the planets in the universe, more than . . . blah, blah, blah. In her usual style, she snuck in a sentence about how cruel the world had been to her, but that she had survived it all to be such a wonderful mother.

Now we're all sitting in the room, ready to start the meeting with my sisters. The room includes eight of Art's other patients seated in chairs around the room. Half of the patients are smoking, including Art. He will lead the meeting from his desk in the corner of the room.

Art starts by thanking Renee and Faith for coming. He explains how the process will work. First, it would be helpful for Carter to hear from each of them. After each, Carter would have something to say. "Your feedback is most helpful if you are as open and honest as you can be. Say what you want, however you want to say it."

Renee looks at Faith, so Faith starts. "I'm really glad you are here. I had no idea that you were struggling. I hope this treatment brings us closer together." She chuckles nervously, looks around, and says, "Thanks."

Art says, "Faith, what do you remember about your childhood with Carter? He says your mother was also an alcoholic and drug addict."

"Sure, she was. But Carter and Renee need to see the good side, too . . ." She says her usual speech about Mom's singing, selling poppies, and making fudge.

I say, "Thank you for coming. It means a lot to me. I'm sorry that I've done this to myself and that we don't have a closer relationship, Faith. I'll work on that."

Art asks, "Faith, what about Carter back then?"

She laughs. "Oh, he was a little devil. He was spoiled rotten. Mom never blamed him for anything. He was always down at Cherry Creek fishing." No, Faith. He wasn't.

Art turns to Renee. She's been looking at the carpet all the while Faith has been talking. "Renee?"

Renee looks at me and clears her throat. My heart starts to race. I look down at my shoes.

"Carter, I'm glad you're here. I've been worried about you. Us kids have gone through hell together. I'm sure others in this room have gone through their own hell, too. They can understand you. They can help you. Mom never helped us kids to help each other. I need you to stay alive so we can do that. I love you, dear brother."

Art senses that's enough. "Thank you, Renee."

He turns to me, indicating it's my turn.

I just sit there. I have so much to say, but nothing comes out. I feel so ashamed, I just stare at my shoes. I heard what Renee meant because we share the same soul—she meant that if I didn't reach out and make the most of where I'm at, I might die, at least in my soul. That would be letting down all of us kids, not just me. She deserves more than my silence now. I look up at her and feel the same love and care that I've felt from her since I was born.

I look at Renee. "I love you, too. I'm so sorry for the pain I've caused you. I never wanted to be like our mother, but here I am. I didn't come home because I didn't want you to see me like I was."

I turned to both of them. "The best thing I can do for me—for us—is to quit killing my soul. We lived with someone who was doing that. I promise you both, from now on, I will be safe and will do everything I can to stay sane. I will always tell you how I'm doing. You won't ever have to go through this with me again. I love you."

Renee quietly says, "I love you, too, brother. I'm going to remember what you said." She smiles.

Faith says, "And remember that I love you, too. It's both Renee and me." She laughs nervously.

Art asks, "Anything else, Carter?"

I get up, walk across the room, and hug Faith. She gives me a heartfelt hug. Our fight is over.

I walk over to Renee. She stands and we embrace in a sharing of love and affection that make us the only people in the room.

Art says, "Thank you Renee and Faith. What we just saw was very powerful. My best to the both of you and your families. Thank you for coming."

After they leave, the rest of us stay to discuss what had just happened. I get lots of compliments and hugs, but some warnings, too, that sobriety isn't that easy.

Afterward, Art turns to me and asks, "How do you feel?"

"Connected," I say. "I feel connected."

Respite

Over the next few days after the session, our routine again saved us. Doing dishes. Washing clothes. Playing with the kids. Slowly, the illusion of normalcy crept back in, but now Teri and I felt like strangers. I missed her dearly. Darienne asked me to explain the word "tranquility." Had the universe posed that question just to help us? Ian asked if I'd ever been in a race car. I ached to tell him I had. Instead, I told him the truth. No, I hadn't, but I drove a tractor when I was a kid.

I knew I needed to talk to Teri about the rage, and soon. All kinds of emotions were washing over me, none of them comfortable. Would she confront me about not doing ACoA? Would she lay down the law that I'm not to be alone with the kids? Could I explain what Astrid had said about PTSD, or would that cause even more confusion?

One afternoon, I asked Teri for five minutes to talk to her. I didn't want to ask for more. I didn't want to bring her back to that terrible experience.

"First, I wanted to apologize for asking about your therapy so much. I know better, but I let myself believe that you might be leaving me, so I needed to constantly be reassured. So I kept asking. That's disrespectful. I won't do it anymore."

"Carter, why would you think I'm leaving you?"

Did she sound guarded, like I knew something I wasn't supposed to know yet? I remembered Astrid telling me that the biggest fear of ACoAs is the fear of abandonment.

"I also wanted to tell you I had a big breakthrough in therapy. I know I've told you that before with the ACoA stuff. I'll understand if you don't believe me this time. All I can do is tell you my experience. I was diagnosed as having something called Post-Traumatic Stress Disorder. Astrid said what happened was I had a

PTSD episode, a blackout. It's different from a flashback, because that's just a memory. In an episode, you feel like you're actually back there in that time. It happens especially with people who've experienced a traumatic event or, like me, many of them."

She said, "I've heard of it for war veterans, but you weren't in the military."

"That's the same thing I said to Astrid. She explained that PTSD can also happen to victims of domestic abuse." I instantly reacted with shame to my word "victim," but damn, I really was one.

"Okay…" She hesitated, as if forming a question, but I wanted to be sure I said my piece.

"Another thing I wanted to say. Back there on the couch, before the episode, you said I was talking bullshit. You were right. I was complaining you didn't share your therapy with me, but I'd been hiding my past from you all along. I'm sorry."

Her face seemed to relax. "Like the night terrors, my body had reminded me of that past. When Mom was drunk—and she was drunk and drugged a lot—she'd eat split pea soup and oranges. There'd also be the smell of her wine and her vomit. Sometimes, she'd be yelling, too." I stopped. Now, I didn't want to get any closer to that experience.

She nodded. Quietly, as if talking to herself, she said, "That's what we were eating. The kids were making a racket, too."

"Yes, those sounds, those sights, those smells—and with my anger—caused a PTSD episode, a blackout. I don't remember anything between sitting on the couch and standing in front of Ian's door. But that's what I have to work on." I felt like such a hypocrite whenever I talked about therapy to her. I'd blown my credibility when I hadn't done the ACoA therapy.

"Love, I went to therapy the first time mostly to get you off my back. But I've tried running from my past and it's not working." The tears welled up in my eyes. I bit down on the side of my tongue to stop from crying. I felt reassured because she had tears in her eyes, too. "You have a right to be angry, very angry, at me. I have good reasons, but I don't have good excuses. I'm sorry." I reached out and squeezed her hand, then got up to leave her alone with what I'd said.

"Carter? Who's Danny?"

I turned back to her. "You asked me that before. What are you talking about?"

She frowned in confusion. "When you were shouting at us, you said things that made no sense. You said I never looked at you, but, Carter, I look at you all the time. That I lie and steal, but I don't. That I'm not a good mother like Danny's, but you compliment me all the time."

"I said all of that?" I walked over to her and got down on one knee. I took her hand and said, "I used to shout all that at my mother. Danny was just a friend of mine when I was a kid. I'm so sorry."

"Is that the PTSD stuff?"

"Yes. I'm sorry. I don't believe any of that about you. I promise you I'll work hard on that and I'll have a lot to tell you about. I just want some help from Astrid about how to do it and how to do it soon." I felt like there was a ghost, a demon, deep inside of me. That evening after the kids were in bed, Teri patted the couch cushion next to her, so I sat back down and turned to her. She took out some sheets of paper and said they were notes from her sessions.

"My therapy is going really well. I'm learning a lot about myself. I'm not ready to say much yet, because I've still got a lot to learn."

"What do you think of therapy?" I asked cautiously, hoping not to scare her into silence.

"I didn't know what to expect. I was scared when my first session started, but sad when it ended. How about you?"

How do I answer that?

"To me, therapy is like someone spliced a dream sequence into a high-speed chase in a movie. Then, while you watch, someone stands behind you, giving you a deep-tissue massage."

We both chuckled. I waited.

"Sandra's having me talk about what it was like growing up. I talked about how, as the oldest of four, I was always trying to be good and responsible. I talked about how even though we didn't move as often as a lot of military families, people were still always coming and going, so I had to make new friends every year. I learned to adapt to whoever was around, but kept to myself most of the time. I talked about how I'm still that way."

I couldn't help but smile. She was not just talking about herself; she was talking about what she was thinking about herself. I wished I'd had her courage.

"She's also having me talk about how much from my childhood I take into my relationship with you. I realized there was a lot of it—avoiding conflict, hardly any talk about emotions. It wasn't on purpose, but it was so natural for me. There are some things I want to say to you. It'd help if you just listened for now. I need to feel like all of this is coming from me, that I'm not worried about what you'll say or do. Okay?"

I felt like I was a high-wire again, but this time, I'd looked down. This could be a long fall. I sat back. "Okay. I'll just listen." I felt my heart beating harder, my face getting hotter. This was an important time for me to stay calm and just listen. She deserved that.

She said, "I might cry, but I want to just get this out. Don't worry, okay?"

I nodded.

She picked up her notes and studied them. "I've struggled with you detaching from us. It's like you go somewhere in your mind, even when you're in the room with us. I feel like I'm not important enough for you to be with, to listen to. Worst of all, I got used to that. I forgot what it's like to have a partner to talk with. I want that back." Her tears started—she was hurting. She took a deep breath. She still hadn't looked at me.

"I walk on eggshells around you sometimes. You get so irritable. It's like you have so much anger inside that it starts to leak out a little bit at a time. I'm afraid the whole torrent will let loose, like it did that night. It seems like your physical rages stopped when you spanked Ian, but your emotional rages just kept on going."

Now she was looking up at me, like she wanted me to explain all that. Where would I start? I just nodded back. She looked down at her list again.

"I wish you trusted me more. Sometimes the topic of your childhood will come up and you either change the subject or you walk away. It's obvious there's something you don't want to talk about, so I just don't say anything. I don't want you to be uncomfortable, but like you said earlier today, there's something in your past that you need to talk about, for yourself and for us." She smiled and reached out to touch my hand. She was reassuring me. There was a huge net to catch me under my high-wire.

She glanced at her list. "Another thing, sometimes you seem so touchy about my moods. If I'm quiet for a while, you'll keep asking me if I'm okay. You'll bring me water or ask if I want to go out. I mean, I should like it, but . . ." She looked up at me. "I'm okay. Okay?" She chuckled, like she knew this wasn't the end of the world, but just the same, it was a problem.

"Carter. I hope you don't feel like I'm beating up on you. I've got all this on my list and wanted you to know." That was a lot. I hoped she was done.

"Teri, I'm glad you're telling me all this. I hope we can share this kind of stuff as it happens rather than much later on." I knew that could be a biting remark, but I was getting pissed. I felt like, if I was that bad, then why was she still with me? I've got to calm down.

"Just like I can handle my own moods, I can handle what needs to be done around me. Sometimes, you act like you're responsible for everything around you. If it doesn't go just right, you apologize, like it was all your mistake. I feel like you think I'm incapable or fragile. I'm not. I've been taking care of most things here while you were working long hours."

She didn't need to convince me. She'd just said more about herself than I had in my ten years with her.

She continued. "I'm working to change, just like you are. I haven't had therapy before like you have, so a lot of this is new to me. It's helped me to understand how people can benefit from it and what it means to get help. It can be scary. Maybe now, I understand more of what you will be going through in it."

I held my breath while she turned the page on her tablet.

"I made a list of some of the great advice I've been getting. Wanna hear it?"

I opened my eyes even wider and nodded. I felt like a kid hearing *want some ice cream?*

"Speak my truth—trust my gut. Know what I want, regardless of what he wants. The better I take care of myself, the better for both of us. Our growth is our children's growth. There's more, but those are the key ones for me now. What do you think?"

"Teri, I feel honored. I feel humbled. I feel inspired. I feel so damn lucky." I just stared at her, wanting to listen to her for the rest of the day.

"Thank you. Okay, then. I've also been thinking it'd be good for us to just get out as a family. There's a railroad display at the museum at Bandana Square. Let's go there on Saturday. We could head over there after lunch. Let's do that."

The following Saturday, we headed for the museum. Twice, I took her hand, once when we stopped to read a sign about trains. Another time when she was in front of a colored-glass window, admiring its beauty. So much of the beauty that I saw in my life came from what Teri had shown me: clouds, flowers, children, music, the layout of fine food on a dinner plate.

When we got home, I approached Teri. "I'd like to tell the kids about Mom. Just top-level stuff and why I get so angry sometimes. Maybe that will help them understand the rage. I won't go into any scary details. What do you think?"

"I think that would be a very good idea."

So we gathered the kids in the living room, Teri and I on the couch and each of them in chairs across from us.

"I want to tell you something about my childhood. When I was little, my mom was an alcoholic and drug addict. That means she drank too much and took too many drugs. That made me real sad a lot. It also made me very, very mad. Sometimes when people are very angry, if they don't talk about it, then that anger builds up in them. Sometimes it comes out later on, so much and so fast, that it scares people. That's what happened with me when I yelled at you and Mommy in Ian's room. So I'm working with someone to get that anger out. Someday, I'll tell you everything about when I was a kid, okay?"

Darienne said, "Okay." Ian said, "Okay" too, but his face was red and his lips were quivering. I went to him and leaned down. "Are you okay, little guy?" He nodded. I hugged him and kissed each of them on the head. We needed to do something together and soon.

I asked, "Will you play kickball with me tomorrow?"

It had always amazed me how children could change moods in an instant. I wished it worked that way with me.

So the next day, there we were in our backyard, the four of us: Darienne, Ian, Teri, and me. We laid out bases, first, second, third, and home. A strong kick could score a home run. It was so much fun, we laughed more than we scored. I must have played like that when I was a kid. Why couldn't I remember it? I'd rather be doing that than lost in my head, thinking about *thinking about* how to have fun.

There were times during our play when my mind was completely quiet. In my life, that was always the time I felt the best.

Bury Your Demons

It's March 6, 1976. I'm back in Belfield for the weekend, taking a break from my studies in Bismarck. I love being here, where I'd been rescued from my childhood nightmare.

I walk into Renee and LeeRoy's house. It's after dark. My feet are wet from the cold slush on the sidewalks. I'm standing by the kitchen counter, smelling fresh-baked chocolate chip cookies. Everyone seems to be in bed, so I think I'll steal a cookie.

LeeRoy walks in. "Where have you been? I've been looking all over for you." This is unusual because LeeRoy rarely talks to me, much less ever looks for me. I know something serious has happened. My body goes stiff.

"I was helping Tom move into his new apartment. What's wrong?"

"I'll get your sister." He turns and heads into their bedroom.

A minute later, Renee walks in, wearing her nightgown and slippers. She walks up to the counter and leans on her elbows. She looks at me and rolls her eyes, as if to warn me of a major annoyance. "Mom died."

I hadn't taken Mom all that seriously, but her dying was different. She'd actually done something normal. "Are you okay?"

She groaned. "Ah. I thought I was done with all of that dreariness around her. Mac found her on the floor unconscious and called the ambulance. They got her out of the house, but she died in the ambulance. He called me to get up there and help right away." Ever since I'd turned eighteen, Mom had been living in Williston with Mac. We rarely saw her anymore. It felt like a cleansing.

I put my hands on my hips. "I just want to get in and out of that Williston situation as quick as I can."

The next day, Renee goes to Williston to clean up Mom's bedroom. I go back to Bismarck to get nicer clothes for the funeral. The entire time, I'm haunted by the pathetic presence of my mother. I'm stuck in a horror movie where the zombie follows me around.

I know I should feel grief and despair. I look for those emotions in me, but they just aren't there. I don't feel that she's really gone at all. My anger, fear, and dread are here whether she's around or not. The demon is alive.

Two days later, I'm driving to Williston in a North Dakota blizzard. Snow is blowing so hard, I can barely see the road. It slows me down. I just want to get this over with.

We're staying in a family friend's house the night before the funeral. Renee's sleeping upstairs and I'm downstairs. Mom's in the basement with me. I see her in the shadows. I feel her in my bones. I don't breathe through my nose, because if I do, I'll smell split pea soup. But when I breathe with my mouth, it sounds like, "Carter. Carter." I try to calm myself down. Then I hear the furnace kicking on—or is that someone stumbling into the wall? I run to the bottom of the stairs.

"Renee? Renee! Come here. I think she's down here."

Our friend comes to the top of the stairs. "I'll get your sister." I hear voices in the background. "He sounds really upset."

Renee comes down the stairs. "Are you okay?"

I try to laugh at myself, but I can't. "I'm freaking myself out down here. It's like she's everywhere, like she's not really dead." I'm hoping Renee will just sleep down here, too—that she'll help me get my head straight.

"Carter, I know. I know. I feel the same way. Like she's not really dead. She was such a ghost, anyway. Remember Faith said Mom wasn't there even when she was sober?" This isn't helping;

Renee isn't calming me down at all. She shakes her head. "Her bedroom was such a mess. There were vanilla extract bottles all over the place. Remember when she'd drink those just to get drunk?"

Renee and I sit down on the bed and talk until we're both so tired we can't keep our eyes open. We talk about how Mom would complain about her friends but then compliment them all the while they were visiting. She wondered how the town mortician could do such a morbid job but then she'd be the first to stare at her dead friends in their caskets. She detested lying but she even changed the date on her birth certificate. That one cracked us up.

I don't remember how we ended up talking about how she'd patiently rub us with Vicks VapoRub to treat our colds and congestion. She'd feel terrible if she accidentally killed a bug while trying to save it. She'd stay awake all night sewing a garment the one of us needed the next day.

In the funeral home the next day, the funeral director pulls me aside. He isn't wearing his paid-for mournful face yet, but he's dressed in black, just the same.

"We had to make a special casket for your mother. She must have weighed four hundred pounds." He starts to lead me toward her open casket, but I turn around. I'm not going to look. No way.

After the service, we mill about, trying to drift toward the door. Then a woman tugs on my arm. I turn around and she looks exactly like my mother. The demon's at her own funeral. Same face. Same hair. Same voice. Same eyes. There is something very different about them, though. They're actually looking at me. Renee had said that Mom's eyes were like a wounded animal—desperate and sad. This woman's eyes are gentle and caring.

"I'm Nora, your mother's sister." Standing there, I ache to cry, to grab her, and not let her go. I'm no longer in a hurry.

I don't know what to say to her. I'd never met her before. Mom always said that her sister Nora and her brother Oscar had been so *cruel to her, that she kept us away from our relatives. We'd always suspected those claims were just drunken delusions.*

I shake Nora's hand while staring deep into her eyes. "Thank you for coming, Nora. I'm sorry I never met you before."

"I am, too. Your mother was such a talented poet and artist, but she . . ." She looks down with tears in her eyes.

I put my finger under her chin and raise her head, then look into those eyes again. "Mom did the best she could with what she had."

"I agree. I want to get to know you kids. I don't know how much Elvina told you about Oluf and Esther, your grandparents. I'd like to sit down with you and tell you about them sometime."

"I'd love that."

She turns and walks away.

All that's left now is to see the burial so I know the demon is dead. Then I'm on my way home. The funeral director approaches Renee and me. Now he's got the paid-for mournful look on his face.

"We think the weather is just too bad for doing the burial right now. I'm sorry. We'll have to do that when the blizzard stops."

I look at Renee. She's already shaking her head.

She says, "We don't have to be there when you do it."

I add, "Just make sure you bury her."

"You Need More"

A week after my session with Astrid, it was cold, gray, and damp outside. The fog was thick, like my brain. I'd spent the week festering that I had yet another diagnosis, this time, PTSD. Yesterday, I felt fine about it. Today, not so good. If that pattern persists, then tomorrow I'd feel fine again. Astrid had said that recovery could be a long and rocky road. Another time, she'd said that ACoAs like their quick fixes. Those two situations weren't all that compatible, and I was already feeling the frustration.

I walked into the lobby, almost tripping over a kid playing on the floor. I managed to make it to Julie's desk and sign in. She didn't even look up at me. This all was so different than the first visit. Did I walk into the wrong building? I sat down and fidgeted while I waited for Julie to call my name. When that finally happened, I got up for her to walk me back, but instead she stayed at her desk, still looking at her computer. So I walked back myself.

I tapped on Astrid's door. She opened it and we exchanged perfunctory smiles as I headed to my spot on her couch. Why is the sandalwood so strong today and isn't it hot in here? She grabbed a box of tissues and pulled her chair over to me, but not as close as last session.

In a nasal voice, she said, "You'll have to excuse me, I've got a cold today. If it gets too warm in here, just tell me." She reached for a box of tissues and blew her nose.

"I'm relieved the tissues are for you. I thought you were planning a big confrontation today." I laughed at my own joke. She didn't.

"How was the journaling?"

"Well, I did some, but I kept finding myself working on the letter to my mother. Can I share it with you?"

She raised her eyebrows like she'd suddenly remembered. That wasn't like her. She was sicker than I realized.

She gave a strong nod, as if to apologize. "Sure."

I wished she would've seemed more excited. I pulled the letter from my pocket, unfolded it, and read:

Dear Mom,

I'm in therapy with a great therapist. Her name is Astrid and she's saving my life. She's helping me to see you and me more clearly. She's helping me to remember that I was a little boy once.

You talked baby talk to me and called me "Bim Bim." We played checkers and you let me win. That made me mad. It felt like you cheated, but I loved playing with you just the same.

Renee and Faith told me that you grew gardens and sold poppies for veterans. I never saw you do that. I wish I had. It would have made you more real to me.

There are so many things you did to me— especially at night. Mostly, though, I wish you had gone fishing with me. I wish you had heard my concerts.

You need to know that you hurt me deep into my soul. You made me take care of you and do things that no little kid should ever have to do. You turned me into an angry person, like a wolf who attacks.

You had chances to sober up and stay that way, but you didn't. Now, I've done terrible things to my own family, but I'm going to do something about it.

I'm grown up now, but I'm still a little kid inside and that kid is crying. He doesn't want to do to his kids what you did to him. He wants to stop the madness.

I'm trying to learn to forgive you, to love you, and to love me again, but right now, I hate you. Maybe that will change during my therapy.

Carter

I finished, folded the letter up, and put it back in my pocket. I sat there and stared at the floor. Now I knew what Astrid meant when she'd said "facing my past." For me, reading the letter was a good start.

"How did it feel to read it?"

"I felt like a sad and angry twelve-year-old kid. I think I sounded like one, too." I felt those two conflicted feelings, but the anger was winning out—I was angry when I came in and the letter just made it worse.

She nodded, blew her nose, then headed to the trash can to toss the tissue. On the way, without looking at me, she said, "Now, what would you like to get out of today?"

What would I like to get out of today?

I snapped. "I'd like to stop this session right now. You're the shrink. You tell me what I should get out of today."

"You're very angry today. What's going on?" She picked up the trash can and moved it closer to her.

"I'm sorry, Astrid. It's just a shitty day. It brings out the anger in me." It dawned on me. "I'd like to work on my anger."

"You chose to deal with your mother by getting angry and fighting, so I'm not surprised you do that as an adult, too. There are all kinds of techniques to deal with anger, but you need more."

More? She'd better explain that—and now.

I snarled, "Be gentle with me. Remember, I have PTSD. I could blow up at any time."

She didn't appear fazed by my sarcasm. She looked at me for a few seconds.

"Are you angry at what I said?"

"Damn right, I'm angry. I felt insulted when you said there was more needed for me. Want a minute to blow your nose again?"

"Carter, I could share all kinds of tips for dealing with anger. Deep breathing. Counting to ten. Learning your triggers. Praying. Exercising. But as I said, you need more. Anger is a common in people who were traumatized. It rides over all the other feelings. What's underneath anger, though, is fear. How did you feel when I said you needed more?"

"I felt terrified of what that might mean."

"I understand. You felt terrified and so you responded in anger. You asked for help with your anger today. Until you face the fears and feelings of your past, your anger will always be there."

She rolled her chair back to her desk and grabbed a sheet of paper and handed it to me. "I've found you a PTSD support group that can help you with that. The facilitator's name is Mike. I told him about you and gave him your number. It was all in confidence of course. He said he'd give you a call. What do you think?"

"As far as what I think, I think it's a very good idea. As far as what I feel . . ." I gathered my courage and asked, "Where does this leave you and me in the therapy?" I sounded pathetic.

"I've asked Julie to call you to make sure that we touch base in one month. It could be just over the phone. We can decide." Then she paused. "I am so proud of you, Carter." She wasn't just smiling. She was beaming!

I got up, beamed back, and on my way to her door, I hugged her.

Share and Share Alike

I mentioned to my friend, Bob, that I'd soon be joining a PTSD support group. He laughed and said, "I bet they'll all be Vietnam vets. When they find out you weren't in the military, they'll either completely ignore you or they'll be really pissed."

His comment sent me reeling. It touched my biggest concern: that I'd be sitting in a room full of vets hearing jargon that makes no sense to me. When I did speak, I'd be ignored because I "was never really in a war." I'd be judged because I hadn't served my country. I just wanted to read a book about PTSD. Maybe that would be enough to cure me.

A few days after I'd seen Astrid, I got a call from Mike. "Hello, my name is Mike and I'm the facilitator of your PTSD group. I wanted to welcome you to the group, Carter." His voice sounded velvety—low, full, and smooth. Exactly like my best friend, Tony, from Belfield.

Mike continued, "Astrid told me a bit about you. I wanted to congratulate you on your work. She said that you agreed you were a victim of trauma and had PTSD. That's a big first step, Carter. She said she'd seen you three times so far and would be seeing you some more. She said you were ready to practice being vulnerable and sharing your story. That sound about right?"

"It does, Mike. Astrid was very helpful." Did she tell you that I'd never served?

"Good. I wanted to tell you a bit about me and the other members. Then I'll talk about the group itself, too. I'm military, retired. As far as members, there's you, Spanky, Grunt, Cuss, and Whatever. We use nicknames, but it's up to you. We've all been in therapy at one time or another for PTSD. I told them about you and they're fine with you joining." He went on about the timing and frequency of meetings, where we meet, and the ground rules, especially confidentiality. "Any questions?"

"No, you covered it all."

We shared our goodbyes and hung up.

The following Wednesday, I went to my first group meeting, ready to do battle against PTSD. There were six of us in the meeting including Mike. He wore blue jeans and a red plaid shirt. If he'd had an ax, he'd be a lumberjack. After reminding the group of the ground rules, he said, "Let's do a quick check-in."

When my turn arrived, I launched in. "I'm Carter and I'm glad to be here. I want to take action against my PTSD. In the past, I tried to change merely by reading some articles and that didn't work out too well." Like popcorn, comments popped up from the group like "been there, done that" and "didn't work so well for me either." I'm beginning to like this group after all.

Mike asked if anyone had anything they wanted to share since the last meeting. Grunt held up his hand. "I want to remind everyone there's a stand-down at the VA next week. All of you are invited." Evidently, I was the only one who didn't know what a "stand-down" was.

Whatever held up his hand. "I got another letter from the VA declining my increase in benefits. It's such a hassle. Whatever. It's like a firefight in country, right?" What's a firefight?

Cuss held up his hand. "I did get that truck driving job. Goddamn. New boss loved that I drove supply in Nam." Everyone clapped, me included. "But I'll be moving up north, eighty miles. So, shit. I don't know if I'll make it to meetings, regular or not."

Already, I was aching to flee. I promised myself that when I heard the next military term, I'd be outta here. This was not at all like the sessions with Astrid. But then the next guy raised his hand.

"Hi, I'm Spanky." He looked right at me. "Were you in the military?"

Here we go.

"No, I wasn't." Please! Make an issue of this and I'll rip you a new asshole!

"I thought so. You didn't mention what outfit you were in when you introduced yourself. I wasn't in one either. I grew up with alcoholic parents and my dad beat the shit out of me. I belong here. I'm glad you're here, too."

I'm in a room with five other guys and already my eyes are stinging.

Spanky asked, "So what were your triggers?"

"Smells. Split pea soup, oranges, wine, and vomit." To anyone else, that sounded like a bad recipe. "Yours?"

"Beer, blood, fists, and screams." He said it like reading from a grocery list.

Mike asked, "Anyone want some individual time today? Remember, the less you want to talk, the more likely you really need to." It was quiet for a few seconds.

Spanky raised his hand again. "In our last meeting, I told you about struggling to build my life after divorce. It's been almost a year. Well, I've met someone." He shifted in his seat, looked around and laughed nervously. Group support rose in a tide. "Way to go, man." "No shit? All right!" "It's about time. Whatever."

"But I'm scared shitless. Every relationship has fallen apart and they've all been my fault."

Mike asked, "What did you learn about yourself in individual therapy?"

"I go through the same cycle with women. I'm just naturally in my head a lot. She notices and asks questions about me. I try get her off my back. She keeps at it. I blow up. I don't hit like Dad did. I just yell, do a lot of name-calling, and storm out the door. Eventually, I feel guilty, come back, and apologize. Both of us act like nothing happened and I go back in my head. It happens over and over again until one day, she tells me she's gone. I can't let that happen this time. This new gal might be the one for me."

Mike said, "Does that cycle look like what happened in your childhood?"

"Oh, shit yeah. That was our life. Mom would harp at Dad for this or that. One time she said he should get therapy because the war—World War II—changed him. He smacked her so hard she fell against the table and broke her glasses."

Spanky's story felt so much like mine that I just sat there, staring at him. How can these people help me if we've all got the same problem?

Mike asked, "How can we help you, Spanky?"

"Help me stop the cycle." He turned to the rest of us. "I gotta get out of my head. I gotta tell her what I'm feeling when I'm feeling it. Ask me if I'm talking to my new gal. Ask me if I'm showing up for her. Help me stick to it. I gotta stop this." Everyone stepped up. "Count on me, man" and "Fuckin' A, man. I'm here for you" and "Yeah, you gotta quit spacing out."

Mike turned to me. "Carter, I want to be sure you feel comfortable asking for help today. We're all equals here."

What was that phrase Astrid had said? Fight, flight, or freeze?

"No, I'm good."

"Anyone else?"

Grunt held up his hand and Mike nodded at him.

Grunt said, "A buddy from my unit in Nam is coming to visit next week. Every time we get together, all he talks about is the war. I try get him onto something different, but it's the same stuff. He calls it the Devil, like it's a real person. Devil did this, Devil did that. It wasn't the Devil; it was the war. Get over it. I'm thinking about just telling him that I've had it. I can't be around him anymore."

Spanky said, "My dad was Hades, the Greek god of hell."

Cuss said, "I called the war *the goddamned Grinder.*"

I said, "My mother is the Demon."

Grunt said, "Yeah, but you all know better. That's just a name. This friend of mine has gotta admit he was a victim in the war like the rest of us grunts."

Mike said, "I think we're survivors more than victims." He got agreements all the way around.

He went on. "I hear traumatized people come up with names of all kinds of characters for the traumatic experiences they were in.

I've heard Hitler, Stalin. Even Cancer and the Kill Machine. One guy said it was a way to make clear and understandable what was otherwise foggy and insane. It's how we choose to understand what we can't understand—the trauma. But we can get so wrapped up in the name that we don't face the trauma itself."

I asked, "Then what do we do?"

Mike asked, "What do the rest of you think?"

Cuss said, "The war was a fucked-up mess caused by a few politicians. Some people were killed, others were wounded, and others went insane. But a lot of guys came home and a lot them are doing okay. Calling the war *the Grinder* made me feel like everyone was killed. They weren't. To me now, it was a war."

Spanky said, "Before my dad died, we went fishing. He sat there in the boat talking the whole time, almost like he was talking to himself. He talked about so many good times we'd had—times I'd forgotten about. I told him there were bad times, too. He looked right at me and said, 'I was a real bastard. I hate myself for that.' After that, I never called him Hades again. That name was damn convenient when I was angry and wanted to vent, to get revenge. But it blocked me from seeing who he really was."

Mike said, "It sounds like, to rid the effect of our trauma, we have to face our Demon, our Hades, our Grinder. We have to see our trauma for what it really was—the facts. What caused it, the bad and the good. We have to see our role in it—and there might need to be some forgiveness in there, too."

In his words, he'd said the same thing Astrid had: I needed to face my past, accept that the human mom had an illness, see the good in her, and forgive her. Okay, I'm convinced. Yet, I have so many questions. Where do I start—or am I already doing it? If so, then how will I know if I'm on track? When will I know if I'm done with it? Or isn't there any end to it?

My Time in the Barrel

Two weeks later, I was already in my second meeting. I'd spent two weeks blaming myself for not speaking up in the first. Would that happen this time?

After starting the meeting, Mike turned to me. "Carter, I'm hoping we can hear from you today. It's up to you, but in this group you get out what you put in. How do you feel about it?"

My heart pounded harder. Should I pass? Should I say just enough to appease everyone? I'd try and see what happened.

Grunt looked at me. "Carter, looks like it's your time in the barrel." They all laughed. I did, too, even though I had no clue what he'd just said. Another military term?

They want me to share? Then I'll get help with . . . sharing. "I'd like help with sharing."

Mike asked, "What about sharing. Can you say more?"

"In my therapy, it seemed like everything involved facing my past and sharing my story. My therapist kept saying that meant being vulnerable and listening to people."

Grunt said, "I heard that a thousand times, too. But it's true, man. That broke the logjam for me."

Spanky said, "Me, too. But it's hard—real hard."

Whatever said, "Me, too. I wish I would've started a lot earlier, but . . . whatever, right?"

Mike didn't say anything. He didn't have to.

I said, "I told my therapist my story. She said I'd listed it to her like a boring travelogue. I'm not sure what else she expected—to drag her back home to my childhood, so she could actually see what happened?"

Mike asked, "Have you told your story to your wife yet?"

"What does that even mean 'tell your story'? Jesus Christ, it's like I'm condemned to hell unless I 'tell my story.'" Now my heart was racing.

None of them answered. I felt like they all knew a secret I didn't—like they were watching me, a rat in a cage trying to find my way out. They knew where the door was and I didn't.

Mike asked, "Carter, why don't you share your story with your wife?"

"First, I can't explain it. Words can't describe it." Some other group members said "no, they can't" and "you had to be there."

"I won't have people judging me because I was a character in a shit show. No way. And I hate, I despise, I get sick when people feel sorry for me. My mother groveled in that weak, petty slime and I won't." Tears started to well up. I was biting the side of my tongue so I wouldn't cry.

Mike said, "We're all equals here, Carter. We aren't judging you. Any other reasons?"

I took a deep breath and sat back. "Like I told my therapist, I don't want to relive it. I can't go back there again. It all becomes too real if I talk about it. Where would I even begin? Even I don't understand it."

Grunt and Spanky were sitting on the edge of their seats, nodding at me. Spanky was rocking back and forth. Whatever was looking off to the side like he wanted no part of this.

Mike said, "What your therapist said about needing to be vulnerable and sharing your story? Right now, you're doing that—and you're showing us the hard work that it takes to do it. You're turning to face your past, Carter." He paused. "If you lean back, close your eyes, and think of other reasons not to share, what comes to mind?"

I did as he suggested and the tears trickled down my cheeks. "If I start talking, the floodgates will open and it'll all come pouring out, the fear, the anger, the rage—the sadness and shame. I'll become the person I was back then." I felt like rocks had been piled on top of my chest and I was slowly taking them off, one by one.

Mike asked, "What would be your biggest reason for not sharing? If you imagine yourself telling your story to your wife, what might she do that would hurt you the most?"

I felt like he'd asked me to face an oncoming truck. "She'd get up and leave."

"Where would she go? What would she do?"

Now I felt like I was standing naked in a North Dakota blizzard. My breath was coming in gasps. "She'd leave me. Don't you get it? She'd know I wasn't normal." I sounded like I was pleading.

Mike said, "Over the years, the biggest reason I've heard for not sharing our pain is that we'll be judged and then abandoned. It's a reasonable fear, but I've never seen it come to pass. It's like a big lie we tell ourselves." He turned to the other members. "Each of you had shared your story with a loved one. What happened?"

Spanky said, "It took a lot more than that for me to start. We were in the kitchen in a big fight about something with the kids. I don't even remember. Then she said something about my not having the courage to be present, to be a real father. That just blew me up. I spent the next five minutes telling her about what my real father had done to me. I told her I didn't want to hear a word about it again. Then I stormed out. Six months later, she was gone." He sat back. "If I had to do it again, I'd do it different." He was staring right at me.

Grunt said, "I told my wife in the car during a long drive. I had a captive audience. Damnedest thing, I kept looking at myself in the rearview mirror and didn't like what I saw. So I just started talking. She just sat there, looking straight ahead and listening. Afterward, she didn't talk for a long time. I guess she needed that time to take it all in. Then she said she knew something awful had happened back in Nam, but she wanted me to tell it when I was ready. She said that meanwhile, she'd thought about divorcing me because of my anger, my lying, my spacing out. She was so much smarter than I ever gave her credit for." He nodded to the group.

Whatever said, "Like Grunt, I just felt phony, but I couldn't look in a mirror like he did. Anyway, one time we were moving things out of the basement and I came across a picture of my unit in Nam. Two of them were KIA. My wife wrapped her arms around me and she said, 'It's time.' So I spilled it all out. The sights, the sounds, the smells. I broke down big time. Once I started talking, I thought I'd go on all night. She held me the entire time. Felt like I'd lost fifty pounds." He smiled.

Mike added, "I was all of that, too, and I was exhausted from it. I wasn't learning from life; I was hiding from it. I wasn't healing and my body kept reminding me. I was having nightmares, night terrors, and blackouts. Finally, the pain of being stuck was more than the pain of just facing my past." He paused. "Carter, what are you hearing from all of us?"

I sighed. "I heard that I could lose her if I don't tell my story, because I'm lying now, hiding my past and spacing out like Grunt. I've had big blow-ups, too, like Spanky. There were times I thought about just dumping it on her so she'd finally know. I can imagine the relief that Whatever felt just from just coming clean. I'm hearing if I share with her, I need to ease her into it, to give her time. She might be scared by it too, so I need to be there for her."

Mike said, "Remember, we each have our stories that we've struggled with. What can you share with us?"

I surprised myself and rolled right into my answer. I told them of the lying, stealing, and broken promises. Even the attacks and the rages, the knives at night, the enemas.

Afterward, Mike said, "That was a long list. Anymore?"

I felt so at home in this group. "Yeah. I fought back and fought back hard." I told them about the poison, the gun, the bruises, and my own rages at my mother. When I realized what I'd confessed, I looked around, afraid of what I might see. No one had moved. No one had said anything. They either didn't believe me or they'd already heard something like it. It didn't matter to me.

Grunt asked, "Do you have flashbacks, man?"

"I do. They pop up whenever. They're vivid memories of what actually occurred. It's like what took me ten minutes to do back then, took me a minute in a flashback. Time is completely different. Funny thing is, I remember the flashbacks, but I don't remember much else. It's all a fog. My PTSD episode was different. Then, I felt like I was actually back there, reliving it."

Mike turned to the group. "Did you notice the similarities again between a vet's experience and that of a child in trauma? Carter was in close-quarters combat when his mother flailed at him. He was in an ambush when his mother came through the curtain. He was setting his perimeter when he locked his bedroom door. He was fighting his enemy when he fought his mother. His weapons were his hands and his mouth. Notice when the ambushes and skirmishes occurred? At night, just like our firefights. Notice how he felt even more alive when he was back there than he does now? Notice how he mentioned the fog—the fog of war?"

Whatever looked at me. "I'm sorry, man. Until Mike just said all that, I didn't buy it, that you and Spanky were in a war, not like Mike, Grunt, Cuss, and me. But I was wrong." He looked at Spanky. "I'm sorry, man."

Spanky nodded and smiled back.

Mike looked at the rest of the group. "Each of you has gone through the challenges in first sharing your story. What did you learn about the harm of not doing it?"

Grunt said, "I was stuck in a cycle of lying and hiding. I thought I'd fooled everyone else, but they'd figured me out—my wives and my family, anyway. So I'd move onto the next relationship until they got tired of me. Meanwhile, my not sharing was telling them that I didn't trust them with my truth." That sounded familiar.

I felt like I was on a roller-coaster, slowly moving up the rail.

Spanky added, "Like Carter, I hated pity. But I was okay with my own self-pity. I reveled in it day and night. I played the victim card, big time. I blamed my father, my wife, my boss. You name it.

Blaming them gave them all the power and I had none. Telling my story to my therapist gave that power back to me."

That sounded too familiar. The roller-coaster was still slowly moving up.

Whatever sighed. "Me? All of that. The worst part? I felt phony. I couldn't look in the mirror. No matter how many friends I had, I felt lost and alone. Still do sometimes." Now, the roller-coaster was suddenly speeding down the rail. I felt exhilarated by the members' acceptance, excited about growing with them, and terrified about where all this might go.

"Carter, what are you hearing?"

"If I talked to you all day long, I couldn't add anything new. I'm all of that." I started laughing. "I just realized I've never felt so normal."

We all laughed.

Mike said, "I hope you don't feel we're pressuring you to share right away. Each person is different."

"If I did share, I don't know how I'd do it." I shrugged my shoulders, then shook my head. "I'd have to say 'I'm sorry,' too."

Mike turned to the group. "What did you learn from sharing, especially with your loved ones?"

Grunt said, "I just said 'I'm sorry' to my wife, and that was a big mistake. I'd been selfish and irresponsible around her for years. She deserved more than a simple phrase from me. It got worse when I just kept talking, trying to clear things up. What did I know, right?"

Spanky said, "My therapist said it can be traumatic for someone to hear about what happened to their loved one, so don't put any more pressure on them. Share so they know your story, not to make them do something for you. When you do start to talk, don't dump it all at once. Start slow and ask if they have questions as you go along."

I raised my hand. "Stop. Mike, I gotta write this down." He handed me a tablet and pen. I wrote down what I'd heard.

Whatever said, "I wished I'd had that advice. I'd add, don't babble like I did. Know what you're gonna say before you say it. Then stick to it, but say it in your way. Don't make it a speech."

Mike waited for me to catch up with my note-taking. "Just the act of sharing your story is a big deal. You did that with us here today and you did just fine. I'd add, though, that you probably don't need to share all the details that you did with us. Just share the experiences, what affected you the most and how you felt about it. What are you hearing, Carter?"

I read back my notes from my tablet. "This is extremely helpful. Thank you."

But could I really do this with Teri?

Mike said, "How do you feel about sharing with your wife? What kind of help might you need?"

I inhaled deeply and slowly exhaled through pursed lips. "I've been hiding a story since I left my childhood home in 1968. If I share, that changes everything. I don't know. My life ain't all that bad right now."

Whatever said, "You look like you're staring down the abyss. But what do I know, right?"

The Enemy Is Us

My sister Faith is on the bed in her bedroom. She's coiled into a little ball with her arms around her knees, pulling them tight to her chest, and trying to tuck her head between them. She's wearing a green nightgown and bathroom slippers. She's moaning, "Mom, just leave me alone," over and over again.

I rush in. "Mom, stop it! You're scaring her. Leave her alone!" Mom doesn't listen to me. She's at it again, raging at Faith. That means she's probably on drugs, not drinking, otherwise she'd be passed out on her own bed by now. Her left knee is on Faith's bed and her other foot is on the floor. She's leaning over Faith, pointing her finger at her. She's wearing a large cotton summer dress with tiny white and blue squares in rows. It has wide straps over her bare shoulders. She's wearing bathroom slippers and the heels of her feet hang over the back of her slippers. Her hair is rolled up in the back. She calls it a chignon. She's big now. She's gained weight.

Her voice is rapid and sharp. "You don't care about anyone but yourself! I do everything for you. You do nothing for me. I'm your mother!" Mom's finger is still poking at Faith, but now it's even closer.

I'm thirteen and tall for my age, but a bit chubby. I get close behind Mom and grab the right strap on the back of her dress and pull as hard as I can. She falls back and lands on her right side on the floor. It makes a loud thud.

I yell, "Get out! Now!" I'm standing over her, pointing to her bedroom.

She manages to sit up. Her glasses are still lying on the floor and the piece that goes behind the right ear is broken off. With her right hand, she picks up the pieces. She loves those glasses. Then she slowly rolls to her right, not looking at me. She never does. She slowly gets up on her hands and knees, each arm and leg moving one at a time. She stands in slow motion and starts moving toward her bedroom. She's not the raging animal anymore. Now she's the zombie that I'm so used to.

I follow her. "How can you call yourself a mother after attacking your child? Is that what good mothers do? Or are you too drugged to know what you did? When you sober up, you'll blame this on us, too? I don't love you. I feel sorry for you. Why don't you die and save us all a lot of trouble?"

She doesn't turn around. It doesn't matter. She's not worth looking at.

Then I go outside to get away from Mom and Faith, from my yelling, from the memory of breaking Mom's glasses. Faith, Mom, and me. Feels like we're in the same nightmare and can't get out of it. It's all of us.

It's Storytime

February 1992. It's miserable outside but cozy inside. Teri tucked in Darienne and I tucked in Ian. Between the rooms, we both said, "Good night, Darienne. Good night, Ian." Each child answered in turn. A beautiful closure to a beautiful day.

Teri put their dirty clothes in the hamper. She did it like a pure and natural practice, like she was privileged to be part of it all.

Me? Since the meeting about sharing, I'd felt like it was my assignment to share with Teri. I resented the weight of it. Just look at today—my life now was even better than I had realized. My goal now should be to appreciate it even more.

She came up to me. "I wanted to thank you for today. Thank you for being such a great dad. Thank you for being such a great partner. Our children can grow up knowing we always showed up for them, right?" She kissed me, then headed into the kitchen to clean up.

I headed into the bathroom and then washed my hands, remembering "you're such a great dad" and "we always showed up for them, right?" I kept washing my hands, but I couldn't get them clean. Then I looked up. There in the mirror was my image.

Still looking in the mirror, I said, "Teri, can I talk to you?"

She came over. "Sure, we can talk. Are you all right?"

I couldn't take my eyes off that face in the mirror. "No. I've got some things to tell you about—things I should've told you long ago." It felt like the words hadn't come from my mouth, they'd come from my soul. I turned to her.

She put her finger on the side of her chin and frowned. "Okay, should I be worried?"

"No, just stay with me, please?" Forever?

"I'll boil some water and pour us some tea."

I headed into the living room, feeling like I was dancing on the edge of a cliff. After all this talk about sharing, the group's stories, and that damn mirror, maybe it wasn't such a sudden shift after all. Like Mike and Whatever, I'd grown so tired of being stuck, of living in fear, of feeling phony.

Where should I sit with her? I glanced at our couch. I remembered her sitting on it right before my rage. I remembered her sitting on the old couch in the condo, insisting I get therapy for night terrors.

She asked, "Where would you like to sit?"

Still looking at the couch, I said, "On our couch, please."

She set our tea on the coffee table and we sat down. I turned to her on my right and took her hand with mine.

"Carter, your hand is freezing. It's trembling. What's going on?"

"You were right in so many ways. When you said I needed to apologize to Lonny for my outburst. When you said I needed therapy for night terrors. When you said we needed family vacations during the chaos of our schedules. When you called me on my bullshit, when I said I was being truthful with you. When you insisted I get therapy for the rage."

She whispered, "I'm glad you feel that way."

"I'm sorry. I've been so selfish with you. I've been detaching while you've been sharing. I've been dishonest with you while you've been honest with me. I've been telling lies of omission—hiding a past that's deeply affected who I am and what I do with you. I've been hiding emotions that could have encouraged our love and our relationship to blossom so much more. I've been cheating you out of a partner who's always there in his mind and his heart. I want to tell you why I've been that way. You didn't deserve any of that. I have reasons, but I don't have excuses. I'm so sorry." My mouth was so dry it made small clicking sounds. She reached for my tea and handed it to me.

Still holding her hand, I said, "Love, if this is hard to hear, let me know. That's fine. I want to go at your pace, not mine. Know that none of this is your fault. You've been the one who's been right in so many ways. What I'll talk about is not a list of problems to solve. It's more for us to understand about me and our relationship. Okay?"

"Okay, but I'm a little nervous." She offered a quick smile.

"Remember when I told you about the ACoA traits ten years ago? I mentioned my blow-ups, isolating, not feeling safe, not trusting, sensing violence. But I didn't tell you why I had those. I just said Mom was an alcoholic and a drug addict. Remember?"

She nodded. "Yes, I remember. I always felt like something was incomplete about all that."

"That's what I feel the worst about—the lying to you. I tried to make you think that reading a book was enough. I knew better. I didn't tell Astrid all about Mom when I saw her about the night terrors. I hid it from her. Teri, I learned about lying real young. Mom lied about stealing from me. She lied to get drugs. She lied when she told me she'd stop drinking. She lied that she'd go fishing with me, go to my concerts. She lied that she'd tell me who my father was. She lied when she denied abusing us." Now I was feeling hot and my fists were clenched. I was so damn mad at Mom.

"Was that why you got so angry about not telling the truth to your employees? You seemed more upset than I would've expected."

I nodded. "Yes, that's why." I felt relieved. She'd understood.

"I'm so sorry about my anger, my irritability, my snapping at you all." I steeled myself. "And my rages. I grew up with it. Rage and anger were how I dealt with Mom. I got real good at it. Too good at it. I wasn't just angry at Mom. I hated her. The whole house revolved around her binges. She'd go on for days. Renee moved out and Faith was good at just staying away. I kept Mom away with my anger. But when she ignored me, I'd go into a rage."

Should I tell her about almost freezing Mom, the enemas, the poison, the gun? I ached to come clean. But I didn't want to repulse her, to scare her away. I'd lose her.

"I learned from Astrid that when a person has been abused, there are all kinds of confusing feelings. Anger is the one that's easiest to feel. I felt it a lot and sometimes at myself." I was getting angrier. My muscles were tightening, I was talking faster. I took another breath.

"That helps explain why you got so angry at Lonny when he ignored you. I never understood why you got so enraged. You didn't even remember some of what you'd said to him."

"Yes, that happened with Mom. It's why I did the bruising." Had I meant to say that out loud? Would she think I'm an abuser, that I'd hurt her or the kids? I was losing track of what to say...of what to think. My ears started ringing and I kept holding my breath. I was starting to panic.

"What about bruising? You started saying that and then just stopped."

"Love, remember the times I was so afraid of taking care of Darienne when she was an infant?"

"Yes. You were really hard on yourself."

"There were times when Mom was so drunk that she didn't know what she was doing, and I'd have to get her back to bed. Sometimes, she'd fight back at me. Sometimes, I'd grab her so tight there were bruises later on. I kept thinking of that when I was moving Darienne's little arms and legs around. Love, I'd never hurt Darienne. You gotta believe that. I . . . ." My chaos of emotions was vanquished by panic and guilt. Panic that, after hearing all this, she wouldn't want me around our kids. Guilt that I'd bruised Mom and marked Ian.

"Are the bruises why you were so upset when you spanked Ian? You were frantic that you'd done that?"

I took a huge breath and nodded. "Yes, that's why. It came from Mom always telling me that I was mean, that I was cruel. It was her standard line whenever she didn't get her way."

"How old were you?"

"I don't remember. I think it started when I was old enough to fight back, probably six or seven, until I left for Belfield when I was fifteen. I'm sorry for not showing you my emotions. That was because there used to be so much fighting back then—yelling, screaming, furniture tipping over. I saw Mom go after Faith sometimes and would have to pull her away. We didn't know how to deal with conflict. We just fought hard. Mom always told me that big boys don't cry. She said it all the time, so I just stayed alone and kept my emotions to myself—and I got used to it. But I was scared, sad, and lonely a lot."

I bit harder on the side of my mouth. I couldn't cry now. I needed to get the story out. But was I telling her too many details? Mike had warned me. She reached with her other hand and started stroking the back of mine.

"You said the word 'safe' before. What do you mean by that?"

I was glad she asked. It meant she was listening. She cared.

"When Mom was drunk or drugged, she'd sometimes come into my room. She never meant to hurt me, but she'd carry a knife. She meant to kill rats, that's all. Other times, she'd wander in and I'd get her back to bed. It kept me up and exhausted at night. Our toilet was in her bedroom. Sometimes at night, if I was using it, she'd think I was someone else and she'd come at me. I'd get nervous and scared and wide awake."

"Is that why you had the night terrors, talking about your mom in your room at night?"

"Probably." It felt good, helping her to put the pieces together.

"I grew up deeply ashamed of Mom. Deeply ashamed of myself. I read once that guilt is feeling bad about something you've done to somebody. Shame is feeling bad about yourself just being in the world. That was me. Mom kept telling us not to tell anyone about what goes on in our house. Our lives were always a secret. I called it the Big Ick. The secret got out when she walked by the school grounds in her nightgown, drunk. It's another reason I detached so often, why I liked to be alone. I felt so ashamed. I didn't want anyone to find out about us, about me."

She released my hand and started stroking my cheek.

"Don't do that! Don't feel sorry for me."

She jerked her hand away as I kept talking.

"I'm sorry. I hate pity, I hate self-pity. I want to seem—I want to be strong and always on top of things. I want to be . . . normal."

"You want to be normal, but I don't know what normal in the world really is, Carter. You've always been Carter to me. The man I know and love." She shrugged, like she was confused.

I felt so torn. I wanted to just say it all, but I couldn't bear her leaving me. I couldn't talk about what might repulse her. I sat back, pried my hands open and squeezed my thighs. I exhaled slowly.

"Whew. I'm done," I said.

"Why didn't you tell me all this before? I don't understand."

"There are so many reasons." I told her of my many fears of not knowing where to start, not understanding it myself, not being able to explain it. Fears of being judged, pitied, and abandoned. Feeling my sadness and shame, my reliving it. "I believed a big lie. That if I'm flawed, I can't be loved." I looked down at the floor and yearned for the safety of my private hole back at Cherry Creek.

She stood up and moved in front of me. She raised my chin and said, "You will always be loved, flaws or not. You're Carter, and there's so much more there to love." She pulled me up and into the safety of our embrace. We cried together—cleansing the room and our lives of the fears and misunderstandings that had built such a wall between us.

***

Over the next eighteen years, Teri and I grew personally and professionally. Each of our therapies guided us to more sharing, confidence, and courage. Teri learned to trust her wisdom and speak her mind. I learned to accept the unconditional love that had been there all along.

In 1993, I graduated with my MBA. During the program, I developed a vision to create a series of support groups for stressed-out managers. Groups would operate much like the support group I was in. Each member would get individual time to be open and honest—authentic—with their peers. Groups would not be as professionally facilitated, but members would be trained to do the critical basics.

Soon after graduation, I enrolled in a PhD program to do the research to carefully design the groups. I quit my full-time job in 1995, graduated with my PhD in 1996, and in 1998, I started a company, Authenticity Consulting, to begin teaching people how to develop and facilitate their own groups. Teri joined the company in 2001 and it continued to grow, spawning groups around the world. Darienne and Ian graduated from high school, got married, and moved on with their lives.

I had read that recovery from PTSD can take months, years, or decades, depending on the severity of the trauma. My recovery, so far, had been stalled by my belief in a big lie that flawed people can't be loved. That big lie was dispelled when I'd shared my story with Teri—and she'd stayed in my life after all. The coming years would challenge me with an even bigger lie, one that would confront me with my biggest illusion yet—myself.

Self-knowledge is the first step to maturity.

– Jane Austen

Part 5
Revelation

(1994 – 2022)

"After 30 years or more of floundering around and screwing up,
you will finally know, and when you get serious,
you will be dealing with the one thing you've been
avoiding all along – your wounds."

– Anne Lamott

A Crack in the Dam

In July 2010, we were congregating in Renee's living room in Bismarck, North Dakota. Thankfully, her air conditioning was at its best. It was ninety-five degrees and muggy out there. Sticky and oppressive.

There were twelve people in the room, some in chairs and others on the floor. The group included Teri, Darienne, Ian, and me, Ian's wife (Lotus), Renee, Faith and several of their daughters and grandkids.

We were exhausted and yet joyful. We had just returned from the large Veeder family reunion back in Watford City, one hundred eighty miles away. My grandmother, Ella Veeder Buell, had seven siblings and many of their descendants were at the reunion as well. Since the first grade, I had carried the shame about my mother in that town. I believed everyone in town knew about her. At the reunion, I stood on the stage and introduced myself and my family. To be in the reunion was an honor for me.

We'd met many relatives and asked many questions. "Did you know Roger Buell, my father? I know very little about him." We got many answers. "Yes, I knew Roger. He was a natural leader, out front in any group, always kidding around."

We'd answered many questions. "I'm Carter McNamara, Roger Buell's son. He was Ella's son. I grew up here until 1968 when I moved to Belfield."

The best question, though, came from Kerry Veeder. "When did you know you were related to us?"

"Around 1990, for sure. But my sister first told me when I was ten."

She countered, "We went to high school together, you and I. Why didn't you tell me then?" She'd looked so non-judgmental and sincere that I found myself answering her honestly.

"I felt too ashamed to tell anyone. I'm sorry."

Back at Renee's, we were debriefing.

"Do you remember when . . . said . . .?"

"Yeah, who was that?"

"That was . . . wait, I don't remember. Dad, was that your first cousin or second cousin, once removed?"

"So that's the town you hated so much? What's wrong with it? It's just another town. I don't get it."

I was on a high. I loved everyone in the room, including myself. All of this was so far removed from what I'd grown up with, from what I had fought so hard not to be part of. I was feeling proud and seen—feelings I was not all that familiar with.

In every crowd of friendly exchange, there are lulls in the conversation. It's when some organic force suggests that everyone take a breath—that they all should just look around, take in the companionship and appreciate it.

During one of those lulls, Faith blurted out, "Carter, I am so sorry that I left you alone with Mom when I moved out. It's really bothered me all my life. I feel awful about it."

Words can move people to tears, win wars, and authorize contracts. Faith's words felt worse. Suddenly, I was jerked back from the validation of the reunion to the Big Ick in my hometown— to split pea soup, oranges, wine, and vomit. I suddenly shifted from standing on a solid rock to falling into a deep, dark pit, like when Darienne died.

I looked at Renee. I could see from the look on her face that she'd been shot back as well. A face radiating in joy was now stern in the effort to stay here in the present. I was very protective of Renee because she'd saved my life so many times in so many ways. Goddamn it, Faith! Did I say that out loud?

I felt as if I was sitting there naked in front of everyone, as if everyone was staring at me, first with curiosity, then with abject pity. I wanted to scratch deep into my skin to cleanse myself. I thought about just sitting still, not saying anything. What's the worst that could happen? They'd assume Faith was off her medication—and surely, she must be on medication to have blurted all that out. I thought about asking Faith to explain what she was talking about and then I'd deny any knowledge of it. No, that wouldn't work because, despite Faith having her own sense of timing, she was honest and sincere. Any strategy to blame her would likely backfire, leaving people to believe I was heartless—and should've been abandoned, anyway.

I sat back and took a deep breath. I remembered hearing members of the PTSD group talk about sharing their story and I remembered sharing some of mine with Teri. Back then, I'd felt honest and inspired. Now, there was another way to cleanse myself and it wouldn't require deep scratching.

I turned to Faith. "I don't blame you for leaving. Frankly, I'm glad you left. It was a lot easier for me to handle Mom without your being there. I forgive you. We've moved on. This reunion was a big part of it. Let's enjoy ourselves for what we've come through." I'd spoken the truth. When Faith lived with Mom and me after Renee had moved out, she had a way of disappearing. I didn't blame her because Mom was constantly picking on her. After she started diet pills in 1965 when I was twelve, I had what were essentially two dazed and confused creatures frequently fighting with each other.

Maybe we can tamp out this conversation right now if Renee says just the right thing in just the right way. I turned to her, holding my breath and she delivered.

"God, yeah. Carter was the only one who could deal with Mom. She was terrified of him. He was the only one who fought back." She'd said that the best thing that could've been done, had been done. She knew enough not to say anymore.

LeeRoy walked in from the garage where he'd been having a cigarette, saving me from this conversation. "What are all you people doing in my living room?" he said, laughing. The rest of us followed suit. The moment had passed.

The next day, on the drive back to Minnesota, I was reflecting on that scene in the living room. I gasped and glanced at Teri. "Do you realize Faith admitted that Mom was awful? I just realized that. I mean, she apologized for leaving me alone with Mom, right? She wouldn't have said that unless she knew living alone with Mom was not safe. That's a big confession for her." I turned back and looked at the road. "What brought about the sudden change in her?"

"I wondered that, too. Maybe it was the kinds of conversations the three of you have been having lately?"

"What do you mean? We only talk when we visit Renee. Those visits only happened two or three times a year."

"Yes, but you seem more open with your sisters, especially in the last three or four years since Astrid and the PTSD group. Before then, if the topic of your mother came up, you'd just say 'I had a different mother.' These last few years, you've mentioned how your mom woke you up to care for her and clean her bed. Now, if Faith tries to get you to remember the good, you at least speak up. You remind Faith that your mom raged on her, too."

"You're right. I remember saying those things. You're right, too, that I want to share more now." I glanced at her. "It's like I'm on a mission now to find the truth." We laughed at the irony of that.

"Maybe she didn't know what it was like living alone with your mom. Maybe she felt guilty and just wanted to say 'I'm sorry.'"

I nodded and my eyes teared up. I looked to the left and wiped them away, hoping she wouldn't see.

"It's okay to cry, you know. I see a lot that you don't see." She said it as a playful accusation. "Faith is a wise woman. I remember the first time I met her, she said your mother was sick with alcoholism and drug addiction. She had an illness."

"Yeah, I remember. So what?"

"Remember what Astrid said in one of your sessions? She said your mother had an illness and that your recovery depends on you accepting that and forgiving her."

I felt like I'd been looking for my glasses and they'd been right there on my head, all along. "Are you telling me that I need to listen to Faith a lot more?"

"That's exactly what I'm saying. She's trying to see both sides of your mother now."

***

In the interval of 2010 to December 2019, I continued my efforts to face my biggest fear: facing my past and sharing my story. I told Teri more details that I was ashamed of, including about the poison and the gun. I remained too ashamed about the enemas and almost freezing Mom. I remembered Teri's tactful suggestion that I try to see both sides of Mom. I remembered Astrid's advice to see Mom as having an illness and to forgive her to get the demon out of my head.

I realized how closely Mom's troubling behaviors matched many of the symptoms of ACoA and PTSD. The more I thought about that, the more I wondered what childhood trauma she might have experienced. Over the years, I shared my thoughts with Renee and Faith, who had been wondering the same. That helped us to see Mom more as a troubled human being than a demon intent on abusing her children.

In 2009, Laverne and I discovered that Roger Buell had left behind another son, my brother, Roger Krumel. Like Laverne, he and I shared similar features. It was uncanny how we also shared such similar interests in history, politics, and philosophy. We decided to do a DNA test to conclude if we actually were related. The results verified we were indeed biological brothers. That also verified for me that Roger Buell was actually my biological father.

On February 21, 2011, Elijah Ciembronowicz, our first grandchild, was born. That afternoon, I was headed to buy a drink in celebration. Suddenly, in the middle of the road, was a black wolf, a rarity. It blocked the road. It turned to me and met my gaze, rolling its head from side to side. Then it turned to the right and disappeared into the woods.

Laverne died in October 2012. During a visit shortly before she passed, I told her to tell Roger Buell in heaven that I forgave him.

She teared up and said she would. My brother, Roger Krumel, and I continued our loving and lively conversations until he passed in December 2017.

In 2013, I gathered the courage to visit Watford City again. Earlier visits had brought back dreadful memories, especially when I'd driven by the location of my childhood home. I was pleased to see now that it had been torn down and replaced with a much more modern home with plants in the windows and toys in the backyard. Unfortunately, the trees—the canopy I'd sometimes hidden under—had been removed. They'd done their job for me when I needed them to.

On a bittersweet note, Ian and I became estranged during a major disagreement in the summer of 2019. I don't feel comfortable trying to convey his point of view. Suffice it to say that I miss the kind of relationship that I thought we had.

Apology in a Dream

I'm walking south along the west side of the school in Watford City. I had moved away and am an adult now, so I don't go to that school anymore. When I get to the corner, I turn to my left to head east. I live half way down the block on the right side of the road.

It's evening and a few cars are moving along the street. The lights are on in some of the homes. It feels like a small-town neighborhood at dusk.

I am a visitor to my childhood home now, and don't feel the dread and despair at all. I don't feel the Big Ick.

Rounding the corner, instead of our small white house with its red shutters, there's a large, dark brown A-frame home facing the street.

On the main floor is a large square window on either side of the front door. Each is larger than you'd expect for a house that size. Behind each, there's a light giving off a soft, warm, yellow glow.

The second floor is formed by two roofs, each starting from the top of the first story and coming together at the top, forming a large "A." It has two large, back-to-back, triangular windows. Behind the windows is a chandelier giving off the same soft, warm, yellow glow.

It's beautiful. I'm surprised to see it, but still, I know that it's my home somehow. I've been away somewhere for a long time, but I don't know where.

I open the front door and there's a spiral, dark brown staircase that starts in front of me. I hear a woman's pleasant voice say, "I'm up here." I don't recognize her voice, but I know I'll get a warm welcome.

At the top of the stairs, I stop when I see a woman sitting on a stool with her back to me, facing an artist's easel. She has red hair like my mother's. When I lean to my left, I can see she wears the same cat-eye glasses as my mother. She has a paintbrush in her right hand and a cigarette in her left. She's moving the brush around on a canvas in front of her face. I can't make out the picture she's painting.

While she keeps painting, she says, "I'm glad you're here. I wanted to talk to you. You know all that pain back then? I wanted to tell you 'I'm sorry.'"

She said it like she truly believed that I deserved it. Yet she said it simply, like she was apologizing for picking me up late from school. She didn't say any more.

I felt touched that she'd apologized to me, that it was important to her to do that. I wondered, though, how she knew that she'd hurt me. She hadn't looked at me or said anything more, so she still seemed so strange. Then she turned and looked directly into my eyes. She was my mother, after all.

I woke up feeling the same yellow glow inside.

"Teri, I dreamt about Mom last night. I dreamt she apologized to me. I've never dreamt anything like that before. It was wonderful."

Teri has a feeling for beautiful things from another world. She said, "I bet your mother feels as good as you do." She gave me a long hug.

"It's Not About the Details"

January 2021. I was on our couch watching an episode of Ken Burns' series "The Vietnam War." I'd seen the ten-part series before. It was being rebroadcast on public television now, and I was eager to see it again.

Teri was on the couch next to me. During a break, she turned and pointed at me. "Carter, I notice when you watch war shows like this, you sit like that."

I looked down and around. What? Then I noticed what she was talking about. I was sitting with my feet up on the couch, my body turned toward the television, my knees up against my chest and my arms wrapped tightly around them. My chin was resting on top of my knees and my eyes were fixed on the TV. I could not have been a smaller—a more protected—cocoon. I immediately felt self-conscious and started to unwind myself. I didn't want Teri to see me looking like my body was crying out, "I'm in pain!"

It was difficult to describe how I felt when watching that series. I felt like I was not alone. It felt so good to know others shared the same experiences but struggled to talk about them.

During another break to ask for donations, she said, "Carter, I'd like to talk with you sometime soon. There are some things I'm noticing that I'd like to tell you about—good things. Let me know a good time for you."

I reacted with some concern, but more with curiosity. "After this episode, sure, we can talk. I'd like that."

"Don't you want to sit for a while after this? Think about what you saw in this episode?"

"Yeah, that would be good. I'll come and get you then. Thanks, love."

I was always sad when an episode ended. It felt like a good friend had just walked out the door. I'd try to remember the dialogue, the looks on the people's faces. I'd try to remember how I felt.

A few days later, after another episode, I turned to Teri. "Yeah, Teri, let's talk."

She reached over and pulled my feet over her lap so we could be closer to each other. "I've been noticing some things about you these past few months. I think it's interesting."

I was excited to hear more. If she'd opened that way years earlier, I would have been terrified. It's amazing how things change.

She squeezed my legs. "I apologize if I sound like I'm sharing a grocery list or something." She laughed that genuine laugh that I'd grown to relish. "I notice you are so fascinated by the Vietnam series. I hear how the soldiers talk about what they've seen and felt during the war. Carter, they sound just like you when I ask you about your childhood. Your voice gets flat like theirs. In one of the episodes, they mentioned the 'thousand-yard stare.'"

Now she's starting to choke up, but that's okay.

"That is the stare that you have if I ask more than one question about your childhood. Your eyes gloss over and you're looking right through me, way into . . . somewhere else. Do you know that? That you do that?"

"No." Was I sounding like that now already?

She looked like she wasn't surprised at my answer. She went on. "You recently dreamed about your mother. You haven't dreamed about her for years, right?"

"No, I haven't."

"I wonder if there's something going on in you that you should listen to?" She waited.

I nodded. I felt like I was getting on a roller-coaster again. Where would this end?

"The small green note that I noticed on your table by your end of the couch. The one with 'I F U' on it. I asked you what that meant and you said it was an abbreviation for 'I Forgive You.' I asked who to forgive and you said your mother—then you said 'and maybe me.'

I asked why forgive yourself and you said you weren't sure. You said you made the note back in 1992 when your support group facilitator said forgiveness might be needed. You weren't sure what it meant. You said you pulled it out after dreaming about your mother's apology. Carter, I wonder if your spirit is telling you something there."

I felt jealous that she was tuned to a wavelength that I wasn't. If my spirit is telling me so much, why doesn't it speak on my frequency?

"Another thing. You've been talking about your mom more than usual. When we were in the garden last fall, you suddenly mentioned your sisters said your mom used to garden. I didn't mention it before because you always get quiet somehow when the topic of your mother comes up."

"I'm sorry, love. Thanks for your patience." I was convinced she was onto something, but she had more.

"I've noticed when we visit your sisters, you all end up talking about your mother. You used to get up and walk away. Or you'd say something like 'I had a completely different mother' and then you'd get quiet. You used to get frustrated with Faith when she'd try to get you to remember the good. Lately, you agree with her, and sometimes she agrees with you."

By now, I wasn't thinking about each item she'd shared. I was feeling deep gratitude that she'd noticed those numerous changes that I hadn't.

"When we were sorting out books in the basement, you put your mom's poetry book on the top."

"Love, I appreciate everything that you've noticed about me. I . . ." I didn't know what else to say. But this deserved more than silence. "What should we do??"

She squeezed my legs again. She looked at me with such love. "You seem ripe for something. I wonder what it is." She'd been noticing things about me that I hadn't. She had a sixth sense about things and I respected that.

"What do you mean ripe for something?"

"I don't know."

"Teri, you can't just stop with that. What do you mean? If I'm the one who's lined up to do something, then what the hell is it?"

"If you don't know, then we'll have to wait and see."

Suddenly Seeing Mom

In February 2021, out of boredom with the pandemic, we started cleaning out old files. Also, I hated clutter and cleaning out files felt like scratching an itch. Teri and I were in each of our offices going through old papers.

"Teri, I just now came across more of Darienne's poems. I'd filed them away and couldn't find them before. They're right here! We should frame them and put them on the wall." Her poems always touched my heart with their insights and imagery.

"You do that, love."

I found a poem called "At Eventide" and read it. It was beautiful!

"Teri, there's a poem here that you've got to read. This one goes on the wall first." I handed it to her. She took the poem and began to read it, but stopped.

"Carter, this isn't Darienne's. This is your mother's. I've always thought that your mother's poetry is beautiful. I've said before that you should share her poetry with Darienne."

"You did? I don't remember that."

"That's because whenever anyone mentions your mother, you always just shut down. Why don't you share her poems with Darienne? They're part of her legacy, you know." She handed the poem back to me. What else had we lost out on because of my anger at my mother? Teri had suggested that anger was slowly seeping away. What will happen now?

I immediately emailed the poem to Darienne. Within the hour, she emailed back, "This is very good. What other poems of hers do we have?" The universe was sending me a message, "It's time to open up, Carter!"

I hadn't kept copies of Mom's poems, but I did have a small self-published book that contained thirty-eight of them. I went to

Faith, keeper of Mom's flame, and asked for whatever she had. She had stacks of them along with twelve stories that Mom had written. She wanted to make sure they weren't lost or damaged.

We realized if we put all her materials online, they could easily be shared with all of her grandkids, with anyone. So, we began the tedious task of transcribing them into online files. We also created a website, elvina-granlie-mcnamara.com.

One day, while deep in the transcription, Teri set down a poem. "Carter, this is so fascinating, looking so closely at each poem, each story. What's it like for you?"

I set down another poem and looked at her. "She feels so real to me now. I can't describe it. It's like she's another person—a healthy person—sitting right next to me. She's a stranger to me, but we're related by blood. I keep wondering how this thoughtful and hopeful person became such a raging alcoholic and drug addict."

"Me, too. It's like she's two completely different people." She picked up a stack and rifled through them quickly. "So many of these poems were written in her youth. They're so full of hope and promise. She writes about fertile fields of crops. Her great love for her father." She looked at me. "Did you know he migrated alone from Norway when he was only sixteen? Imagine that. She wrote about her mother being so stern, but also so very caring. Her mother not only took care of the children and the chickens, but also her husband's drinking habits." She set down her materials and opened her arms. "This is amazing. What are you finding?"

"I was touched when she wrote about her hopes to be a writer. She wrote about her favorite writers, poems, and stories. She gave some serious thought, even as a teenager, to creation, evolution, and how the world worked. I'm blown away."

"Yeah, and she still worried about things that typical teenagers do, like what color dress to wear and whether the boy in class noticed her. I keep wondering what this might feel like for you—it's such a different look at your mother."

I stared at my stack. What were my feelings?

"Teri, when I think of her hopes and dreams, I feel more compassion for her. I feel less anger. I feel less blame. I keep wondering, what kind of trauma changed her into such a . . ." I was going to say a demon. ". . . an alcoholic and drug addict? We've gotta talk about these with Renee and see how she feels."

She set down her stack, looked at me, and waited to hear more.

"Astrid once said to me that I had three saving graces: you, Renee, and my Old Soul. I once wondered if my Old Soul was really my dead mother and father trying to help me. Now, I wonder if my mother is also giving me grace through her poetry."

"It seems like you're seeing her as a human being now rather than some powerful demon. Maybe it's easier to forgive a human than a demon."

"You know, I've been working on forgiving her ever since that note with the 'IFU' back in 1992. I read somewhere that forgiveness is what you do for yourself, so you can let go of your anger and move on. My anger at her is gone. So I realize now that I've already forgiven her."

Teri nodded with a soft smile.

I picked up Mom's picture, looked at it and said, "I forgive you."

So why didn't I feel like I was done with her?

Sartre Was Right

It's the fall of 1976. Philosophy classes make my mind soar up to fifty thousand feet, then down to five and back up again. At times, it's breathless. Frankly, I treasure how all the concepts don't always have to apply to real life. Sometimes it's great just to exercise our brains for the sake of the exercise.

This philosophy class is so thought-provoking. Brandt is such a great teacher. He explains a concept, then looks around at all of us to see if anyone is confused. "Any questions? If so, that's all right. Others probably have the same question, too."

Then he slowly paces left and right across the front of the room, scanning the students for interest. His elbows are down, close by his side, with his forearms bent up and the palms of his hands turned up. It's like he's inviting some spirits down from the skies.

Today, the lecture is on existentialism. Brandt explained that existentialists believe that every person is responsible for their own life, their own actions. Today's lecture is on Jean-Paul Sartre. Sartre believed that if people avoid that responsibility, then they are living in bad faith—they are being inauthentic. Inauthentic people might feel phony or continually guilty about something. Brandt adds that one example of avoiding responsibility is escaping into addiction to anesthetize yourself, to avoid reality.

Brandt's words keep ringing in my ears. Feeling phony? Continually guilty? I feel almost like someone is accusing me of something. Do I feel that way about myself? I don't. At least I don't think I do. What is that about?

Brandt keeps talking while I look back over my life. When have I been inauthentic? My mother certainly was, but what about me? I've overused in the past to self-anesthetize, but that's understandable given all the crap I put up with from Mom. I've got to push this out of my mind. Whatever . . .

I tune back into Brandt's lecture. "Can anyone think of another example of Sartre's bad faith?" He gently calls on another student, one who rarely talks. This might be interesting.

The student asks, "What about a person trying to escape responsibility by continuing to blame someone else for that person's actions?"

There is that haunting feeling again, but this time, stronger.

Who's Really to Blame?

It was March 2021 and we were on our way to Bismarck to talk to Renee about the poems and the website project. During the past month, we'd sent the web address to Renee and Faith. Faith had thanked us and raved about how it was such a gift to our family. Renee was more modest in her appreciation.

Still, during the drive, I was haunted. Renee had long since settled into her own way of dealing with Mom: with compassion, but still from afar. How would it go, talking with her about poems so deeply personal to Mom? What wounds might that reopen? Also, since forgiving Mom, why had I still felt so confused? Shouldn't the apology have cleared the air?

We pulled into Renee's driveway in the early evening and unloaded our stuff. Her house smelled like caramel rolls, like it always did when we arrived. We'd joke that they had no calories. Those sweet, decadent sensations. She'd also made strong coffee this time—not the Belfield brown water that they called coffee. We welcomed each other with hugs. We each grabbed a coffee and roll, then sat down at her kitchen table.

After some small talk about the weather and the drive, Renee said, "Well, I tell you. That website was amazing. There must be more than sixty poems in there and . . . what, ten or twelve stories? I didn't know about most of them. I agree with Faith. They're such a gift to our family, especially to our kids. I hope you both feel so proud."

"Teri and I talked about how very human she seemed all of a sudden. I used to think of her as being some kind of demon. In therapy, I learned that the real demon was the way I chose to see her. I'd created the demon in my own head. But even in knowing that, I still couldn't completely let go of the demon. Those poems made her completely real to me and not a demon at all. I was able to forgive her after reading those poems."

"You forgave her? I don't know if I could do that."

"Yeah, I did. But I don't know. There's still something . . ." I looked off to the side. What was it?

When I hesitated, Teri asked, "But what?"

"I don't know. It's just something . . ." I looked back at them. "Anyway."

Teri said, "Yeah, the poems changed how I saw her, too. I never met her, but she seemed so much larger than life, the way you both talked about her. Carter said they helped him accept her as having an addiction—an illness—also while trying to raise four kids alone."

Renee said, "I was worried that if I started reading them, I'd have nightmares again. I've read a few of them, but so far, no nightmares. Maybe I'll read the rest of them someday."

I asked, "So are you okay?"

"Oh, sure." She really seemed okay. That was such a relief for me to hear. Then she asked, "What was most interesting about her poems for you two?"

I looked at Teri. She looked at me.

I said, "Mom poured her heart out in her writing. It all felt so genuine, not like the whining she did with us kids. That honesty in sharing feelings took real courage. I didn't have that kind of courage. I shared some of my painful stories with you two. But I said them like they were headlines in a newspaper, with no feelings at all."

Teri asked, "You said just some of the stories? What other stories were there?"

I felt a bit defensive, knowing I had held back some stories. "There were others, sure. I gave her enemas, probably twenty or thirty. I don't know." I looked at Renee. "You must have, too, right?"

"No, I never did that. I can't believe she did that to you."

Teri asked, "I never knew about the enemas. I can't imagine that."

I shrugged. "Oh, it was routine. Warm the water, hang the bag, open the valve, squish—you're done. You know?"

Teri said, "I don't know. I can't imagine doing that as a kid, or as an adult asking a kid to help me do that. How did that feel?"

I sat back. I felt embarrassed and ashamed. "How did it feel? How do you think it felt? It was the first time I knew I would never be a kid again. I would never feel pure again. That I'd fallen into a cesspool of slime that I'd never get out of again. That's how it felt. Is that what you wanted to hear, Teri?"

Teri reached out her hand to touch me.

"Don't touch me. I don't need your pity."

Teri jerked her hand back.

Renee asked, "That must haunt you all the time. What else haunts you, Carter?"

"I'll tell you what haunts me—what haunts me the most." Now, I was on a roll. "I almost froze her one time. I shoved her out in the shed so she'd leave me alone to do her sheets. Then I went back to bed and forgot about her. When I remembered her, I rushed to get her out. She was shivering in the corner, curled up in a little ball, covered with her coat. She was so white. She kept whispering, 'It's so cold. It's so cold.'"

As I spoke, I suddenly saw an image of my mother. I saw an eighteen-year-old, writing a poem of innocence and hopefulness. I saw a human being, not a demon.

I rested my elbows on the table and buried my face in my hands. "I'm so sorry, Mom! It's my fault. It's always been my fault, not yours. I shouldn't be blaming you."

My torment shifted to confusion. What's always been my fault? What was I blaming her for? Why was I saying that? Then I remembered Brandt Henderson at the front of the room, talking about bad faith.

Time stopped.

Now I knew why my forgiving her wasn't enough. My jaw dropped. I looked slowly at Teri, then at Renee.

"What I did to Mom was bigger and for much longer than everything she did to us! I scapegoated her for most of my life. I blamed her for all of my problems. Whenever I'd hurt someone, I'd privately blame Mom. I'd dump it all on her. I'd tell myself, 'It's not my fault. It's my mother's. She abused me, so I get a pass.' I steeped myself in self-pity. That's why I despise self-pity. It's because I wallow in it. I needed to keep Mom alive as a demon in my head, so I could keep blaming her. I'm such a phony."

I felt a giant bubble ready to burst. It started in my belly and rose up through my throat. I wrapped my arms around myself and started sobbing. Convulsing, gasping, rocking back and forth, struggling to catch my breath.

Then I panicked. *Please, God, don't make me vomit!* But it was too late. I staggered to her bathroom where I dumped my guts—dumped the guilt, disgust, and self-loathing I'd been carrying deep inside for decades.

Teri came in behind me and touched my shoulder, but I put up my hand, silently asking her to leave me alone.

Finally, I was still. I tried to get fully conscious by cleaning up the bathroom. Then I crept back into the living room. Teri was saying, "I've never heard him blame himself before. I thought it was all at your mom for what she did to all of you."

Renee kept saying, "I had no idea. I didn't know about this."

By then, I was composed enough to speak. "God, this feels so good to admit that to myself, to you. It feels so right. Neither of you had any idea because I had no idea myself. It never would have happened without the poems, without you two—the two people I trust the most in the world. Thank you."

"But Carter, you've admitted that to yourself now. That's a big breakthrough," Teri said.

"I've got myself to blame. And now I've got to forgive myself for that."

Renee added, "I agree, Teri. And Carter, I mean, I understand what you said. If it's forgiveness that you need, then I forgive you."

I looked at Teri and she nodded. Each of them hugged me. My mind was blank, but my heart was wide open.

"I'm exhausted. I need to lie down."

Teri wrapped an arm around me and guided me to our bedroom, then laid down with me. I turned to her and whispered, "I'm sorry for the rages back then. Those were my fault, not my mom's."

"The rages? I forgave you. A long, long time ago."

"Thank you."

Now I've got two more people to apologize to.

Two Kinds of Forgiveness

Years ago, when I'd confronted Lonny, I would've blamed my rages on my mother—telling myself that she had instilled that anger in me. Now, I knew better. They were my fault and I needed to take responsibility, especially for my actions as an adult. I needed to apologize to my kids. I'd start with Darienne.

Email from Carter to Darienne McNamara, dated Mon, May 24, 2021 at 8:03 AM

Good morning, Dawder.

I wanted this to be an email, rather than a phone call, so you can deal with it when you're feeling some quiet and peace of mind.

Last night, I remembered a scene from my childhood. It was a common scene in our house in Watford. It was Mom raging at Faith again.

She'd have Faith in a corner, terrified and shaking, even though she was probably twenty-one years old. Still, at eleven or twelve, I'd run between them and rage back at Mom and Mom would skulk back into her bedroom and disappear.

I know I raged at you and Ian when you were little. This is why I'm emailing you. You two shouldn't have experienced that kind of evil.

I hope you can forgive me. I'm sorry.

I love you.

Email from Darienne McNamara to Carter, dated Mon 5/24/2021 at 12:42 PM

Hi Daddy.

I'm sorry you have demons that haunt you like this. I know you weren't fishing for pity and that you don't want pity, but that's my first thought, so I'm stating it.

My second thought is: yes, I forgive you.

As I see it, there's two types of forgiveness. The first I'd describe as intellectual, as in "it's understandable what you did because x, y, z" so rationally you know you shouldn't be angry, or you know it only hurts you to stay mad, not the other person. For your own sake you rationally convince yourself to stop being angry about it. Sometimes it takes work to forgive someone intellectually because it conflicts with your emotions, which would be the second kind of forgiveness—what's in the heart, not the head.

With emotional forgiveness, the key is whether you feel anger or not. You may not feel angry, even if it makes perfect sense to be angry. It may not make rational sense to forgive someone, but it's just a question of whether there's anger in your heart or not. Sometimes it stays there, sometimes it just doesn't.

I forgave you on both levels a long time ago.

I love you, too.

Darienne

Apology Offered

It was July 2021. Teri came in from the backyard wearing her dirt-stained gardening hat and gloves. It warmed my heart, nonetheless. I was sitting at the kitchen table, wearing pajama pants and a torn T-shirt, still feeling frustrated.

"You look perturbed, Carter. What's on your mind?"

"It's been two months since I apologized to Darienne. I still want to do that with Ian, but I don't know how to do it. I haven't talked to him in two years. I keep hoping he'll want to do family therapy. Right now, I don't know if he'll even talk to me."

She took off her hat and gloves, poured a glass of water and sat down. "I agree you need to be careful, but you don't need to be perfect. Let's write down some ideas and organize them as we go along."

"Thank you," I said, relieved. I picked up my pencil and got ready to write.

"Let's start with how you invite him. I'd do an email, so it's written down—clear and consistent. Text him to see the email, too. As far as the message itself, right up front, say why you want to talk to him. It's so you can apologize for your rages, right?"

I nodded.

"Then suggest a time and place to meet. I think you'd both feel more comfortable if it's not together yet. Do a Zoom call."

I nodded.

"Be sure to say he doesn't have to do or say anything. You just hope that he'll listen."

"I like that. I'm worried if anything is expected, then he won't come."

That evening, I drafted an invitation for a half-hour call. I also listed some talking points to look at during the call. I ran both past

Teri and she tweaked them a bit. Then I emailed the invitation and texted him, asking him to please see my email.

Two days later, he emailed back that he would be there. That's all he wrote.

An hour before the Zoom call, I was on the couch, looking out the window, trying to remain calm. Teri walked over to me and handed me a sheet of paper. On it, she had drawn a heart. "That's to remind you to stay focused on what's in your heart." She handed me another sheet, a picture of the North Dakota Badlands. "That's to keep you grounded during the call."

I got up and hugged her. "Offer some pauses so he can speak up if he wants to. Whatever he says, don't get caught up in shame or defensiveness. I'll be in the room if you need me during the call."

An hour later, I dialed into the Zoom call. After some technical glitches, his face appeared. For an instant, it felt like old times, like I could say "hello" and then crack a joke. Instead, I glanced at my talking points, looked up, and began.

"Ian, thank you for coming."

He had the camera off to his right, but looked straight ahead.

"Thanks for inviting me."

"I want to apologize to you for my rages when you were little." I paused. He kept looking straight ahead.

"I was in therapy to try to understand why I was so angry all the time. The therapist helped me remember that I used anger and rages to keep Mom away from me when I was little. That's how I dealt with stress then." I paused. "I used those same rages to deal with stress when you and Darienne were little. Do you remember times like that?"

Still looking straight ahead, he said, "I remember you used intellectual rhetoric to make me feel small."

I paused to be sure he was done.

"That must have been terrifying for you." I thought I detected a slight nod. I waited.

"Ian, I'm sorry I put you through that—having those frightening feelings." I paused. "I'm working on forgiving myself. I

274

hope you can forgive me someday, too." I paused. "I'm still hoping that we can do family therapy when you're ready."

Ian said, "I need to focus on my primary family right now."

"I understand, Ian. That's what I wanted to say in this call. Thank you for coming, son."

He glanced briefly at the camera, then down and to the side to disconnect our call.

Teri sat next to me. "I thought the call went as well as could be expected."

"I had hoped he'd look at me and say something." I shook my head. "I have no clue now whether he's any closer to doing family therapy with us like we hope he'll do. I don't think I should share any childhood details with him now, either. I have no clue how he'd take it."

"You've done all you can do. I hope it's healing for both of you." She squeezed my hand and walked into the kitchen, leaving me alone with my thoughts. She was right. I'd done all I could do.

Closure

At the time of this writing, May 2022, I've come to some closure of this story. I've apologized to Teri, Darienne, and Ian for my rages. I gained forgiveness from Teri and Darienne. It remains to be seen if and when that will ever come from Ian. I hope it will for both of us.

What remains is to apologize and gain forgiveness from two other important people: my mother and myself. Since it's up to me whether this forgiveness is granted or not, I want to be careful about how I decide. I'm just not sure how to do that.

I've read that when ACoAs are unsure or confused, they often leave their emotions behind and go into their heads to try make sense of it all. I feel that happening to me now. I want some logic behind this process of forgiveness. I'll try that now. I've chosen the following five-step process. I'll start with gaining forgiveness from my mother.

First, I have to admit what I did to my mother. I kept her in my head as an evil demon so I could conveniently blame her when needed. Instead, she was a mother with a severe illness that she had not chosen to have.

Then, I have to admit the effects my actions had on her. Keeping her as a demon meant continually telling others how bad she was, creating a reputation she might not have deserved.

Then, I have to admit that I was wrong for what I'd done to her. I should've taken responsibility for myself rather than blaming my problems on her, certainly by the time I was a young man responsible for my own actions.

Then, there's the need to offer a sincere apology. "Mom, I'm sorry for the actions I did that hurt you, especially the scapegoating."

Finally, I need to ask her forgiveness for what I did to her. Of course, that's impossible because she's dead. However, if she was alive and recovered from her addictions, I would hope that she would've forgiven herself for her own scapegoating of others which she clearly had done for most of her life. Perhaps, in forgiving herself, she would've forgiven me as well. That's all I have to go on for now.

Now, I need to think about forgiving myself. First, I must admit what I've done to myself. I lied to myself throughout many of the decades of my life, scapegoating my mother for my faults and problems. That worked well in my twenties, not so well in my thirties, hardly at all in my forties and fifties, and certainly not in my sixties. So, bottom line, I lied to myself.

Then, I need to admit the effects that lie had on me. It retarded my development as a truly authentic adult who takes responsibility for my own actions, rather than blaming them on someone else: my mother. Another effect was the feeling of phoniness that haunted me much of my life. Another was the lost joy that I could have had with my family if I had fully shared myself rather than hiding in illusions of safety within my head.

Then, I need to admit I was wrong in what I had done to myself. Clearly, I was. I could have admitted I was wrong in my late twenties if I had fully and honestly completed my ACoA therapy. In that therapy I might have faced myself and my own responsibilities.

Then, I should offer myself an apology. Carter, I'm sorry for not always honoring the wisest part of myself, my Old Soul. It cried out to me with time-tested wisdom when I was crippled with self-doubt and blinded in rage.

So, do I forgive myself?

I remember that forgiveness of others is what you do for yourself, so you can release your anger at them and move on. Am I still angry at myself? I'm not sure.

I know I'm a good man, doing the best I can. That will have to do for now.

"One of the most courageous decisions
you will ever make
is to finally let go of what
is hurting your heart and soul."

– Brigette Nicole

Epilogue – The Healing Place

After my treatment for PTSD starting in 1992, research and treatments about the disorder have expanded significantly. No longer is the disorder seen as occurring primarily among soldiers back from war. The field now recognizes that it can occur among victims of domestic abuse as well. New types of PTSD are being categorized, including complex PTSD that can occur in individuals like myself who have repeatedly experienced traumatic events.

After the apologies, I still had not shared my full story with my kids. That was one of the reasons for writing this book. In a few short weeks, Darienne will have the manuscript—the full story—in her hands. Hopefully, the estrangement with Ian will end soon and he will have my full story as well.

Since my revelation in March 2021—that my anger and blaming were actually at myself—there has been a remarkable path of healing. Like that revelation, several big breakthroughs have occurred at Renee's home, what we've come to call "the healing place." In addition to myself, others on the path to healing have included my sister, Faith, and my niece, LaRae, and my niece, Rhonda, as well as her two children. I suspect that much of that healing, like my own, was seeded and nurtured by Renee herself.

I have never been deeply religious. However, as I've aged, I've become much more spiritual, focusing on the beauty and goodness of the world around me. For me, the most tangible symbol of that world is Teri. She makes this book a true love story. Wolves naturally live in packs. She's helped to bring this wolf back home to the pack where he belongs.

I go home to North Dakota as often as I can. It's my home base. I feel like a soldier home from war. Whenever I'm there, I try to visit my niece Darienne's grave. I update her on what I've been up to. I tell her that I miss her and that I hope she's scooting around the hills, this time with no braces on her feet.

A couple of years ago, I met my maternal first cousin, Dennis Granlie, for the first time. After we'd exchanged welcomes, the first thing he said to me was, "How could someone from your background accomplish what you have?" Immediately, Renee answered for me. "Well, he's always had an Old Soul."

We all have that Old Soul. Nature plans it that way. We just need to listen more with our heart than with our head.

The last time I visited the cemetery where Mom was buried, the warm wind was blowing across the prairie. I stood there watching the waves of grass rolling across the fields. Then, I swear I saw a young girl with bright red hair dancing across a hilltop. She stopped, looked back at me and smiled as if to reassure me. Then she danced on. I'd like to think it was Mom, back at home on the prairie, healthy now, beyond the bounds of any disease.

After what I've been through, if someone asked me how to turn a marriage around, I honestly wouldn't know. If this story somehow inspires people to improve their lives and their relationships, then I deserve none of the credit. They deserve it all. It's not easy.

If I was pressed to proclaim a moral of my story, then it would be this: if someone does not talk about some important aspect of their life, then don't be wary of them. Tell them if they have a story, you will listen. Say that. Then be quiet. And just listen.

Love After Love

The time will come
when, with elation,
you will greet yourself arriving
at your own door, in your own mirror
and each will smile at the other's welcome,

and say, sit here. Eat.
You will love again the stranger who was yourself.
Give wine. Give bread. Give back your heart
to itself, to the stranger who has loved you

all your life, whom you ignored
for another, who knows you by heart.
Take down the love letters from the bookshelf,

the photographs, the desperate notes,
peel your own image from the mirror.
Sit. Feast on your life.

– Derek Walcott, *Collected Poems, 1948-1984*

Acknowledgments

Family

Teri McNamara, my wife – This entire section should be about Teri. It's difficult to name any aspect of my life or this book that she has not contributed to. Most importantly, she convinced me to believe in, and to accept, her unconditional love. She was the antidote I needed for the poison I'd collected from my childhood. She softened me the way a soft running brook smoothes the sharp edges of stones: with infinite patience.

Darienne McNamara and Ian McNamara, my children – My kids brought more unconditional love into my life. When each of them moved out of our home, I had a crisis. After we had just dropped Darienne off for college, I ended up in the Emergency Room in the same town. I had an increased pain in my left side. The doctor did his quick assessments and advised, "You're just stressed. Breathe deep. Take a walk. You'll be fine." After Ian moved out, I ended up in group therapy, talking about how much I missed him— our walks and our talks.

Dion (Mac) McNamara, my brother – If there's a heaven, I hope he's there, eating pork and beans and minced ham sandwiches on white bread. I hope he's watching Roadrunner cartoons and laughing his ass off.

Elvina Granlie McNamara, my mother – She gave the world beautiful drawings, paintings, and poetry. Oh, how I wish I could've known her as that bright, thoughtful, and hopeful young woman.

Faith Bellon, my sister – The Keeper of the flame was right all those years. Our mother did many beautiful things. I'm so happy that Faith and I are more than just siblings now. She's a dear friend whom I look forward to seeing each time I'm back home.

Renee Lowenstein, my sister – She saved my life, physically and spiritually. There are no words I could write that would do justice for the deep love and affection I feel for her. She was my compass for how I parented when I was at my best. She remains one of my best friends, regardless of being my sister.

Roger Krumel, my brother – He came along late in my life. At the 2010 Veeder reunion, we were known as the "DNA duo" because we'd suddenly appeared out of the blue. I'm so sorry that I lost him to cancer too soon after we'd met.

Darienne, my niece – I can still see her looking off to my left, headed for a destination somewhere beyond the coffee table. I never had to wonder where she was going, though, because she always had her tiny fingers locked in my hair. I was coming along with her because that's the way it was meant to be. Thank you for the journey.

Laverne Malott, my aunt – She was the greeter, always with an embrace, a compliment, and a string of questions about what I'd been up to. She never forgot my answers, either.

Chuck Malott, cousin – He was the gatekeeper, a role he doesn't see himself as having, but I do. If that first phone call with him had gone differently, I might still be wondering who my real father was. The entire Malott family welcomed me, as did the Cary clan.

Dennis Granlie, cousin – He has become more than a first cousin for me. He's been the source of more true information about my mother's family. He's inspired me by using his retirement to sail his boat around the Caribbean. He's someone I'd drink a beer with while listening to Jimmy Buffett.

Kerry Veeder Christman and Rose Veeder, cousins – They welcomed me into the Veeder clan. I was nervous at the Veeder reunion, but only for the first five minutes. After that, I felt like I'd known them all my life.

Friends

Andy and Priscilla Watson – They helped show me the skill of being happy as a couple; that happiness is often a matter of attitude and that there will be occasional disagreements, but that doesn't mean the marriage is at stake. What matters most is love and respect.

Andy Horsnell – He's a soul brother in our mutual devotion to self-growth, intimacy, and professionalism. He was the right catalyst at the right time to launch our company, Authenticity Consulting, LLC. More importantly, he remains a stimulating and inspiring dear friend.

Bill Monson – He believed in me during all of my graduate school years while guiding me to focus on what's important for the long haul, rather than just on what's urgent for now. He deepened and enriched my learning during countless dialogues. He has continued to be a personal and professional friend, adding insights and meaning to my life.

Bob Radspinner – He taught me to never take anything too seriously. He taught me the rich heritage of having—and loving—a long-time friend.

Cindy Hanna Ostman, Jimmie Christensen, and Mike Konkel – These three friends from my childhood town, where I'd grown up in fear and shame, welcomed me back and transformed how I see that town for the better.

Chuck Appleby – He came into my life at a time when I was despairing—and probably depressed—about providing my professional services. His enthusiasm lit a fire in my work just when I needed it.

Dave and Sandy Livingston – They reminded me of the importance of living life to the fullest with humor and joy. Dave was the first to ask me, "Why aren't you dead or in prison?"

Lowell Flemmer – A friend of long ago, he reminded me of the critical role of romance. Back then, he meant the majesty of King

Arthur, the power of a beautiful poem, and the joy of shared laughter.

Lynne Kaizer Sears and Regi Schumacher Boulais – Both have permanent places in my heart. They reminded me that love, care, and nurturing are what the heart is meant for.

Michael Olesen – He kept my brain and imagination alive during my often stressful and tumultuous years working at the University of Minnesota. His camaraderie and companionship continued to remind me that the world was much bigger than that job.

Pat and Karen Carver – They reminded me of how precious it is to have curious, skilled, and interesting conversationalists who can share different points of view in a highly respectful and non-judgmental way that makes for an endearing and affectionate friendship.

Ron Makaruk – He is my soul brother in the purest and best sense of the word. When we were together, every thought and word meant more meaning for each of us.

Tony Knopik – He and I would sit up till the early morning hours in high school and share irreverent opinions and insights, usually about ourselves. Our brains were on fire. I had never laughed so often and so hard. I will always carry good thoughts of him.

Others

Cherry Creek – Some places are so beautiful, accepting, and endearing, that we have to remind ourselves they were real. The Cherry Creek area just south and east of Watford City was my magic place where I was safe in my little hole in the ground—in my den.

Editors – Carolyn Holbrook, Debbie Burke, Rachelle Ramirez, Sarah Ratermann Beahan, and Teri McNamara took a rough pile of text and turned it into a coherent story that stayed true to my life experience and my learning. It was like magic, watching them do their craft. Any errors remaining in this manuscript are mine, not theirs.

Beta readers – Andy Watson, Bob Hussey, Diana Sage, Gary Nereson, Katherine Hussey, Ken Kaliher, Michael Olesen, and Priscilla Watson all provided valuable feedback.

How Will They Remember Me?

What will they say about me,
  Those whom I hold so dear?
  What will they best remember
  When I am no longer here?

Will they recall the mistakes I've made,
  Battles I've never won,
  Moments of pain I've caused them,
  Things I have left undone?

Will they censor my human failings
  And wish I'd been noble and strong?
  Will they scoff at the hopes I nurtured,
  The dreams that somehow went wrong?

Or will they be moved by compassion,
  Directed by Heaven above,
  To temper their judgment with kindness
  And soften their memories with love?

– Elvina Granlie McNamara
elvina-granlie-mcnamara.com

Questions for Discussion

1. Carter was the protagonist—the main character—in the story. Who or what was his primary antagonist?

2. What events, experiences, and/or comments referred directly or indirectly to a wolf or the nature of wolf? (There are eight of them. Shoot for at least four.)

3. Why were the sisters (Renee and Faith) not to blame for leaving Carter alone with his mother?

4. Who had it worse in dealing with the mother? Really?

5. Why was it so difficult for Carter to finally share his childhood experiences with his wife, Teri?

6. What was Teri's influence on Carter's recovery?

7. Who were other mentors/advisors to Carter?

8. Why did Teri stick with Carter, despite the long time it took for Carter to change?

9. What were the two big lies Carter had been telling himself? How was each dispelled?

10. What is the arc of Carter's growth and development over the five parts (think of the arc of tension in the book)?

11. What/who do you think Carter's Old Soul really is?

12. What are at least three universal lessons/truths/themes that emerged from the story—that are true for everyone? (Think about the nature of Carter's struggles and his eventual recovery.)

About the Author

Carter has written numerous award-winning textbooks in the fields of leadership, management, and organization development, as well as hundreds of related articles. Those textbooks, which included new approaches to consulting and organizational development, are used in colleges and universities across North America. His author's website is https://cartermcnamara.com.

In the mid 1990s, Carter started the Free Management Library, one of the world's largest collections of free, online resources about personal, professional and organizational development—a venture that was well ahead of its time. During that period, he also developed a group-based, peer coaching model which was adopted by a wide variety of organizations around the world for a variety of uses. He is co-founder of Authenticity Consulting and Action Learning Source, both of which leveraged that peer coaching model. More recently, he founded the Consultants Development Institute, one of the few on-line, self-directed training programs about how to consult to solve complex problems and how to facilitate strategic planning in any type of organization.

He holds a B.A. in Social and Behavioral Sciences, a B.S. in Computer Science, an MBA from the University of St. Thomas, and a Ph.D.in Human and Organization Development from The Union Institute. The University of St. Thomas awarded Carter the "Business Excellence Award" for volunteering over six hundred hours of community service. Carter also received the "Organization Development Practitioner of the Year" award from the Minnesota Organizational Development Network for his many contributions to the fields of peer coaching, Action Learning, and Organization Development.

Carter maintains a deep interest in conveying the similarities between trauma experienced in war and in domestic violence. He remains committed that recovery depends on accessible means for the traumatized to feel safe enough to participate wholeheartedly—authentically—in their recovery.

He relishes his family, rich conversations, and playful humor. He enjoys his retirement in Minneapolis, Minnesota. He and Teri celebrated their 40th wedding anniversary in July 2021.

"Among my Dakota and Absaroke people is a saying
that I can only really translate into English
using a double negative:
'I do not remember a time when I did not know him.'

It is intended to point out and compliment
one who has had a good, significant impact on another,
an impact so great that one's history is changed.

That is what I say to you, Carter,
I do not remember when I did not know you."

– Jon Bell, consultant, Somerset, Wisconsin

For reprint permission, more information on Authenticity Consulting, LLC, or to order additional copies of this or any of our other publications, please contact:

Authenticity Consulting, LLC
4008 Lake Drive Avenue North
Minneapolis, MN 55422-1508 USA
+1.763.971.8890
publications@authenticityconsulting.com